and the Social Worker

PHILLIP FELLIN

SCHOOL OF SOCIAL WORK
UNIVERSITY OF MICHIGAN, ANN ARBOR

F. E. PEACOCK PUBLISHERS, INC.
ITASCA, ILLINOIS

CONTENTS

PART ONE

Approaches to Understanding Communities

CHAPTER 1

Defining Communities and Community Competence

To be effective, professionals in the human services need a conceptual and practical understanding of communities within American society. This book is designed to assist these professionals, especially social workers, in the development of a fund of knowledge and a systematic way of thinking about communities. Conceptual frameworks and empirical findings from the social sciences and social work, as well as information from journalistic reports in the mass media, are presented in this book. This knowledge about communities will contribute to the achievement of social service goals through social work practice.

DEFINING COMMUNITIES

A community exists when a group of people form a social unit based on common location, interest, identification, culture, and/or activities (Garvin and Tropman, 1992). For the purposes of this book, communities are classified into three major groups. These groups are distinguished by common locality, or place, by non-place characteristics, and in terms of an individual's "personal community" (Davidson, 1986). Locality-based communities are characterized in terms of three dimensions: (1) a functional spatial unit meeting sustenance needs, (2) a unit of patterned social interaction, and (3) a symbolic unit of collective identity (Hunter, 1975). Communities of "place" vary along these dimensions, as well as in terms of size, density, and heterogeneity. Locality-based communities are often referred to as neighborhood communities, community areas, local municipal communities, and metropolitan communities. Generally the population size and geographic area of these communities increase from the neighborhood community to the metropolitan community.

Locality-based communities are usually overlapping, such as neighborhood communities within municipal communities. Consequently, people generally reside in multiple communities of place, that is, communities within communities. While we give attention throughout this book to the various types of locality-based communities, our principal analysis of a community as a social system focuses on the municipal community—commonly referred to as a town, a city, or a suburban community—and on neighborhood communities. We use an ecological perspective to examine locality-based communities, with consideration given to the demographic development and social stratification of American communities. This is followed by a social systems perspective, which is guided by Warren's (1963) definition of community as "that combination of social units and systems which perform the major social functions having locality relevance." This definition of locality-based communities guides our examination of the major subsystems which carry out community functions.

In addition to membership in locality-based communities, many people belong to one or more "non-place" communities. These may be referred to as "communities of identification" and "communities of interest" (Longres, 1990; Garvin and Tropman, 1992). Identificational communities are based on some feature of common identity or belief, such as ethnicity, race, religion, lifestyle, ideology, sexual orientation, social class, and profession or type of employment. Thus, it is not uncommon to hear people refer to themselves as members of the African American community, the Asian American community, the Jewish community, the Catholic community, the Polish community, the Italian community, or the gay community. These communities are regarded as communities of interest, especially when members have a common identity and also engage in some level of organizational activity, such as happens in professional groups, sports clubs, religious groups, and ethnic organizations.

Locality-based communities, especially neighborhood communities, often coincide with identificational/interest communities. For example, people who identify themselves in terms of a common background of race, religion, national origin, or social class, may live in residential areas which have a high proportion of people with one or more of these characteristics. In many large American cities, such as Chicago, Los Angeles, New York City, Boston, Philadelphia, and Miami, the names given to community areas or neighborhoods are often associated with specific ethnic, racial, or religious groups.

A somewhat different use of the term *community* focuses on the membership of an individual in multiple communities. Thus an individual's "personal community" consists of all of the communities—locational, identificational, interest—in which one engages in social interaction, in use of services and resources, in employment activities, and in leisure time pursuits (Davidson, 1986). This definition of community broadens the scope of potential social interactions and social resources, including both formal and informal helping networks. With this formulation, the personal community serves as a context for the social worker's development of interpersonal treatment and social service intervention goals, as well as the goals of community practice which seek to change organizations and communities.

DEFINING COMMUNITY COMPETENCE

The concept of community competence provides a framework for understanding the functioning of the various communities which make up the social environment. Community competence is a major attribute of a good community, as it consists of the capacity of a community to engage in problem-solving in order to achieve its goals. A number of "good" community qualities serve to enhance the creation of a competent community.

More specifically, a competent community may be defined as: "one in which the various component parts of the community are able to collaborate effectively in identifying the problems and needs of the community; can achieve a working consensus on goals and priorities; can agree on ways and means to implement the agreed-upon goals; can collaborate effectively in the required actions" (Cottrell, 1983). The idea of community competence is expanded upon by Barbarin (1981), who emphasizes that the capacities of social systems, and of the individuals and groups within a community, constitute a dual dimension of competence. In Barbarin's terms, "Community competence refers both to the ability of social systems to respond to differential needs of the varied populations they serve, and the ability of citizens or groups to use existing resources or develop alternatives for the purpose of solving problems of living."

ENHANCING CONDITIONS OF COMPETENCE

A number of conditions may enhance the competent functioning of a locality-based community. Some of these are individual or group attributes and behaviors, such as the degree to which: (1) residents have a commitment to their community; (2) there is a self-awareness among the various community groups of their own values and self-interests; (3) there exists a level of articulateness that allows for effective communication about community issues between the diverse segments of the community; and (4) residents participate in identifying goals and implementing them. Systems components often found in a competent community are (1) procedures for handling conflicts which arise between various groups in the community and (2) the capacity for managing extra-community relationships with the larger society, while at the same time maintaining an appropriate degree of local autonomy (Cottrell, 1976).

Another way of describing a competent community is to locate qualities which are valued in a community, qualities which are considered "good." For example, Martin Luther King, Jr. used the term, "beloved community" to "describe an ideal town or city, which would flourish without racism, poverty, or violence" (Logan, 1993). Most citizens would agree with this view of a good community. Still, community qualities are value-laden in that they may not be regarded as "good" by all residents. It can be expected that people share some values and interests and differ with regard to others. Examples of such values appear in Warren's discussion of "What is a good community?"

- People should deal with each other on a personal basis, rather than an impersonal basis.
- There should be a broad distribution of power within the community.
- The community should include a wide variety of different income groups, ethnic groups, and religious and interest groups.
- There should be a great deal of local neighborhood control.
- The community should encompass the greatest possible degree of cooperation in policy-making and the least possible conflict (Warren, 1980).

Warren (1980) raises the caution that few communities have all these desirable qualities at the same time. Thus, as people move to maximize the benefits of one community characteristic, such as autonomy, they may have to accept a reduction in benefits from other areas, such as extra-local, state, or federal funds. Similarly, broad decision-making involvement in a community may not be compatible with effective, efficient, and timely actions on the part of the community's political system. The small size of a community may allow for primary group relationships that might be much more limited in large cities. Yet smaller size may also limit the potential for heterogeneity of community residents.

Finally, there may be times when fewer of these usually desirable community qualities might result in a more competent community. For example, Warren (1980) has alerted us to the potential benefits of apathy and ambiguity, especially on controversial issues which are extremely divisive. In Warren's words, "We need apathy. We need people who will clamp the lid on excessive partisanship." Furthermore, there may be times when groups are ambiguous about issues or unable to clearly articulate their differences. In such cases a level of ambiguity may allow for consensus on points of agreement, rather than an emphasis on disagreement, and thereby lead to community action rather than inaction or overt conflict.

IMAGES OF A GOOD COMMUNITY

As people think in terms of how good their community is, they develop images. These are based on objective characteristics of communities, as well as subjective opinions and feelings. These images may affect the way residents relate to each other, as well as their involvement in the informal and formal organizations of a community. A number of ingredients may contribute to an individual's positive "picture" or "image" of a community—for example, the opportunity for primary group relationships, the attachment of citizens to their community, the absence of serious social problems, the presence of solid, functional, safe neighborhoods, the presence of opportunities for education and employment, a positive physical and cultural environment. Many citizens describe a good community in terms of a "good place to live," a "good place to work," a "good place to raise kids," or a "good place to retire"—with each citizen having a somewhat different definition or image of what is "good," depending on personal factors such as age, gender, ethnicity, race, social class, sexual orientation, and religion.

Professional planners, politicians, and human service workers are likely to evaluate a community in terms of how goals are established and whether or not they are attained. For example, professionals may consider a community to be competent when (1) its governmental officials determine priorities, such as controlling juvenile delinquency, drug traffic, violent crimes, civil disorders, creating new employment opportunities, building convention or sports facilities, and (2) when action is taken to obtain funding to undertake efforts to reach these goals. Thus, one measure of competence is the extent to which goals are actually achieved: Are social problems being controlled or reduced? Are United Fund campaigns successful? Are job opportunities created? Are occupational barriers for ethnic minorities, economically disadvantaged people, disabled people, women, and gay and lesbian people reduced or eliminated?

The task of the human service professional is to understand the impact of the competence and "goodness" of the community on the social functioning of individuals, families, and small groups. The professional's role is to assist people in relating to their environment and effecting changes that will be beneficial to all community residents. Ideas about "good" and "competent" communities provide a context for identifying social practice goals and strategies. Obviously few, if any, communities are "ideal," or so "good" and "competent" that no social problems need solving and no individuals are in need of help in their social functioning. In responding to these problems and needs, social workers become more effective if they can identify and understand the factors which enhance or detract from the competence of a community.

PLANNED COMMUNITIES

The ideas of "community competence" and "good community" are usually directed toward the evaluation of communities which have been functioning for some period of time. We are interested in the features of competence which make these communities work well, or which need improvement for better functioning for local residents. Social workers are especially concerned with ways to minimize or eliminate barriers to community competence for special population groups. Another approach to creating "better" and "stronger" communities is through the development of "new towns" or "planned communities." There are many historical examples of alternative communities—such as utopian communities, communes, garden cities—which emphasize the proximity of living together and the sense of shared values. Currently, there are a number of examples of planned communities in American society. These communities represent the "images" of good communities on the part of urban planners, architects, and the people who choose to live in them. At the same time, many public-housing developments have become examples of communities with negative images and identities, especially when they have high rates of crime and violence and lack the social cohesion often found in traditional working-class neighborhoods.

Suburban communities developed from the late 1940s—for example, Levittown, New York, and Park Forest, Illinois—represent one model of a planned community. This model included increased household and area space, parks, schools, nearby commercial establishments, churches, and neighborhood associations. A somewhat similar development occurred in the creation of planned retirement communities, especially in states with mild climates, such as Florida, Arizona, and California. Newer versions of planned communities which have emerged in the 1980s and 1990s will be cited here as illustrations of attempts to create competent, good communities.

Old-Style Towns

One example of the development of an old-style town is Rancho Santa Margarita, a community in Orange County, California, designed to include "medium-priced homes, shops, industry, and plenty of open space within a well-defined area, so people can get out of their cars and actually meet each other" (Hirsch, 1991). The goal of this community model is to "create a self-contained community where all activities—working, shopping, playing—are woven together like the strands of a spider web." At present the community population is about 15,000, with an anticipated population of about 45,000. The developers of this community have used ideas from urban planners and psychologists, such as Maslow's hierarchy of needs, to create a community which "looks at wellness as a lifestyle need." Priority is placed on affordable housing, shared open spaces, jobs, small yards, porches and patios, general stores, walking paths. As of 1991, this new town "is still more promise than reality," as it seeks to possess three major dimensions of community, that is, a geographic place which provides for sustenance needs, a high level of social interaction, and residents with a strong community identity.

Another example of old-style towns is found in community projects such as Seaside, Florida, developed by an architecture firm headed by Andres Duany and Elizabeth Plater-Zyberk. Their image of a "good community" is one in which people are less reliant on cars, as in many pre–World War II traditional neighborhoods (Morgenthaler, 1993). These architects advocate strict building codes, streets which diffuse traffic (not cul-de-sacs), a mix of commercial and residential areas, mixed housing and apartments, and mixed age and income residents. The ideal of this community model is for residents to have the option of shopping, eating, and working within walking distance.

New Town Within a City

A rather different model of new town development is found in a proposal for a new semi-autonomous municipality within the City of Detroit, Michigan (Cannon, 1990). While some old buildings and homes would be preserved in a 740-acre area of the city, most of the area would be newly developed. The "new town" of about 7500 people would have its own mini-government, a Community and Development Enterprise Zone Authority, with control over its government, schools, and services such as police and fire departments. The development of this "new town" would require cooperation and resources of various levels of government, including the City of Detroit, the state, and the federal government. The overall goal would be to create "a community of mixed incomes, ages, and races with an independently run, first-rate school system," "a place where practical family values can flourish in an atmosphere free of drugs, prostitution, pornography, gambling, and other criminal activities" (Cannon, 1990).

A quite different model of a new community has been developed in Winslow, Washington, on Bainbridge Island. This is a village for about 70 people with co-housing rather than single units, designed by future residents, pedestrian-oriented, with privacy and substantial facilities shared by all the residents (Giese, 1990). Exemplars of this type of co-housing community can be found in Denmark, Sweden, Norway, France, and West Germany. The houses in Winslow are in the style of traditional Bainbridge farmhouses. All are attached and clustered in three neighborhoods, one with large units and two with one-bedroom apartments. There is a "common house" with dining options and meeting room, library, day-care center, and laundry, as well as a guest house. Each unit has a kitchen, but communal dining is an option. All decisions about the community are made by a consensus of the residents.

The various types of "planned communities" described here represent attempts to rebuild traditional community structures which are associated with characteristics of "good communities." Keep in mind these community types as well as more traditional and emerging urban, suburban, and rural communities as you examine ecological and social systems perspectives for understanding communities in American society.

ECOLOGICAL AND SOCIAL SYSTEMS PERSPECTIVES

No single theoretical framework for understanding communities provides an adequate basis for practice by human service professionals. There are, however, two sets of theories which contribute to the study of communities: human ecology and social systems theory. These perspectives, which are well developed in the social sciences, are being widely used in social work circles in the conceptualization of the social environment (Germain, 1991; Meyer, 1983; Longres, 1990; Chess and Norlin, 1988). These "systems" approaches provide several kinds of knowledge about communities.

The *ecological system* perspective focuses on the population characteristics of a community (size, density, heterogeneity), the physical environment (land use), the social organization or structure of a community, and the technological forces in a community. The ecological perspective seeks to explain the salient features of population groups within a geographic area, such as social class, racial and ethnic composition, age structure, aspects of family composition, and division of labor within the community.

This perspective draws our attention to the interdependencies of people, services, and their local environment and to community interactions with other communities and the larger society. Of particular interest are patterns of spatial organization, e.g., the location of business and commercial areas, residential areas, health and welfare services, and parks. An ecological perspective also helps us understand community changes, such as movements of population groups, patterns of migration and immigration, succession and segregation, and the growth dynamics of communities. It provides a framework for judging when such changes are beneficial or detrimental to residents and the community as a system. From an ecological perspective a competent community enjoys a productive balance between its inhabitants and their environment, allowing for change in an orderly, nondestructive manner and providing essential daily sustenance requirements for its citizens.

The *social systems* perspective involves social institutions relating to one another within a community system, providing social functions of production/distribution/consumption, socialization, social control, social participation, and mutual support for individuals and for the community as a whole (Warren, 1963). Special attention is given to the formal organizations which operate within the major parts of a community system, such as the economic, political, educational, and social welfare and health care subsystems of a community. The social systems perspective focuses on the interaction of these community subsystems on a horizontal level within a community and on a vertical, extra-community level. The conditions which enhance community competence can be viewed from a social systems perspective, with a focus on both the community system as a whole and the activities of the various social units which make up its subsystems. From this perspective, a good community is one where the various subsystems operate for the benefit of all citizens.

In exploring communities from these systems perspectives, one may look upon a community as an actor. Questions of when, how, and why communities act, and what environmental forces influence the ways in which they act, can be explored. How communities handle conflict, maintain or regain equilibrium, react to change, achieve community objectives, and satisfy their members are to be considered. The ways in which various social arrangements and organizations within a community operate need to be examined—in particular, the functions of primary groups and social institutions in serving community residents. Finally, knowledge about communities as systems becomes more meaningful when it is placed in an historical or developmental perspective and understood within a context of social change, trends, and projections for the future.

BARRIERS TO COMMUNITY COMPETENCE

Competent communities are not easy to create or maintain. Sometimes communities are adversely affected by societal forces outside of their control, such as economic recessions and state and federal policies. Communities vary in the extent to which they have local resources, employment opportunities, organizational leadership, and sound educational, health, and social welfare programs and services. They also vary in their innovative capacities and their efforts to improve community conditions. One of the most significant barriers to community competence involves the values, attitudes, and practices of people toward special population groups. Thus, communities vary in regard to their level of discrimination, prejudice, oppression, acceptance, and tolerance. Many American communities lack an appropriate response to the "differential needs" of such groups as ethnic minorities, women, physically and mentally disabled people, and gay and lesbian people. The greater the inequities in employment opportunities, health and social service resources, and social status, the less effective and functionally competent the community is with respect to its total population.

Barriers for Ethnic Minorities

Institutional racism is a major force which fosters a lack of a community competence. As Longres has noted, "Racism can exist independent of the attitudes and beliefs of individuals. When it is built into the norms, traditions, laws, and policies of a society, racism is said to be institutionalized." Discriminatory policies and practices toward racial groups may be found in any of the subsystems of a community and may come in many forms: economic discrimination, insensitivity to the special needs of minorities, distorted characterization of minorities by the mass media, and provision of inadequate or inferior services to minorities (Longres, 1990).

Social workers need to recognize the barriers and limitations imposed upon minorities of color, especially when this occurs in human service organizations. As Barbarin has noted, an increase of community competence requires a twofold focus:

- an awareness on the part of community agencies about the cultural diversity brought to a community by different minority groups;
- a minimal level of sophistication on the part of minority group members concerning ways to access and to make systems more responsive to their needs (Barbarin, 1981).

Some communities have this type of organizational awareness and individual sophistication. Those that do not can benefit from the efforts of citizens, especially human service practitioners, in reducing institutional racism. Good communities can be created, communities that support cultural diversity and social support systems which respond to the needs of all cultural, racial, and ethnic groups.

Barriers for Women

Communities often place women in a disadvantageous position and impose burdens upon them which restrict their full participation in community life. Communities that are successful in improving environmental and social conditions for women are more competent than those which are not so successful. A number of special burdens or barriers for women have been identified in the feminist literature

(Choldin, 1985; Mazey & Lee, 1983). The spatial organization of the community may place restrictions on women whose primary role is motherhood as well as on women who are employed outside the home. The location of workplace in relation to residence may limit the employment opportunities of women or impose heavy time burdens and transportation difficulties (Ferguson and Carlson, 1990; Shellenbarger, 1993). The scarcity of public services such as day care centers and transportation limits the opportunities for women employed out of the home. Limited transportation systems force many women to use cars for transporting children to school and recreational activities, thus curtailing their other personal, professional, and community involvements. Discrimination in organizational policies and practices continues to limit the roles of women and their participation in workplace benefits and community activities. Communities vary in the extent to which workplaces provide equal opportunities for women in regard to hiring, pay equity, and advancement.

Some groups of women, such as the elderly, female heads of households, low-income women, and young suburban mothers, have special problems in urban communities. Elderly women in both suburbs and central cities are often restricted in their activities by inadequate transportation, isolation from the broader community, fear of crime, or the location of health and social services away from the neighborhood. Employed women who head households with children are especially disadvantaged in urban communities in terms of transportation to work and job choices. Low-income women have special problems in urban areas because of the lack of affordable goods and services and the poor quality of rental housing.

In some instances, however, women in inner-city neighborhoods have health and social services more readily available in their local communities than suburban women. The suburban community is not always the ideal environment described in the mass media. Some young suburban mothers are restricted to a social life within the immediate neighborhood, especially if they lack cars. Social life becomes localized for women with young children, even if they are of elementary school age. This is especially true for female-headed families, often described as "latch key" households, with women employed out of the home and school-age children left unsupervised.

Barriers for the Physically and Mentally Disabled

The special problems of people with physical and mental disabilities have been identified in the Americans with Disabilities Act of

1990. These problems come from discrimination on the part of individuals and the actions of social institutions. The act noted that "discrimination against individuals with disabilities persists in such crucial areas as employment, housing, public accommodations, education, transportation, communication, recreation, institutionalization, health services, voting, and access to public services." Some communities have demonstrated competence in removing some of these barriers by policies and programs directed toward assuring "equality of opportunity, full participation, independent living, and economic self-sufficiency for such individuals," including alteration in architectural designs, provision of special transportation arrangements and facilities, and development of job training programs. These community efforts are now supported by a federal act which mandates the elimination of discrimination against individuals with disabilities. The act establishes standards for the workplace, an area where the need for equal opportunity in employment matters is great, and for which local communities have had little influence.

Barriers for Gay Men and Lesbians

Gay and lesbian people represent a community of identification which is discriminated against in many local communities. Some communities view gay and lesbian persons as belonging to a minority group, a group which is often denied civil liberties, excluded from social participation, subject to violence and stigma, and not provided equal employment opportunities. In these communities, efforts are made to overcome discrimination against members of the gay and lesbian community through legal means, voluntary associations, and the media. In other communities gay and lesbian people are viewed as members of a deviant group, whose lifestyles and behavior are deemed to be deviant and unacceptable. In such communities, discrimination may be legal, and there is likely to be a high level of homophobia (Longres, 1990). For example, in 1992 the voters in the State of Colorado approved legislation against gay rights. However, the State Supreme Court found that the "law appeared to violate the equal protection clause of the U.S. Constitution" and required that a "compelling interest" be demonstrated before any implementation of the law (Johnson, 1993). At the same time the Colorado communities of Denver, Boulder, and Aspen have ordinances which protect gay and lesbian people from discrimination in relation to jobs and housing.

Barriers to full participation in community affairs by gay and lesbian people appear to be less problematic in some communities. In these communities, some neighborhoods become communities of location for gay and/or lesbian residents. Often the municipal community gains a reputation for being hospitable, accepting, and sensitive to the needs of the gay and lesbian population. This hospitality and/or tolerance is especially evident in certain cities, as well as in some vacation communities in the United States (Kaczor, 1993). At the same time, these communities recognize the diversity of members of a gay or lesbian community, such as variations in social class, ethnic or racial identity, religious affiliation, and lifestyles. Where recognition of diversity is lacking, gay and lesbian advocacy groups have attempted to educate the public. An example of such education is found in the placement of posters in the New York City subway cars, showing actual gay and lesbian people, not models, from various ethnic and professional groups (Elliott, 1993).

Barriers for Cultural and Religious Groups

Discrimination, oppression, and prejudice are related to groups other than those we have just specified. In some communities, white ethnics with southern or eastern European heritage may face barriers in housing and employment. In some communities, membership in some religious groups, such as Catholic or Jewish, is associated with discrimination and prejudice. Sometimes a mix of culture and religion constitutes a barrier to equal opportunity. For example, Soifer (1991) has argued that Jewish people in the United States constitute a cultural-minority group which continues to suffer from anti-Semitism. A major problem for all of these cultural and religious groups is the perpetuation of myths and stereotypes which reinforce negative individual and community attitudes and behaviors towards members of these groups. Knowledge about cultural and religious groups in the community is necessary for social work professionals in order for them to discover special needs and to provide culturally sensitive services.

SOCIAL WORK PRACTICE AND COMMUNITIES

An understanding of various types of communities is useful for practice at both "macro" and "micro" levels of social work intervention. Practice at the "macro" level involves professional roles in changing organizations and communities through community development, social planning, social action, social welfare administration, social policy development, and social program evaluation (Netting, Kettner, McMurtry, 1993). Community practice in particular involves tasks of developing cohesion among community groups, helping people improve their capacities for performing various community roles, mobilizing people and resources to improve social conditions and services, and promoting the interests of disadvantaged groups within the community (Chess and Norlin, 1988). Textbooks on social work practice at the macro level emphasize the need for understanding communities as the context of practice, the target of intervention, or both (Cox et al., 1987). A useful framework for conceptualizing communities in relation to practice is presented by Netting, Kettner, McMurtry (1993). This framework includes a number of tasks the social worker should complete in order to gain knowledge focused on the following topics.

- Identifying the target population
- Determining community characteristics
- Recognizing differences (oppression, discrimination)
- Identifying structure (locations of power, resource availability, resource control, service delivery)

Knowledge about these topics can be found throughout various forthcoming chapters of our book, such as the demographic development of communities, social stratification, and the community political, economic, educational, and social welfare and health care systems. Our focus on ecological and social systems perspectives provides a framework which is compatible with the macro practice tasks identified by Netting, Kettner, McMurtry (1993).

Practice at the "micro" or direct-service level seeks to restore, maintain, and enhance the social functioning of individuals, families, and small groups. In working toward these goals the social worker gives attention to the immediate social environment and to the transactional relationships between person(s) and environment. According to Hartman (1989), social workers occupy a unique position between "client and community," as they seek to help people improve their lives and to "overcome their marginality and to become fully functional and rewarded members of their communities." Thus direct social work practice gives attention to person-in-environment and to social change at the community and societal levels of the social environment. Most often, then, practice in direct service agencies involves practice at both the "micro" and "macro" levels of intervention.

Competent practice at "micro" and "macro" levels requires that the social worker understand communities as a major element of the social environment. Knowledge about communities is needed for assessing the impact of the environment on the individual's social development and behavior. The social worker must know about resources located in the various communities which make up the client's "personal community," and about community conditions which may constitute barriers to an individual's personal and social opportunities. For effective practice at community, organizational, and policymaking levels, a working knowledge of the processes of community development, social integration, and social conflict is needed. An understanding of these processes is enhanced through knowledge about locality-based communities as well as communities of identification and interest.

COMMUNITIES AND THE MISSION OF SOCIAL WORK

There seems to be little consensus within the social work profession as to the proper balance between "micro" and "macro" practice in serving individuals, groups, organizations, communities, or society. As already noted, Hartman (1989) argues for practice which involves work at the boundaries of the client and the community. Specht (1989) contends that social work places too much emphasis on the practice of popular "psychotherapies," and he urges a return to the "true" mission of social work, the building of "a meaning, a purpose, and a sense of obligation for the community, not one-by-one. It is only by creating a community that we establish a basis for commitment, obligation, and social support." Through the use of groups, community associations, and voluntary associations, Specht urges "a vision of social work that enables us to direct our energies to the creation of healthy communities. This is how we make healthy people." In a contrasting view, Wakefield (1992) takes the position that Specht's vision of the mission of social work is too narrow, and that the mission appropriately includes psychotherapeutic interventions. At the other extreme, Saxton (1991) responds to Specht's position by claiming that "The original vision of social work is not, as Specht implies, a perfected community. The mission of social work is an enhanced quality of life for individuals." This rather complex debate over the mission of social work and its practice methods is ongoing, but there is a general recognition that knowledge about organizations and communities as a part of the social environment is essential for both "micro" and "macro" levels of professional practice.

PRACTICE WITH POPULATIONS-AT-RISK

Professional practice in the human services requires knowledge and appreciation of cultural and social diversity. This provides a foundation for practice which is sensitive to "the experiences, needs, and responses of people who have been subjected to institutionalized forms of oppression" (CSWE, 1988). These persons have been labeled "populations-at-risk" and include, but are not limited to, such groups as people of color, women, gay and lesbian persons, and groups distinguished by age, ethnicity, culture, class, religion, and physical and mental ability. Whenever possible, we introduce knowledge about community related to these groups.

In recent years there has been an attempt to define feminist social work and to incorporate a feminist perspective into practice (Nes and Iadicola, 1989; Bricker-Jenkins and Hooyman, 1986; Van Den Bergh and Cooper, 1986). For example, Nes and Iadicola (1989) have examined three models of feminism (liberal, radical, socialist) in order to ascertain their implications for social work practice. These authors have identified some of the major differences in feminist perspectives and have matched them to models of social work practice. Some aspects of these perspectives are related to communities, such as the nature of the social order, the nature of inequality, views of a good society, and strategies to achieve a good society. The reader familiar with feminist perspectives will have a basis for incorporating ideas about gender issues presented in this book into their overall understanding of communities and feminist social work practice.

REVIEW

Three major types of communities are identified as locality-based, identificational/interest, and personal. Reference is made to the ecological and social systems perspectives which guide the examination of these three community types. The idea of community competence provides the central framework for consideration of communities. One of the essential characteristics of a competent community is that it acts effectively for the benefit of its members. These actions lead to the creation of a good community, one which has opportunities for rewarding social relationships; for sustenance, employment, housing, education, health, and social services; and for individual participation in community decision making. Such a community provides for social control, conflict management, and desirable living conditions for all its citizens.

Competent communities provide care for those who cannot care for themselves. They attempt to reduce institutional racism, sexism, and homophobia, promote cultural and racial diversity, and create equal opportunity and support for the civil rights of all citizens. Special efforts are made in these communities to reduce the barriers to the quality of life and the full participation of groups often discriminated against, including, but not restricted to, members of ethnic, racial, cultural, and religious groups, women, physically and mentally disabled persons, and gay and lesbian persons.

The practice of social work at both "micro" and "macro" levels of intervention is briefly discussed, as the purpose of understanding communities is to assure that the social worker has knowledge about this part of the social environment. Special attention is given to the need for this knowledge as a context for practice with populations-at-risk.

PREVIEW

Locality-based communities constitute our beginning point of reference for understanding communities as social units. We start with an overview of ecological and social systems perspectives about communities in Chapter 2. An ecological perspective guides Part Two of the book, which includes the presentation of the demographic development of communities in Chapter 3, the social stratification of communities in Chapter 4, neighborhoods in American communities in Chapter 5, and the emergence of social class and ethnic minority neighborhoods in Chapter 6. Content on communities of identification and interest is woven into these chapters.

Park Three of the book is based on a social systems perspective, with attention given in Chapter 7 to the relationships of locality-based and identificational communities to voluntary associations. Locality-based communities serve as the basic frame of reference for examination of social welfare and health care, education, economic, and political community subsystems in Chapters 8 through 11. Part Four includes a discussion of community processes of social conflict and social integration in Chapters 12 and 13. Finally, Chapter 14 concludes the book with a consideration of the implications of knowledge about communities for social work practice.

Newspaper feature articles are included in selected chapters of the book as vehicles for student exercises (Fellin, 1992). These news reports have been included to allow the student to gain skills in applying concepts about communities to "real world" events. The reports were selected in order to raise issues for discussion and application, not to promote a particular point of view. The news reports are intended to "provide insights that complement and give substance to the scientific literature" (Bachrach, 1990). They contain information and opinions from people not accessible and/or not included in studies conducted by academic researchers, and are intended to introduce a "human interest" dimension to the student's learning. These reports form a basis for testing one's understanding of the conceptual frameworks through the application of this knowledge to community "cases."

SUGGESTED READINGS

Cottrell, Leonard S. (1983). "The Competent Community." In Roland Warren and Larry Lyon, eds., *New Perspectives on the American Community.* (1983). Homewood, IL: Dorsey Press.

Cox, Fred, John Erlich, Jack Rothman, and John Tropman, eds. (1987). *Strategies of Community Organization.* Itasca, IL: F. E. Peacock Publishers.

Hartman, Ann (1989). "Still Between Client and Community." *Social Work* 34:5 (September).

Nes, Janet A. and Peter Iadicola (1989). "Toward a Definition of Feminist Social Work." *Social Work* 34:1 (January).

Netting, F. E., P. M. Kettner, S. L. McMurtry (1993). *Social Work Macro Practice.* New York: Longman.

Rivera, F. G. and J. L. Erlich (1992). *Community Organizing in a Diverse Society.* Boston: Allyn and Bacon.

Specht, Harry (1990). "Social Work and the Popular Psychotherapies." *Social Service Review* 64:3.

Van Den Bergh, N. and L. B. Cooper (1986). *Feminist Visions for Social Work.* Washington: National Association of Social Workers Press.

Wakefield, Jerome C. (1992). "Why Psychotherapeutic Social Work Don't Get No Re-Specht." *Social Service Review* 66:1.

Warren, Roland (1983). "The Good Community: What Would It Be?" In Roland Warren and Larry Lyon, eds., *New Perspectives on the American Community.* (1983). Homewood, IL: Dorsey Press.

EXERCISE

Use the various definitions of community in the text to describe the Ravendale area. Draw from this news report to illustrate ways in which the residents have displayed features of a competent community. Identify some of the social conditions in Ravendale which enhance or hinder community competence.

DETROIT GHETTO AREA TRIES SELF-RELIANCE, AND LEARNS ITS LIMITS

By John Bussey

The talk over a dinner of fried chicken, green beans, and coffee, served in a grade-school gymnasium, was awkward. The 100 or so neighbors gathered here barely knew each other. On this cold winter night in 1986, they were drawn together by a free meal and fear.

A slight man in a tie and jacket, a preacher, approached the podium. "I have a vision," said Eddie Edwards, "that Ravendale is going to be a jewel of this city. . . . We've been operating under a welfare mentality too long. *We* must do something to change the conditions of our neighborhoods."

A colleague took the microphone and thundered at the audience: "You let us raise another generation that can't function, and it's all over. The burden is on *you*. Our national government doesn't know what to do."

It had the self-conscious ring of a Republican prayer meeting, all this talk of self-reliance. But this was a different world: the east side of Detroit, a violent, drug-soaked ghetto, a paradigm of America's urban pathology. More by necessity than design, Mr. Edwards was heeling to the new conservative ethic in America. He was challenging the poor to help themselves. Here, long before George Bush began to ballyhoo his "thousand points of light," one of them began to flicker.

The black minister that night christened the surrounding 38 blocks "Ravendale." He beseeched its residents to organize to fight crime, find jobs for the unemployed, and clean up the streets. Ravendale, he said, would transform itself, demonstrate to other ghettos how to do the same.

The audience applauded enthusiastically. "My roots are here," said Herbie Crowell, a retired teacher sitting near the back of the room. "I intend to stay and fight."

Two years later, a return to Ravendale shows the potential—and the limits—of self-help in the ghetto. The community has achieved remarkable things. But even as the poor have willingly manned the dike against blight, the tide has risen relentlessly.

Asked whether Ravendale has changed at bottom, Greg Smith, bundled in his Detroit police overcoat, pauses and then tells a story. It is after midnight on a recent Friday, and his squad car has been patrolling Ravendale's ill-lit streets.

"We had a radio call a couple months ago about a four-year-old child crying on a porch," he begins. "We arrived and, sure enough, there's this kid crying. We asked him—kiddingly— 'Where did your mother go, to buy crack cocaine?' He said, 'No. She went to buy some weed.' He actually knew the difference," the policeman said, shaking his head. "It was unbelievable."

*   *   *

Hands jammed in his pockets against the cold, Eddie Edwards walks down Camden Street and takes a head count. "I think we've had a significant impact on this block," the 32-year-old minister says, motioning to two freshly painted houses and one completely renovated home, painted a cheerful blue. "Contrast that to this block," he says, crossing the street, "where we don't have block leadership. Eight abandoned houses."

They sit, broken and scavenged relics of a once-healthy blue-collar neighborhood. Twenty years ago, first- and second-generation immigrants from Belgium, Germany, and Italy owned and lived in these houses. The newcomers were drawn by jobs in the auto plants and aspired to the middle class. That was before economic collapse and white flight cut this city's population in half. Now a gray, two-story home sits vacant, its door ajar, broken glass lining the upstairs window like jagged teeth. Nearby, other houses sag in abandonment.

"Our goal is to let the residents take back control," says Mr Edwards. "That's what makes it important: getting people mentally ready to accept responsibility."

The minister, a soft-spoken man who used to work for the phone company, is the fulcrum in Ravendale, the leader critical to its self-help campaign. He grew up in Detroit, and was ordained at the Fountain of Truth Missionary Baptist Church on the East Side. Intense and deliberate, he resembles nothing so much as a corporate administrator, a man who knows the virtue of patience. He founded a youth ministry called Joy of Jesus and, in 1983, moved it into a boarded-up Catholic church in Ravendale. Thus began his campaign.

"If we come in as a church and say, 'You are somebody,' people will start looking up instead of down, and when they start looking up, they'll start getting up," he says. "I don't think my expectations were too high or my vision too lofty. Frankly, I'm just astounded with what we've accomplished."

Simply reaching residents in this fractured community was challenge enough, as a reporter's visits to the project in 1987 and 1988 revealed. Several chicken and spaghetti dinners followed that one two years ago, as Mr. Edwards and Gene Kempski, a former bank manager who became the program's operations chief, coaxed residents out of their homes.

The first objective was to find leaders from what remained of the stable working class in Ravendale, a name the organizers found on old subdivision papers. Willie Howard, an inspector at a Chrysler plant, stepped forward. So did Toni McIlwain, a secretary and former welfare mother; Ed Bell, a drug counselor; Fred Williams, a steel factory supervisor; and a handful of others, employed and unemployed.

Their efforts would receive little attention from the broader public. Yet their simple goals were dramatic indeed for a community so isolated and steeped in fear.

Simple Wants

The group, mostly black, began plotting strategy on Saturday mornings in a classroom at the ministry. In the evenings, volunteers went door-to-door to talk with Ravendale's 4,000 residents. The survey revealed simple desires: more jobs, less crime, somewhere to shop. "I see parents being parents," a resident called out at one community gathering. "I see a community free of fear," said another, to much applause.

Unifying symbols began to appear: Ravendale bumper stickers, T-shirts and buttons. "Ravendale: A Community of Unity," read one banner. "Catch the Vision," another. Mr. Edwards kept urging his volunteers: "We've got to do it ourselves."

At meetings, residents would self-consciously stand to report on progress in their committees. Mr. Williams, head of the transportation committee, hoped to find a used bus for the neighborhood. Mr. Bell, in charge of security, planned a Little League; Ms. McIlwain hoped to form new block clubs—small groups of neighbors who watch out for one another's homes.

By the summer of 1987, the project had visible momentum. Fliers and a regular community newsletter went out, cajoling residents to join up. Ms. McIlwain even paraded through the streets with a bullhorn, announcing Saturday meetings.

"A lot of people are afraid to start block clubs," she said one afternoon, as she walked door-to-door drumming up support. "They're afraid their neighbors may be the ones ripping them off." She climbed the broken steps in front of one house and knocked. A man answered but, frightened, wouldn't open the door. The conversation was shouted, his response barely audible. Finally Ms. McIlwain yelled: "I can't give you this paper with the door shut." The man, in his 30s, relented and opened it a crack—but kept the chain-lock fastened.

Some Gains Achieved

Efforts like this paid off. Twenty-three of the community's 38 blocks now have block clubs. After Mr. Edwards complained, the city raided crack houses in Ravendale, tore down some abandoned homes, and towed away 75 junked cars littering the streets. Leaders such as Willie Howard, head of the beautification committee, helped organize neighborhood events, clear alleyways, plant shrubs, and sell security lighting. And Habitat for Humanity, a national housing group, pitched in, renovating three homes.

Volunteers painted 32 houses with donated paint, trained the unemployed for interviews, and found jobs for 150 of them—an extraordinary feat in this economically gutted city. Mr. Bell's Little League was a smash hit: 120 youngsters signed up the first summer, 150 the next.

The group eventually got the bus, which volunteers on Mr. Williams' transportation committee use to drive the elderly to stores. The ministry got a health clinic to provide medical service on a payment plan, and helped persuade the police department to build a "ministation" in the neighborhood.

So, thanks to the Ravendale program, Cynthia Doakes, 36, a clerk in the city water department and the divorced mother of two, has a new home. She's renting the blue house on Camden Street that the ministry bought and renovated with the help of a local church. Inside, the house is spotless. "The furnace is new, the carpeting is new—this is an answered prayer," Ms. Doakes says.

And, thanks to the program, Luther Johnson, a clean-cut 24-year-old, has a career. Two years ago he was in a dead-end job at a fried chicken restaurant earning $120 a week. Then he came to a Ravendale employment clinic. "The first day, I came up here and was chewing gum, had on gym shoes, no tie," he says. "They chewed me out. I hate ties. Now I know that sometimes you have to wear one."

The clinic helped him land a job with a maintenance company. Two years and several promotions later, Mr. Johnson is earning four times his old salary and talking about owning his own company one day. His future, he says, is "very bright."

Little Outside Support

Despite its visible gains, the Ravendale project has existed hand-to-mouth, threatened daily by financial collapse and physical exhaustion. There wasn't the groundswell support Mr. Edwards had hoped for. Coaxing initiative out of third-generation welfare families proved more difficult than he had expected. Mr. Kempski, his assistant, notes: People "would come out and eat the spaghetti and chicken, but when you have a project, the folks all go home."

There was little but piecemeal response from city hall. Neighborhood Renaissance, Inc., promised hundreds of thousands of dollars of support in the exciting early days. But the group, now more an adviser than a fund raiser, scraped together barely enough money to pay Mr. Kempski's modest salary and a few program expenses.

Few area businesses and churches have chipped in. St. Ignatius, a Catholic church, has no presence in the project, even though it stands just across the street from Joy of Jesus. St. Ignatius has its own problems. As crime and drugs moved into the neighborhood, white parishioners moved out, and now the local diocese plans to close the church.

"I drive down these streets and say, 'Can we really expect these people to turn this around?'" says Ray Lubien, a deacon. "It's like a gas candle that's running out of gas: The flame just keeps getting smaller and smaller."

Burdening the Leaders

The burden of Ravendale's "renaissance" fell back on a half-dozen community leaders. But how much could Mr. Edwards realistically expect from volunteers who also had home and work responsibilities? At a leadership retreat in the fall of 1987, a weary Willie Howard complained: "Every time people need something—from a toothpick to a step ladder—they come to me."

Twelve people initially signed up to work on the employment committee, but soon only three were showing up for meetings. Mr. Williams once convened a meeting of his transportation committee and found only his wife, Mr. Edwards, and Mr. Kempski attending. Distressed by the lack of foot soldiers for the cause, some key organizers left. One quit after a tiff with Mr. Edwards. Another was lost to crack.

As for Mr. Howard—well, he simply got tired. Raised in the tenements of Detroit's lower east side, Mr. Howard, now 47 years old, was the first black on his block in Ravendale in 1973. He pushed his three children through high school and into college—and watched his neighborhood decline. The Ravendale program inspired him. Soon he was juggling assignments on six different neighborhood projects.

Wearing a crucifix that hangs from his neck, Mr. Howard sits at the kitchen table of his small, well-kept home and opens file folders of Ravendale fliers and surveys he prepared. "I found myself going to three or four meetings a week," he says. "There was a lot of talk, talk, talk. But I didn't see any force of people getting on the bandwagon. The organization is beautiful, but I can't burden myself with the problems of the world and worry about my problems too."

One day last year, he stopped going to meetings.

Staying Idle

Others share his sense of futility. Among them are those who worked to find Jesse Simmons a job at McDonald's

Mr. Simmons, a short-tempered 20-year-old who dropped out of high school, lost that job in record time. His supervisor asked him to get his shoulder-length hair cut, "and I didn't want to," he says between basketball games at the ministry gym. "I'm not going to get my hair cut for any job. I'll get my hair cut when I want to." He's still unemployed.

So is Peggy Taylor. Dressed in a red sweat suit, the welfare grandmother sits on a folding chair in her run-down home on Maiden Street. At 52 she seems steeped in the welfare culture; she lacks the confidence, the skill, and the momentum to find a job. "I don't want to scrub floors or do any domestic work," she says. "I don't want that."

Last summer, Ravendale residents volunteered to paint Ms. Taylor's house. Their morale sunk when they found three men—her sons and a nephew—on a couch watching television, ignoring the workers outside.

There is little solace, too, for those who hope for safer streets. Crime in Ravendale remains violent and indiscriminate. A few months ago, a narcotics cop was shot while raiding a suspected crack house. A couple days later, someone fired a shot—no one seems to know why—through the front window of Diana Johnson's home on Elmdale Street.

The bullet made a clean, nickel-size hole in the window, traveled across the living room, where the family was gathered, and slammed into a wall, leaving chips of blue plaster scattered over the hardwood floor. While a police officer with a flashlight searched the backyard, a near-hysterical Ms. Johnson exclaimed to a visitor: "I don't know who would do this. All we do is go to church and sit in the house."

Hope for "Little Miracles"

Mr. Kempski, a short, indefatigable and ever-optimistic man, acknowledges the pace of progress in Ravendale hasn't lived up to predictions. Family chaos was more widespread than he expected, contributions from outside sources less forthcoming. Most of the money for the program has been raised through Joy of Jesus or donated by religious groups like World Vision. It is the ministry's small paid staff—not the residents—keeping the project alive.

"You can be in work like this and feel alone," says Mr. Kempski. "Evil is moving faster than you are and it's overtaking the kids. But it's the little miracles I look at—changing people's lives. If you can condition yourself to be satisfied with the little miracles, then you can stay here, you can do this."

Mr. Kempski counts the self-help project about half complete, the chief task—mobilizing the community—already achieved. Full success will come, he says, when residents take over the administration and Mr. Edwards can move his campaign to a new neighborhood.

Even by optimistic estimates, though, that day is a good way off. For the social tide in Ravendale, as in so many inner-city neighborhoods, runs against the organizers. Sixty-nine homes stood empty and crumbling in Ravendale two years ago. Community members helped rebuild nine. The blight spread nonetheless. While they were renovating those nine, an additional thirteen were abandoned.

CHAPTER 2

Systems Perspectives for Understanding Communities

In this chapter we examine basic concepts of ecological systems and social systems, two different but complementary frameworks for understanding communities. These systems perspectives establish a basis for understanding the structure and processes of locality-based communities. Both perspectives contribute to our knowledge of ways in which social interactions of individuals, groups, and organizations are patterned within a community. The application of systems models to communities involves consideration of the various social units which make up a community—that is, "(1) all individuals enacting community roles; (2) all of those social groups and other such social units that enact or perform community-related functions; and (3) all formal organizations . . . that perform community-related functions" (Chess and Norlin, 1988).

COMMUNITY AS AN ECOLOGICAL SYSTEM

Human ecology provides an interesting theoretical perspective for examining a community as a system. From an ecological standpoint, community may be defined as: "a structure of relationships through which a localized population provides its daily requirements" (Hawley, 1950). This definition is grounded in Hawley's definition of ecology as "the study of the relation of populations to their environment."

The focus of this definition is on "spatial organization," that is, "the distribution of people and services operating in a system of interdependence." It also implies an organizational feature commonly described as a "division of labor," the interaction of occupational groups and technology in a stratification structure which results in interdependence of the parts of the community and between communities (Hawley, 1950; 1986).

The community as an ecological system operates at two levels, the biotic (subsocial) and the social. As in plant and animal ecology, a pattern of interdependence develops among humans who "share a common habitat" (Poplin, 1979). These patterns or relationships at the biotic level are not considered to be deliberate or rationally determined but are viewed as impersonal and symbiotic. Such patterns can be observed in a community structure which is developed through the process of competition. This underlying structure of a community provides a foundation for a social level of organization, involving social relationships which can be described in terms of consensus and communication.

The ecologist's definition of competition is somewhat different from the common use of the term. This view of competition maintains that since groups and institutions within a community depend on one another a symbiosis must develop, that is, a living together. This development comes from a "cooperative competition," which allows for an accommodation to the interests of diverse groups rather than the elimination of groups through a destructive competitive process (Poplin, 1979). A major area of competition in communities is over the use of land, as individuals, groups, and social institutions seek what might be called an "advantage of place" for commercial, industrial, institutional, and residential purposes. Social units are described as dominant when they have the power to control the use of the most valued land in a community. In addition to competition, a number of other processes are associated with an ecological perspective of community. These include processes such as centralization, concentration, segregation, invasion, and succession (McKenzie, 1926; Poplin, 1979).

Centralization describes a clustering of institutions and services in a central location, such as a business district or a transportation or communication center. Such centralization in the early development of a central city leads to its domination of the surrounding hinterland. The concept of decentralization describes the process by which individuals or organizations move out from a central location, for example, movements of businesses to new suburban shopping areas.

Concentration describes the influx of individuals, especially through migration, into an urban area. The process of segregation describes how individuals, groups, and institutions, distinguished by characteristics such as race, ethnicity, social class, or religion, locate in separate physical locations. Segregation is an ongoing process whereby groups isolate themselves from one another, as in the development of white suburban neighborhoods. When one group moves into an area occupied by a distinctively separate group—e.g., African Americans into white neighborhoods, business into residential areas—this is called invasion. The term *succession* is used to describe the state of the area once invasion is completed.

Early ecologists in the Chicago School, Park, Burgess, and McKenzie (1925), believed that ecological processes led to predictable patterns of land use, spatial distribution, and community organization. These patterns were described in terms of concentric circles, or zones. Five zones were identified: central business district, zone of transition, zone of independent working men's homes, zone of better residences, and commuters' zone (suburban residential areas). Describing the spatial organization of a community in terms of zones or sectors highlights the heterogeneity and homogeneity of urban areas (Choldin, 1985). Some zones attract homogeneous population groups. Ecologists label these zones "natural areas"; examples include skid rows, Chinatowns, rooming house districts, industrial areas, and ethnic neighborhoods. These areas are seen as "natural" because they are unplanned and result from the process of selection and competition related to land use. Research on communities since the development of the concentric zone hypothesis indicates that most growth in cities has not continued to develop in a concentric zone pattern. Nonetheless, "natural" communities with common culture and concerns continue to form within the urban community.

APPLICATION OF AN ECOLOGICAL PERSPECTIVE

An ecological perspective allows us to describe the community in terms of social geography, the distribution of people, organizations, and resources in space. This perspective calls attention to the physical layout of the community, that is, the location of residences, industrial units, commercial and business areas, services, churches, hospitals, recreational areas, social agencies, and schools. It allows for the observation of changes in the use of space, in the distribution of people, and the movements of people over time. The concepts of centralization, invasion, succession, and their measurement are used to describe these changes.

A first step in describing the physical environment and showing the land uses of a community is through mapping. This approach is vividly presented by Suttles (1968) in his classic study on *The Social Order of the Slum*. Suttles' map of the Addams neighborhoods displays an area in Chicago characterized by mixed land use patterns of industry, public housing, private housing, schools, churches, small businesses, playgrounds, and vacant lots. Another map pictures this same area in terms of its ethnic sections as defined by local residents, segregated for the most part into sections of Italians, African Americans, Mexican Americans, and Puerto Ricans. This determination of ethnic boundaries has been called social mapping (Green, 1982), as there is a focus on the cultural characteristics of geographic areas of a community.

Another approach to mapping the community is to identify various kinds of boundaries within a community, such as school districts, health districts, census tracts, religious congregation boundaries, social agency service boundaries, and subcommunities with names. For example, the city of Chicago is divided up into seventy-six community areas, each with a name designation (Taub et al., 1984). For purposes of delivering mental health services, communities have been divided into catchment areas, defining service boundaries for local community mental health centers.

An example of using an ecological approach related to social work practice is found in the development of mobility skills training for people in need of community mental health services (Taylor and Taylor, 1989). Mobility skills involve the ability to move around freely in the community and to arrive at one's destination. Training in these skills begins with a map, followed by the development of cognitive maps, that is, mental representations and associations of how to get to places, using signs, buildings, streets, bus lines, landmarks, and so forth. Such training is expected to facilitate the client's access to and use of services through mastery of travel within a community.

A somewhat different use of mapping is illustrated in the use of an ecological perspective to locate neighborhoods at high risk for child maltreatment, such as child neglect, child abuse, and child sexual abuse (Zuravin and Taylor, 1987). In this application, data on incidence rates are used to present "incidence mapping," "a clear visual impression of distribution patterns by displaying on a map the incidence rate for each specific subdivision of a larger geographic area." One technique of presentation is to print the actual rate on each part of the geographic area; another is to identify areas by color or by geometric pattern. An alternative way of presenting data on high risk is to use spot mapping, which "identifies distribution patterns by placing a dot on the map at the specific address of each incident." A major purpose of mapping in this illustration is for service planning at the community level.

COMMUNITY AS A SOCIAL SYSTEM

Social systems theory provides another useful framework for understanding American communities. While the theory is unusually complex, its major concepts guide us in identifying the structural and functional attributes of a wide variety of communities. We begin with the idea that a social system involves the interaction of two or more social units, that is, the interactions of individuals in social groups such as families, neighborhood groups, or peer groups, and the interactions within and among social groups and social organizations. It is therefore important to identify the particular social system we wish to understand. In the instance of a locality-based community, we are interested in understanding how the system is functioning. This involves examination of the various subsystems within a community, such as the economic, political, educational, health, and social welfare systems. We seek to understand the activities of the various social units which make up the subsystems in order to determine how well these subsystems are carrying out their community functions. The major social units within each of these subsystems are formal organizations, such as businesses, governmental units, churches, schools, health care organizations, and social welfare agencies. Informal groups, including families, social groups, and groups attached to formal organizations, also contribute to the functioning of community subsystems and the community as a whole.

An important feature of social systems theory is the specification of the boundaries of the system in relation to its environment. To illustrate, a central city or other municipality in a metropolitan area may be defined as a community system, with boundaries which are likely to be both geographical and psychological. The environment includes other municipalities as well as state, regional, and national entities with which the municipal community interacts. One of the central functions of such a community system is boundary maintenance. A community engages in activities which will assure its continuance as a separate entity or social organization. Boundary maintenance is exemplified by physical boundaries and legal, political boundaries. For communities of interest, there are social boundaries, such as membership criteria that are related to lifestyle, social class, ethnicity, or racial identification.

A second feature of a systems model concerns the interaction of the system with "outside" systems beyond its own boundary, such as other communities and society. This outside system, designated as the suprasystem, provides inputs into a community system and receives outputs. Thus this interaction provides for inputs into the system, such as culture, money, material resources, and information (Cress and Norlin, 1988). Outputs may be thought of as the results of the interactions within a system, such as the goals of a community or its subsystems. These goals are related to employment, health, safety and security, social welfare, education, housing, and other indicators of quality of life (Cress and Norlin, 1988).

The concepts of input and output of systems are related to the way in which interactions of the units within a social system are patterned. Classical social systems theory, particularly as developed by Talcott Parsons (1951), describes these patterns in terms of systems functions. Patterns having to do with the system's external activities serve adaptive functions and goal attainment functions. Internal activities are viewed in terms of integrative functions and pattern-maintenance/tension-management functions. It is useful to define these terms, as they represent problems a community must solve in order to maintain itself.

Goal attainment is defined by Parsons (1960) as the "gratification of the units of the system." This function deals with the problem of "How to achieve the community's task output of improving the quality of life of its citizens through the provision of facilities and services that will help satisfy common needs and cope with common problems" (Cress and Norlin, 1988). Adaptation is the "manipulation of the environment in the interests of goal attainment," that is, on gaining the necessary resources for the operation of the system. This function focuses on the problem of "How to optimize community goal attainment by modifying the suprasystem or, if necessary, by modifying community structures and goals" (Cress and Norlin, 1988). Integration is the "attachment of member units to each other." This function relates to the problem of "How to optimize satisfaction of the community's maintenance outputs" (Cress and Norlin, 1988). Pattern maintenance involves dealing with the malintegration of the units of the system. This function responds to the problem of maintaining the community in relation to its changing internal environment.

Systems functions are often labeled "task functions" and "mainte-nance functions." Task functions of adaptation and goal attainment involve relationships with the outside environment through the econ-omy and the polity. Integration functions occur in the juridical sys-tem, and pattern-maintenance/tension-management is handled by groups such as the family and educational and cultural units of the community. Communities as systems must relate to changes within and without the system and maintain themselves through systems functions. From a systems perspective, a community constantly seeks a level of stability or equilibrium. Thus when the various subsystems of the community change there is an impact on the total system. When the task or maintenance functions of the subsystems of a com-munity are not carried out successfully, the result is a lack of goal attainment which may lead to community disorganization.

APPLICATION OF A SOCIAL SYSTEMS PERSPECTIVE

In applying social systems concepts to locality-based communities, Warren (1963) specified five functions which a community performs: production/distribution/consumption, socialization, social control, social participation, and mutual support. Our examination of these functions will focus on the municipal community, which is com-posed of subsystems that carry out these major "locality relevant" functions. The major subsystems, sometimes referred to as social in-stitutions, include the economy, government, education, religion, and health and social welfare. These subsystems carry out community functions mainly through formal organizations, such as corporations, governmental units, schools, churches, medical care facilities, social welfare agencies, and voluntary associations. In addition to these for-mal structures in the community, there are numerous primary groups that engage in social activities on a daily basis and often contribute to the performance of community functions. These primary groups in-clude family and other household groups, friendship groups, kinship groups, neighborhood groups, peer groups, self-help groups, and in-formal social club groups.

Let us consider further the five community functions identified by Warren. Production/distribution/consumption activities in urban communities require a high degree of specialization of employment (division of labor) and the presence of complex bureaucratic organi-zations (e.g., business, industry) and consumption patterns (of goods, services, energy). The daily living of individuals is dependent on the performance of the economic subsystem.

Socialization of individuals and groups involves the impact of culture on personality, the learning of values and behavior, and the patterning of social roles. The family and the school are the most obvious social units contributing to socialization of community members, but other forces—for example, friendship groups, kinship groups, television, radio, movies, newspapers, popular magazines, and books— are also involved in the process.

Social control involves a range of pressures on people to behave according to community and societal norms. These pressures come from a variety of sources, some internal to the individual and some from the social environment. A principal source of social control is the local government, that is, law enforcement agencies, courts, and such "control" arrangements as stop lights, parking meters, and no-smoking signs.

Social participation occurs within both informal primary groups and formal organizations. Social participation includes a wide range of activities within and connected to schools, churches, political parties, social clubs, organizational board memberships, recreational facilities, and fund-raising events.

Mutual support involves assisting people in need when the needs are beyond the capability of the individual, the family, or the household. Mutual support occurs in relation to illnesses which require professional help, family problems requiring professional counseling, learning and behavioral problems of children requiring professional counseling, and economic problems requiring income maintenance programs and financial assistance. A primary source of mutual support consists of health organizations and social welfare agencies. The activities of social workers providing mutual support are not limited to social agencies and health care organizations. Social workers are often involved in government and business sectors through social programs involving employment services, job counseling, money management, and job training; in court services, criminal justice systems, and legal aid services.

Communities interact with other communities, and these external relationships have important implications for the way in which a particular community system maintains its boundaries and its equilibrium. But more importantly, community subsystems interact through their formal organizations with similar social units outside the community. These extracommunity relationships are identified by

Warren (1963) as vertical, in contrast to the horizontal interactions within a community. These types of relationships are illustrated by Warren in regard to mutual support. An example of a typical community unit is a voluntary health association; a unit of horizontal pattern: community welfare council; a unit of a vertical pattern: National Health Association.

COMMUNITY AS AN "ECOLOGY OF GAMES"

Concepts from ecological and social systems theory are combined by Long (1958) in order to create a framework for understanding the local community. Long contends that a local community can be understood as a territorial system within which structured group activities occur. Sets of these activities can be viewed as "games"—for example, "a banking game, a contracting game, a newspaper game, a civic organization game, an ecclesiastical game, and many others." The major games are similar to the community subsystems which carry out the functions cited by Warren (1963), that is, production, socialization, social control, social participation, and mutual support. Drawing from ecological theory, Long suggests that there is no overall coordination of the games in the community; rather, they relate to each other in a symbiotic manner. Thus, the subsystems of the community operate in an ordered but unplanned basis, with the general public deciding whether or not the games are being played well. The social order in the community is maintained because the games have expectations, norms, and rules for their players, not because there is an overall political game which dominates the system. This idea of social order has been elaborated upon by Giamatti (1989) in his book, *Take Time for Paradise: Americans and Their Games.* Giamatti compares communities to sports, noting that they are both "deeply conventional," with established rules and social agreements. Giamatti maintains that when conventions "cohere and are abided by" in communities, we have a city where people choose to live, just as people continue to watch or participate in sports in which the rules are adhered to.

An important question arising from the games analogy is, what game or group links the various games together into the social order of the community? Under Long's formulation, the various games in the community are seen as competing with one another, but they are linked through social interaction of leaders in each of the games. Officeholders and organizational executives have an interest in achieving their organizational goals within their own games, and they recognize that interaction with "players" in other games is important. The leaders in the various games are all influenced by the newspaper game, as it seeks to set the civic agenda, the topics, concerns, and ideas that people talk about, have an investment in, and expect the civic leadership to do something about. While the various games may contribute to the overall order of the whole community, Long suggests that the social game may be the most significant group that integrates all the games. The social game is played by leaders in the various subsystems (games) of the community, through such activities as overlapping board memberships, social standing, and social activities.

The games analogy provides an interesting way of thinking about the goals, functions, and activities of the organizations within the various community subsystems. It helps in assessing the extent to which each of the subsystems functions effectively in a community, using a "keeping score" approach to measure community competence. The games perspective points to ways of understanding the leadership and power structure within a community. Taking the social welfare game as an example, each human service organization can be examined in terms of the part it plays in the social welfare game, what score it receives for services delivered and effectiveness and attainment of social goals, how the organizational leaders within the social welfare field interact with each other, and how the organization relates to welfare coordinating agencies and to other subsystems.

Viewing the community as a social system involving a number of subsystems provides a framework for answering a number of questions about communities. Chapters 7 through 11 will help you to formulate answers to these questions as you apply them to a particular community.

1. To what extent and under what conditions do voluntary associations contribute to the competence of the total community, and what functions do these associations serve for individual citizens?

2. To what extent do the formal organizations within a subsystem of the community articulate with each other and with other subsystems through interorganizational relations?

3. In what ways are community actions, as played out in the various subsystems, influenced by vertical relationships—that is, extra-community influences?

4. How is some degree of integration and social order created and maintained among the subsystems of a community?

5. How is the functioning of community subsystems coordinated or influenced by the power and/or decision-making structure of a community. Under what conditions does one or another subsystem become dominant in a community?

REVIEW

The systems properties of communities direct our attention to the social organization of a community and the processes which relate to stability and change. Two systems perspectives, ecological and social systems, guide our study of communities. The ecological perspective emphasizes the spatial properties of a community, the demographic characteristics of population groups, and the interdependencies which develop within and among communities to assure the requirements of daily living. The social systems perspective demonstrates how a community operates to perform locality relevant functions for its members. The principal focus is on the performance of subsystems, and their formal organizations—such as social welfare agencies, schools, churches, businesses, local governmental units. Norton Long's (1958) framework for analyzing a community as an "ecology of games" provides an interesting way of understanding the functioning of these subsystems.

SUGGESTED READINGS

Giamatti, A. Bartlett (1989). *Take Time for Paradise: Americans and their Games.* New York: Simon and Schuster.

Long, Norton E. (1958). "The Local Community as an Ecology of Games," *American Journal of Sociology* 64:3.

Taylor, Brennan and Ann Taylor (1989). "Social Casework and Environmental Cognition: Mobility Training for Community Mental Health Services," *Social Work* 34:5 (September).

Zuravin, Susan and Ronald Taylor (1987). "The Ecology of Child Maltreatment," *Child Welfare* 66:6 (November/December).

PART TWO

An Ecological Perspective

CHAPTER 3

Demographic Development of Communities

Population size, density, and heterogeneity are the most common demographic characteristics used in describing locality-based communities. The U.S. Bureau of the Census divides each geographical area of a community into census tracts, relatively small units for reporting numbers of residents and for describing other population characteristics, such as race, ethnicity, occupational status, education, and age. Tracts vary in size, depending on the density of population in a given area. Tracks are divided into census blocks. The number of residents in communities is closely associated with the terms we use to describe them, from small to large: villages, towns, cities, metropolitan areas.

POPULATION SIZE

The Bureau of the Census (1990) defines a metropolitan area as "a large population nucleus, together with adjacent communities which have a high degree of economic and social integration with that nucleus." There are three major designations of metropolitan areas: Metropolitan Statistical Areas (MSA), Consolidated Metropolitan Statistical Areas (CMSA), and Primary Metropolitan Statistical Areas (PMSA). When major population shifts occur, the Census Bureau may redefine metropolitan areas by the creation of new boundaries.

Metropolitan Statistical Areas, Consolidated Metropolitan Statistical Areas, and Primary Metropolitan Statistical Areas are defined by
the U.S. Bureau of the Census as follows.

> Each MSA must contain either a place with a minimum population
> of 50,000 or a Census Bureau-defined urbanized area and a total MA
> population of at least 100,000 (75,000 in New England). An MA com-
> prises one or more central counties. An MA also may include one or
> more outlying counties that have close economic and social relation-
> ships with the central county.
>
> In each MSA and CMSA, the largest place and, in some cases, addi-
> tional places are designated as "central cities.".... A few PMSA's do
> not have central cities. The largest central city and, in some cases, up to
> two additional central cities are included in the title of the MA.
>
> If an area that qualifies as an MA has more than one million per-
> sons, primary metropolitan statistical areas (PMSA's) may be defined
> within it. PMSA's consist of a large urbanized county or cluster of coun-
> ties that demonstrates very strong internal economic and social links, in
> addition to close ties to other portions of the larger area. When PMSA's
> are established, the larger area of which they are component parts is
> designated a consolidated metropolitan statistical area (CMSA).

Given these definitions, all communities of the United States can be
defined as located either in metropolitan areas (inside MSA's or
CMSA's) or in non-metropolitan areas (outside MSA's or CMSA's). A
distinction is also made between urban and rural populations. "The
Census Bureau defines 'urban' for the 1990 census as comprising all
territory, population, and housing units in urbanized areas and in
places of 2,500 or more persons outside urbanized areas." Urbanized
areas are defined in order to separate "urban and rural territory, population, and housing in the vicinity of large places. An urban area
comprises one or more places ('central place') and the adjacent densely settled surrounding territory ('urban fringe') that together have a
minimum of 50,000 persons.... In all definitions, the population not
classified as urban constitutes the rural population" (U.S. Bureau of
the Census, 1990).

The concepts of metropolitan area, urbanized area, and rural area
highlight the interrelationships among communities, as well as some
differences between urban and rural areas. Separate communities
within an urban area often have exchanges, communications, and interdependencies with one another. Even the residents of the land outside the metropolis, that is, those who live in the "hinterland," the
"outskirts," or the "rural-urban fringe," have connections with the
metropolitan community, which, in turn, may exert some influence

over them. In recent years some metropolitan areas have expanded to the extent that they coincide with one another. In such instances, the entire area may be called a megalopolis. An example of this type of development has occurred with the metropolitan areas of Washington, D. C., and Baltimore, Maryland, with no rural land separating the two cities (Shribman, 1991).

Communities adjacent to, but outside the boundaries of, a central city can be described as *suburban areas*. These often include self-governing municipalities or townships. A community is defined as a suburb if it is an incorporated municipality within a metropolitan area and is not the central city. While suburbs are ordinarily thought of as being largely residential in nature, they now can include mixed land-use ranging from total residential to total business/industrial. Suburbanization involves development of rings that are hetero-geneous in terms of social class and family composition and varied in terms of age of housing, shopping, entertainment, and job opportu-nities.

The Census Bureau has established some standard categories for community size, such as communities of below 2500, 2500 to less than 50,000, 50,000 to less than 100,000, 100,000 to less than one million, and one million and over. An important factor to take into ac-count in examining small communities with under 50,000 population is the nature of the surrounding area. For example, small communi-ties may be adjacent to a central city in a suburban area, outside sub-urban areas but still in urbanized areas, in non-metropolitan areas, or in rural areas. The concept of small community covers a rather broad range of population sizes, leading to a high degree of variation in these communities in terms of social organization, patterns of social relationships, and collective identity.

The various political, economic, educational, social welfare, and re-ligious activities in communities are likely to be quite different de-pending on population size and the nature of formal and informal organizations within the subsystems. Martinez-Brawley (1990) has pro-vided some interesting perspectives on these differences, not only through her presentation of theoretical frameworks for examining small communities, but also through the use of literary and journalistic sources. Martinez-Brawley persuasively illustrates some of the oppor-tunities in small communities for the development of a sense of be-longing, identification, and connectedness. Her discussion of power, influence, and leadership in the small community suggests the differ-ent ways in which these processes operate in communities of varied sizes. Locality and localism have special, traditional meanings for people in small communities, and population size appears to be an important factor in the creation of the small-town culture.

SIZE AND DENSITY IN COMMUNITIES

Population size and density are closely associated in the central city. Density refers to the number of people within a physical space. Population size and density appear to be related to socio-cultural characteristics of a community. Wirth's (1938) classic work, "Urbanism as a Way of Life," is instructive with regard to how population size, density, and heterogeneity affect community life and the social interactions of individuals. Wirth's theory suggests that an increase in population size leads to greater differentiation and interdependence among people, more secondary than primary contacts, and more freedom from informal social controls. Density is thought to lead to a more complex community structure, a more economically specialized population, and often to residential overcrowding, to "friction and irritation" (Wirth, 1938).

Density of population is frequently associated with negative factors of city life, such as "too much noise, too much dirt, too much pollution," and "an environment that is stress-producing" (Krupat, 1985). Krupat has noted that density may lead to crowding, a "psychological or subjective experience that results from a recognition that one has less space than one desires." Crowding occurs in housing arrangements, in transportation, in use of facilities, in neighborhoods, and in the wider community. Urban inner-city living areas tend to be high in density, in contrast to the low density of suburban neighborhoods. Density and crowding are measured in various ways, such as objective indicators of residential crowding: household size, number of rooms, persons per room, and number of persons per bedroom; area crowding, such as population per square mile, number of single-family homes, and number of dwellings in a structure; subjective residential crowding, such as dislikes for dwelling size, layout, and space; and subjective areal crowding, such as feelings about a crowded area (Newman, 1981).

The question of what effect density and crowding has on people and their social relationships has been of particular interest to social workers, social reformers, and urban sociologists, especially from the turn of the century to the present time (Choldin, 1985; Fischer, 1984). Based on Krupat's (1985) review of the research literature, there appears to be no causal effect between high density and social pathology, but "high-density living definitely has the capacity to be stressful," especially for people living in poverty. Two dimensions of urban life that have attracted special attention for social workers are the adverse living conditions of the poor, and the limits on positive social relationships sometimes imposed upon people in communities of large size and density.

RURAL-URBAN DIFFERENCES

Several theories emerged as sociologists attempted to explain social differences between life in cities in contrast to life in smaller communities. These theories were often characterized by the development of "ideal types" of communities, as illustrated in the work of Tonnies (1887/1957) and his use of the concepts of Gemeinschaft and Gesellschaft, and Redfield's (1947) framework of a folk-urban continuum. Using polar extremes to highlight differences, Tonnies described the small, traditional community (Gemeinschaft) as being like a family, as relying on feelings, propinquity, cooperation, and common will (Choldin, 1985). In contrast, his portrayal of Gesellschaft (society) relationships shows how individuation takes the place of communal ties, isolation develops, and social interactions in the city are based on exchange and conflict. A further example of a theory to explain differences in rural and urban communities is found in the work of Redfield (1947), who believed communities changed in a number of their characteristics as they increased in size and became cities. "Thus while the folk (society) is small, isolated, and homogeneous, the city is large, integrated with the rest of society, and heterogeneous" (Choldin, 1985). Here the large community is seen as having negative features of social disorganization, secularization, and individualization. Where a small community is perceived as attractive, the large community is pictured as unattractive.

As urban communities developed, sociologists highlighted differences between the central cities and suburbs in terms of social interactions and lifestyles (Fischer, 1984). The image of life in the suburbs has been described in terms of homogeneity, with similarities in housing designs (tract houses), lifestyles, consumer habits, recreation, social status, education, etc. But what has actually emerged in some suburbs is a somewhat more differentiated picture, showing a wider degree of diversity in social class, family composition, age structure, and ethnic composition. This contemporary image challenges to some extent the early description of suburban lifestyle, focused on the ranch home, the barbecue grill, the manicured lawn, the station wagon, the coffee klatch, the "within walking distance" elementary school, and the suburban shopping area.

Critics of suburban life have pointed out the negative effects of conformity, preoccupation with children and family (familism), isolation, conservativism, and upward mobility that preclude an attachment to a community. However, it is generally recognized that suburbs *per se* do not mold people into lifestyles; people choose them for a variety of reasons and display a way of life of their own choosing—which, in fact, is often compatible with or similar to the lifestyle of others in the same suburban environment. Some feminist writers challenge this idea, suggesting that the suburbs negatively affect the lives of many women (Fischer, 1984), restricting their freedoms and limiting their employment, recreational, and cultural opportunities.

Perhaps most clear is the fact that changes continue to occur in the suburbs. Life in most suburbs, compared to that in cities, offers fewer opportunities for interactions with people of different ethnic/racial status, greater freedom from crime, and generally more pleasant physical space, housing, and environment (Fischer, 1984; Choldin, 1985). Changes are apparent in terms of the aging of suburban populations, the increasing crime rate in the suburbs, the decline in support for school millages, the increasing proportion of female-headed households, and the rising rate of employment of women outside the home. Still, the suburban community remains an attractive residential area for upward residential mobility.

URBANIZATION

Concepts such as ecology, social organization, and socio-cultural lifestyle can be used to examine the concept of urbanization. A first, common-sense definition of urbanization is an ecological one, that is, an increased proportion of the population in urbanized areas due to population shifts from rural areas to urban areas. Closely associated with these shifts is the fact that the basis for the work life of people has shifted from agricultural to nonagricultural (industrial) employment. Second, as small towns become cities, small cities become large, and new metropolitan areas develop, the social organization of these communities becomes more complex and their interdependencies with other communities, and with state and national levels of government, become intensified. Third, the values, lifestyles, and social relationships of people change as urbanization proceeds.

Central city, suburban, and rural differences can be framed in terms of urbanization. A number of changes took place between 1980 and 1990.

1. The number of Metropolitan Statistical Areas increased.
2. The number of central cities in Metropolitan Statistical Areas which have had a decline in population has increased.
3. The number of metropolitan communities which have central cities of over 50,000 in population has increased.
4. The number of industries, commercial centers, and office centers relocating from central cities to suburban and exurban rural communities has increased.
5. There has been some development of regional authority over some aspects of community life, such as transportation, etc., but no major change in political reorganization.
6. There has been an increase in the separation of population groups, especially in terms of populations segregated residentially by race, ethnicity, and/or social class.
7. Large central cities have higher proportions of people of color, the aged, low income and unemployed residents, and clients of public welfare programs.
8. The number of people moving to rural areas has increased.
9. Generally, the density of the population in central cities remains higher than that of suburban and rural communities. However, some large central cities have lost population and have a lower density than in previous times.

PHASES OF URBANIZATION

A useful conceptualization of urbanization emphasizes the productive functions of communities and the ways in which changes in transportation and communication facilitate production. Urbanization is viewed as "the growing organization of specialists who manufacture goods and provide services that are exchanged for products of surrounding regions" (Hawley, 1978). Changes brought about by urbanization are attributed to "technological advancement." From this framework, urbanization has occurred in three major phases in terms of periods of progress in transportation and communication technology. These phases overlap, with the *city-building* phase (the 1830s to about 1925), the *metropolitan phase* (about 1920 to the present), and the *diffuse phase* (about 1950 and continuing).

The city-building phase was facilitated by developments such as the railway system, steam power and ships, and the telegraph, all of which led to a pattern of urban settlements we now call central cities. During this phase communities grew by migration, by natural growth, and from immigration, and there were major population redistributions, especially migration from rural areas to urban areas. Ecological factors strongly influenced the growth patterns of some major cities and the decline of others in this period, producing the development of closer proximity between employment and residence and the increased division of labor in the workforce.

The beginning of the metropolitan phase of urbanization is considered to be around 1920, since this was the first time that the proportion of the total population living in urban places was over 50 percent. In the same period, the areas surrounding central cities showed increases in population through a process called decentralization. This phase came about due to changes in short-distance transportation (motor vehicles) and communication (telephones), the extension of facilities such as water/sewer systems out from the central city, and new opportunities for residential housing in outlying areas. During this phase there was an increase in the proportion of white-collar jobs in the labor force, and a growth in the scale of organizations. Large-scale organizations developed multi-level operations through branches, and new management-labor relationships resulted from the growth of labor unions. Urbanization in this phase involved a movement of industry out of the central city areas and a movement of large numbers of people to suburban residential areas. This migration to the suburbs, which included high proportions of young families, whites, and high socioeconomic status groups, left many minorities of color, broken families, recent migrants from rural areas and foreign countries, and large groups of low-income people in the central cities. Thus it resulted in suburban areas that were "homogeneous residential colonies" with selective, segregated populations (Hawley, 1978).

With all this movement of people, businesses, and industry to outlying areas, there remained some central control and coordination by major central cities within the metropolitan area. But the central cities become less dominant in the metropolitan area as a diffuse urbanization phase emerges (Fischer, 1984). In this phase the zone of dispersion of people for residential purposes is broadened further to outlying areas of the metropolis, and industry and business continue to disperse—along with major entertainment centers such as super-domes, concert parks, national corporate offices, and hotels—to areas beyond the confines of the central city.

A major decentralization has occurred among some of the nation's largest businesses. Many companies have moved their "back office" people to the suburbs, smaller cities, or the countryside. This white-collar workforce is engaged in operations such as accounting, data processing, and billing, which do not require a downtown central city location. The major force which has influenced this decentralization is technological change, particularly the increased use of computers and communications satellites. Equally significant is the economics of real estate, that is, the high expense of downtown office space and the availability of more economical space in the suburbs and the "boondocks." As decentralization occurs, the major expansion of employment opportunities is occurring in the outlying areas of the large metropolitan communities and in middle-size cities throughout the nation (Wald, 1984).

EDGE CITIES

The movement of businesses and people in the diffuse phase of urbanization has created "new" cities, popularly referred to as edge cities (Garreau, 1991). These cities have a large amount of leasable office and retail space, have "more jobs than bedrooms," have an identity as a "place." These places have traditionally been thought of as suburbs, but they have taken on the functions and form of the city. It is unclear as to the extent to which these edge cities have or will become "communities." Garreau (1991) has identified a large number of edge cities connected to some thirty-six major central cities in the United States. He provides a sense of what these edge cities are like by examining the areas of New York and New Jersey, Boston, Detroit, Atlanta, Phoenix, Dallas, Houston, Los Angeles, San Francisco, and Washington, D. C., The large number of cities which have emerged within these metropolitan areas have many of the characteristics of the central cities. However, the architecture and space use are considerably different, as are the transportation patterns and parking space. What remains to be seen is whether or not these cities will develop into communities—that is, will people identify with these places and engage in social interactions within their neighborhoods and the city areas? Will residents of these cities engage in patterns of social participation which lead to a "sense of community"? Or will these cities simply provide spaces for commercial and business activities, with little integration of workplaces with the functions associated with residence, such as school activities, religious affiliation, and participation in voluntary associations?

One of the principal problems for some people living in edge cities and far beyond is the long commute to work. According to 1990 census data, an increasingly large number of people are moving considerable distances from their jobs (Ferguson and Carlson, 1990). While this type of move generally brings with it "better homes and gardens," it also has its downside. People who reside in communities at large distances from their jobs have less time with families, less time to enjoy their homes and their communities, and increased stress from highway driving. A major concern of parents who work a large distance from home is over the care of children (Shellenbarger, 1993). All of the options for child care, such as child-care facilities, neighborhood child care, and workplace child care, appear to have some disadvantages when the parent or parents commute long distances to work.

To summarize, the metropolitan community continues to exhibit social and economic problems of the earlier metropolitan phase, such as the extreme financial difficulties of the central cities, the fiscal strains on municipal services which serve the metropolitan area, increased governmental fragmentation, and an increase in the mismatch between employees and the location of employment (suburban professionals flowing into central cities, blue-collar workers flowing out to employment sites). In this diffuse phase, suburban communities, like edge cities, have residential patterns of racial, ethnic, and class segregation. These patterns continue to crystallize, eliminating for the most part the possibility of "melting pot" communities in suburban areas.

DEMOGRAPHIC CHANGES IN THE INNER CITY

Wilson's (1987) explanation of the relationship of demographic changes to the social dislocation of African Americans in the inner cities illustrates a number of ecological concepts. Wilson seeks to explain differences between inner-city communities prior to 1960 and communities of the 1980s. He notes that "inner-city communities prior to 1960 exhibited the features of social organization, . . . including a sense of community, positive neighborhood identification, and explicit norms and sanctions against aberrant behavior." In contrast, these inner cities became the locale for a ghetto underclass associated with problems of social dislocation, such as high rates of "crime, joblessness, out-of-wedlock births, female-headed families, and welfare dependency." These social dislocations are seen as the result of societal, demographic, and neighborhood factors, especially historic and contemporary discrimination, the flow of migrants, changes in the age structure, economic changes, and concentration effects of living in areas with high rates of poverty (Wacquant and Wilson, 1989).

The high rate of migration of African Americans from the south to northern cities, and from rural areas to southern cities, helped create ghetto communities with large proportions of low-income individuals (Lemann, 1991; Wilson, 1987). This migration, as well as out-migration, led to age-structure changes, with an increase in numbers of minority teenagers and young adults. These young people faced changes in the economy from production to service industries, which left many unskilled and poorly educated individuals without sources of employment. This situation of joblessness was particularly problematic for young African American males. The likelihood of minority members of inner-city neighborhoods residing in areas with high poverty rates became high compared to residential patterns for whites.

Wilson (1987) examines 1970–1980 census data to illustrate this demographic development, that is, the "concentration effects" which come when people live in extreme poverty areas. Wilson gives special consideration to Chicago, showing the increase in poverty areas in the inner city, caused in part by the departure of upwardly mobile minorities. Most importantly, he suggests that these concentration effects lead to social isolation, a lack of positive social networks and social institutions as community resources for residents in the inner city, and a lack of identification with work roles, leading to a lack of connections with the world of work and a view of joblessness as a way of life (Wilson, 1987).

Another illustration of demographic changes in large urban cities comes from the work of Coulton, Pandey, and Chow (1990). These authors studied the concentration of poverty in Cleveland, Ohio, during the 1980s, demonstrating the growth of high-poverty areas to the point that they cover one-third of the land area in Cleveland. Predictions are that the city will have about two-thirds of its land as poverty areas by the year 2000. A map of Cleveland prepared as a part of the Coulton et al. study shows that the traditional areas of poverty are adjacent to new areas, which in turn are linked to emerging poverty areas. Changes in the city were the result of more people becoming poor and more nonpoor moving from the city. Some of the consequences associated with living in poverty areas include excessive rates of death, low birth weight, child abuse, infant deaths, delinquency, and teen pregnancy (Coulton et al., 1990).

The social and physical neighborhood environment in poor areas has been adversely affected, with limited social networks, lack of participation in community-wide organizations, lack of employment due to distances to suburban jobs, high crime rates, and deterioration of housing conditions and loss of property values. The implications for social workers who serve these areas are clear. "Social workers need practice models that combine their traditional approaches to service delivery with economic redevelopment . . . and mechanisms that reestablish connections between central city residents and distant, suburban job locations . . . and programs that will disrupt their growing isolation from the mainstream" (Coulton et al., 1990).

Isolation is lessened when inner-city residents can find employment in suburban areas. This has been accomplished in some major American cities through the development of bus lines which link the inner-city poor with jobs in suburbia (Wartzman, 1993). With federal funds, cities like Philadelphia, Chicago, Washington, Detroit, and Boston, have shown interest in Mobility for Work initiatives, especially the creation of special bus lines for the commute out to jobs away from the inner city. An example of this kind of program is the 201 bus line in Philadelphia, which serves riders to and from jobs in communities near the central city. This bus line was developed to meet the workforce needs of suburban businesses, such as restaurants and manufacturing companies, and facilitates employment of inner-city residents (Wartzman, 1993).

GENTRIFICATION

During the diffuse phase of urbanization, some changes in land use within inner-city neighborhoods have been labeled "gentrification." This process has involved the rehabilitation of old dwellings for household use by individual investors and real estate developers. The concept of gentrification is borrowed from the British experience of "young professional people . . . the so-called gentry, buying and renovating small homes and row houses in several central districts" (Choldin, 1985). Gentrification in the United States represents a competition for use of urban land, with replacement of poor elderly people, seasonal workers, single-room-occupancy residents, by working, middle- and upper-class individuals and families. As a result, some slum neighborhoods have become fashionable residential areas for young, upper-middle-class whites.

While there has been an increase in the number and scope of gentrified areas in large American cities, what may appear to be a back-to-city movement of population actually involves a relatively small number of people. At the same time, gentrified areas illustrate a form of succession when middle- and upper-class whites displace poor people, ethnic minorities, and the elderly from their housing. In some instances, housing and neighborhood rehabilitation has been carried out by low-income residents and ethnic minority groups (White, 1988), usually in neighborhoods where the residents have been living. Examples of communities in which this type of gentrification has occurred are described in Chapter 10 on community economic systems and in the communities described in the chapter exercises. In these instances, neighborhood residents are not displaced but are able to live in more adequate and affordable housing. The major problem of gentrification within urban communities is the lack of affordable housing for people who usually live in rooming houses and single rooms. Housing options for these individuals are drastically reduced by gentrification.

RURAL AREAS AND URBANIZATION

Up to now our focus has been on what has happened to the metropolis and the central city in the different phases of urbanization. Changes have also occurred in rural areas in the transition from a metropolitan phase to a diffuse phase of urbanization. Rural communities and smaller communities grew, especially as evidenced in university towns, retirement areas, and recreation areas. Rural/small town communities begin taking on urban socioeconomic functions, especially when companies move into small communities. There still remain some ecological and demographic differences between rural and urban areas, such as rates of fertility, age composition, family status, education, employment, and income. Yet in regard to social organization, a key question is the extent to which rural communities have become a part of "mass society." Do bonds of "local integration" persist or change to vertical ties to the larger society? Most small rural communities appear to have developed vertical extracommunity ties and are linked in to the larger urbanized society. Thus, in these small communities, local economic, educational, and governmental units have not been able to retain their formerly held high degree of autonomy. There seems to be little doubt that today few communities, even those like Lake Wobegan (Keillor, 1985), remain truly isolated from the large society. For example, most small communities receive federal and state funding of social programs, education, and health services.

In a diffuse phase of urbanization, does the quality of life differ for people in rural areas compared to those in urban areas? In the past there was some evidence of differences in economic well-being, education, health care, housing, and recreation opportunities (Dillmam and Tremblay, 1977). Rural communities experienced more safety, higher environmental quality, and less pollution and noise. There also have been differences in the attitudes and behavior of rural and urban populations, but it has been suggested that we recognize, but not exaggerate, these differences in religious beliefs, personal morals/vices, majority/minority issues, or political issues. Continued urbanization may progressively eradicate some rural/urban lifestyle differences. However, there is some reason to expect that people in urban areas will continue to be innovative and unconventional, and that new differences between rural and urban individuals will arise as old disparities disappear.

Discussions of urbanization typically identify positive and negative consequences of this process, using an ideal view of rural society in contrast to urban society. It may be more realistic, however, to recognize both the advantages and disadvantages of living in rural/non-metropolitan communities, as opposed to metropolitan areas. For some groups, such as the elderly, a rural area has some positive features in terms of family relationships, safety, environment, or pace of life. At the same time, when rural communities are located some distance from metropolitan areas, they may have limited opportunities for health care, employment, and recreation.

Some small towns have been able to provide cultural and business/shopping opportunities for residents in the town and surrounding rural areas. For example, the three communities of Martinsburg, West Virginia, Staunton, Virginia, and Briston, Tennessee, collaborated in contributing funds for a "time share" orchestra (Slevin, 1993). Each community provides about $30,000 for the orchestra, which gives three or four major concerts, smaller recitals, master classes, and musical workshops in the schools.

In another example of small towns receiving services normally available only in urban areas, shopping opportunities have been provided by Wal-Mart stores (Gann, 1993). This company has developed its stores on the edges of small towns, introducing competitive prices on a range of goods, clothing, home furnishings, and medications and other pharmacy items. Local downtown retailers in these communities have lost business to the new, "big stores" in shopping centers outside of the downtown area. In some communities, such as in Vermont, these retailers and residents have been able to use zoning to keep Wal-Mart from opening stores. At the same time, the success of Wal-Mart Stores has stimulated small town businesses to redevelop downtown main street stores and provide improved customer services.

IMMIGRATION AND HETEROGENEITY OF COMMUNITIES

Significant dimensions of the demographic development of communities in the United States are migration and immigration. These processes affect the size, density, and heterogeneity of communities. The effects of migration on communities have been considered earlier in this chapter with regard to population changes in the inner cities of large urban areas. Because the implications of immigration for communities are multifaceted, we will consider this topic in several chapters of this book.

Immigration can be viewed from several perspectives, such as the origin of immigrants, characteristics of education, occupation, age, and family composition, the time of arrival in the United States, and attitudes of residents toward immigrants. A major contrast can be made between "older" immigrants and "newer" immigrants, a contrast which is sometimes described in terms of a "new American ethnicity" (Greer, 1985; Maldonado and Moore, 1985). Based on patterns of immigration of racial and ethnic groups into the United States up to 1924, the time of the National Origins Quota Act, the United States has been regarded as a nation of immigrants. Historically, large waves of immigrants have included western Europeans (1840s to 1870s), southern and eastern Europeans (Jews, Italians, Poles, 1880s to 1920s), Africans, Hispanics from Mexico, Japanese, Chinese, and Indians (Greer, 1985). The concept of ethnicity was closely related to the cultural and social processes of these immigrants: "It saw the typical career of a new population from a different society as one of social and spatial concentration and segregation, as process of acculturation, and finally assimilation" (Green, 1982). Obviously all ethnic populations did not follow this career pattern. People of color, low social rank, and rural backgrounds encountered greater obstacles to integration into American society than other groups. Some ethnic groups had greater difficulty in regard to employment opportunities and social-class mobility.

From the time of the National Origins Quota Act of 1924 to 1965 entry of immigrants into the United States was drastically reduced. Still, the origins of immigrants remained pretty much the same as during the pre-1924 period. However, with the enactment of the new Immigration Act of 1965 (and succeeding amendments) to the present, there has been a dramatic increase in the representation of immigrants from Asia and Latin America, as well as an increase in the number of refugees from Third World countries. Due to concerns over illegal immigration and its effect on national and community economic systems, the Immigration Reform and Control Act of 1986 was enacted in order to control immigration and to accommodate current residents with illegal, undocumented citizenship status (Finch, 1990).

Census data of 1990 display unusually large changes in the racial and ethnic composition of the United States from 1980 to 1990, with nearly one in four Americans of African, Asian, Hispanic, or American Indian ancestry in 1990 compared to one of five in 1980 (Barringer, 1991). A significant part of this growth came from nearly ten million ethnic minority immigrants, especially in the Hispanic population. Equally dramatic in change is the new diversity of the Asian population due to immigration, with fast-growing groups of Vietnamese, Indians, and Koreans. An important feature related to this growth in ethnic populations from immigration is the distribution of immigrants. An analysis of 1990 census data by Frey shows that "Most immigrants are flooding into just a handful of states, while the rest of America is largely untouched by the new immigration" (Tilove and Hallinan, 1993). Of the seven states which received the most immigrants—New York, Texas, New Jersey, Illinois, Massachusetts, Florida, and California—the white non-Hispanic population declined in all of these states except Florida. This change has led some demographers to believe there is a new "white flight" occurring, not just from communities, but from states and regions of the United States. In the light of these population changes, Frey (1993) predicts that "What is really developing here is two very separate societies, two separate Americas."

REVIEW

Taking an ecological view, communities may be classified as metropolitan communities, central cities, suburban municipalities, small and medium-sized towns, villages, or townships. There are considerable differences in metropolitan communities, as they vary in population size, territory included in the communities, and/or the amount of hinterland contiguous to the various metropolitan areas. In the different states and regions of the United States, metropolitan communities show considerable differences in terms of these ecological and demographic characteristics. Migration and immigration have had a significant impact on the demography of communities in the various phases of the development of American communities.

The discussion of the basic types of communities in terms of population size has provided a basis for a general historical view of the emergence of communities in the United States through phases in the process of urbanization. It is important to keep the idea of community size and heterogeneity in mind as we proceed to examine the functioning of American communities, since differences range from the simplicity of the organization and functioning of villages to the complexity of large metropolitan cities.

SUGGESTED READINGS

Coulton, Claudia, Shanta Pandey, and Julian Chow (1990). "Concentration of Poverty and the Changing Ecology of Low-income, Urban Neighborhoods: An Analysis of the Cleveland Area." *Social Work Research and Abstracts* 26:4.

Finch, Wilbur (1990). "The Immigration Reform and Control Act of 1986." *Social Service Review* 64:2 (June).

Lemann, Nicholas (1991). *The Promised Land: The Great Black Migration and How It Changed America.* New York: Knopf.

Maldonado, Lionel and Joan Moore, eds., (1985). "Urban Ethnicity in the United States." *Urban Affairs Annual Reviews* 29.

Martinez-Brawley, Emilia E. (1990). *Perspectives on the Small Community.* Silver Spring, MD: NASW Press.

Wacquant, Loic and William J. Wilson, (1989). "The Cost of Racial and Class Exclusion in the Inner City." *Annals* 501 AAPSS (January).

Wilson, William J. (1987) *The Truly Disadvantaged.* Chicago: University of Chicago Press.

Wilson, William J. (1989). "The Underclass: Issues, Perspectives, and Public Policy." *Annals* 501 AAPSS (January).

CHAPTER 4

The Social Stratification of Communities: Class, Race, and Ethnicity

A prominent feature of the social organization of a community is its patterns of social stratification. Stratification involves the classifying and ranking of people, allowing for the examination of how communities differ in terms of their social composition. Age, gender, religion, race, ethnicity, and social class are some of the most common ways of classifying groups of people. These classifications are used to describe the social structure of a community. In this chapter we explore the meaning of two major dimensions of social stratification in U.S. communities, social class and race/ethnicity.

The examination of the social class structure of a community provides an illustration of an ecological perspective of communities. The focus is on the "division of labor" within the community, the interaction and interdependence of occupational groups, and the technology used to provide sustenance for community residents (Durkheim, 1933). The social classes within a community illustrate a major type of identificational community, one which often overlaps with neighborhood communities of place. Stratification by race and/or ethnicity displays the diversity or heterogeneity of the community in terms of the size and status of various racial and ethnic groups. These groups also constitute identificational communities, which often overlap with neighborhood locational communities.

The study of community stratification systems of social class and race/ethnicity has special relevance for human service professionals, inasmuch as membership in class and racial/ethnic groups affects the quality of life of people in positive and negative ways. Stratification systems allow us to view the ways in which people benefit or suffer as a result of their social positions within communities, through differential life chances, opportunities, access to social and material resources, and social relationships.

SOCIAL CLASS

Stratification by social class refers to inequalities among people, often expressed in such terms as socioeconomic status, family or social standing, and lifestyle. In operationalizing the idea of social class strata it is necessary to determine the criteria used to classify individuals into groups. Examined here are some of the ways in which occupation, income, education, and lifestyle are used to locate people into social class groups.

Issues of classification become apparent as social classes in a community are defined and named. Most Americans are acquainted with the names popularly assigned to social classes (Jackman and Jackman, 1983). These social class names include variations of upper, middle, lower class (Warner and Lunt, 1941); blue-collar/white collar (Lynd and Lynd, 1929); business/working class (Lynd and Lynd, 1929); poor, working class, middle class, upper-middle class, and upper class (Jackman and Jackman, 1983). Often the hierarchy of classes is inherent in the names, as with lower to upper classes. A relatively new class term, underclass, has emerged as a label to distinguish the bottom part of the poverty population from the lower classes.

Some indicators for assigning people to class groups appear to be more objective than others. For example, measures of the concept of socioeconomic status illustrate the use of quantitative dimensions of social class, while measures of class awareness or class consciousness focus on subjective, qualitative factors. Let us now examine how social class, in terms of socioeconomic status, can be measured with data from the U.S. Bureau of the Census (*Statistical Abstracts*, 1992).

OCCUPATION, INCOME, AND EDUCATION

The U.S. Census Bureau defines major occupational categories, with elaborate lists of occupations coded under each category, and makes these data available by census tracts. These occupational categories are:

Managerial and professional specialty
    Executive, administrative, and managerial
    Professional specialty
Technical, sales, and administrative support
    Technicians and related support
    Sales occupations
    Administrative support
Service Occupations
    Private household
    Protective service
    Service, other
Precision production, craft, and repair
    Mechanics and repairers
    Construction trades
    Extractive occupations
    Precision production
Operators, fabricators, and laborers
    Machine operators, assemblers, and inspectors
    Transportation and material moving,
    Handlers, equipment cleaners, helpers, laborers
Farming, forestry, and fishing
    Farm operators and managers
    Other agricultural
    Forestry and logging
    Fishers, hunters, trappers

Income levels of community residents can be measured in a variety of ways, such as the annual income of the head of the household, the combined income of household members, and the income of household adults. Income levels are usually presented in Census Bureau publications according to the following categories.

Less than $5,000
$5,000 to $9,999
$10,000 to $14,999
$15,000 to $24,999
$25,000 to $34,999
$35,000 to $49,999
$50,000 to $74,999
$75,000 to $99,999

$100,000 to $149,999
$150,000 or more

Level of education is measured in terms of highest grade attended. The major census categories are:

Less than 9th Grade
9th to 12th grade, no diploma
High school graduate
Some college, no degree
Associate degree
Bachelor's degree
Graduate or professional degree

Census Bureau data on occupation, education, and/or income allow us to develop social profiles of communities and their sub-communities, such as community areas or neighborhoods. A community profile can be based on a single variable, such as occupation, or with some combination of measures. A classic illustration of how census statistics can be used to describe social class differences in communities is provided in the work of Shevky and Bell (1955). These authors developed a procedure known as social area analysis. This procedure involves the use of three major constructs:

1. social rank (education and occupation)
2. urbanization or family status (type of housing, marital status, children, members of household working)
3. segregation or ethnicity (proportion of minorities in an area compared to the total community population)

Based on scores for these three constructs, social areas emerge which can be ordered in terms of social rank, urbanization, and segregation. Social ranks, in particular, correspond to social class levels and highlight the social and economic differentiation found in American communities and sub-communities.

Community profiles of social class illustrate ways of using aggregate statistics to determine the proportions of people in various social class levels or social ranks. Sometimes we are interested in making an assessment of the social class level of an individual or of a household based on occupational, income, and/or educational level. However, classification becomes problematic when the indicators of these factors are not at the same level. In addition, social class ranking of individuals and households may be influenced by other factors, most notably race, ethnicity, family background, religion, and lifestyle. In fact, individuals in racial, ethnic, and religious groups may construct their own rankings within a social class stratification system. For example, Boston (1988) describes the class structure of African American society in terms of three groups, Black capitalist class, Black middle class, and Black working class. Each of these class groups has subgroups within it, such as distinctions between the old middle class and the new middle class.

What the factors of occupation, income, and education have in common is the fact that they are quantitative, "objective" indicators that point to inequalities among individuals and among population groups. There is little agreement, however, about where to draw the lines to distinguish one class from another and what to call the various class levels. The boundaries of the various social classes are fluid, as illustrated by the variations which occur in the determination of the size of different class groups by city planners, governmental officials, and political figures. Despite these difficulties with the definition of social class, the census data provide a basis for constructing a description of the social class structure of the society, of states, of metropolitan areas, of local communities, and of neighborhoods.

LIFESTYLE

Social class is often associated with the lifestyles of community residents. Indicators of lifestyles include such factors as the value and location of homes, clothing styles, consumer spending patterns, club memberships, restaurants, bars, lounges, summer and winter homes, travel and vacation styles, type of automobile, cooking and food styles, participation in sports, and choices of reading/magazines/books. The most prominent of these factors is the value and location of one's residential dwelling, be it a single home owned by the residents or a rental unit. In some large urban communities, the high price of rental housing and the location of such units is a sign of upper class membership, just as the single-room occupancy housing in a skid-row area a sign of lower-class or underclass membership.

Communities and neighborhoods are often characterized in terms of the lifestyles of the residents, lifestyles which are closely connected to the socioeconomic measures of social class. Thus, the rich are viewed as having lifestyles in upper-class neighborhoods considerably different from the poor living in inner-city ghettos. One aspect of lifestyle which has traditionally been used to distinguish people within social classes is manners, the "social graces" (Levin, 1986). In the words of the French author and art and wine connoisseur Guy de Rothschild

(1985), "Class is an imponderable mixture of good taste, refinement, proper clothes and proper manners." Class is associated with the concept of "society," which refers to a social group usually distinguished by history of family background, marriage, manners, and money (Barron, 1990). Since the time of the *Mayflower* until at least recent years, the major criteria for belonging to society has been a background of white, Anglo-Saxon, Protestant ancestry. The fact that this is no longer the case is documented in the listing of members of society to be found in Social Registers of large urban communities. The lifestyles of members of society in a community may be identified by where they winter, where they summer, where they shop, where they buy their jewels, who decorates their houses, who caters their parties, and who buries them (Barron, 1990). Another sign of upper-class society is found in the types of philanthropic organizations members of society support, such as contributions to the arts and related causes. To be accepted in some upper-class groups, the important thing is not how much money you have, or how much you make, but how much you give, in time and money, to charitable community organizations.

Generally speaking, upward occupational and residential mobility has been associated with change in lifestyle. At the same time, lifestyles associated with the upper classes, such as home furnishings, food tastes, recreation, and clothing, often are found displayed by members of the middle and upper-middle classes. However, while some aspects of these "ways of life" may extend to the working classes, upper-class lifestyles in general are not as commonly observed in the behaviors of lower class or underclass individuals.

There is some indication that classes reproduce themselves, especially the upper classes. An example of this process is examined by Thomas (1991) in his description of "young society" in Washington, D.C. These young professionals, "the nouveau WASP wanna-bes," are "well-to-do thirty-ish professionals" who attended the "right" schools and colleges, are active in the same cultural and charitable organizations and social events. They appear at the same club-sponsored parties, have linkages to young socialites in New York and Boston, and have a high rate of marriage within the same social crowd. Members of this young society have a lifestyle that strongly resembles that of their parents, and in this sense, the upper class has reproduced itself.

SOCIAL CLASSES AS IDENTIFICATIONAL COMMUNITIES

Quantitative measures are not the only ways in which to determine the "class structure" in a community. Social class can also be determined by "subjective" concepts such as class consciousness, class awareness, class identification, and cognitive maps, all images of individuals about their location in the class structure. The concept of social class appears to have considerable meaning in the way community residents think of themselves. For example, using residents' reports on their subjective interpretations of social class, Jackman and Jackman (1983) found that "social class is a major source of group identity for most Americans." Of special interest is the Jackmans' finding that Americans perceive "classes as a graded series of social communities." Their research involved a national sample of respondents who identified themselves as belonging to one of five class categories: poor, working class, middle class, upper-middle class, and upper class. Respondents used not only educational attainment, occupation, and income to determine their class, but also such cultural factors as lifestyle and "beliefs and feelings" in making this judgment. Thus the Jackmans observed that class is of significance to respondents, and "class has a subjective meaning that transcends the economic sphere and incorporates factors normally associated with status groups" such as education, beliefs, lifestyle, and family. In regard to family, the occupation of the male had the most important influence on class identification, even in households with women employed out of the home.

A number of these findings by the Jackmans are related to the social relationships of individuals in the community. People indicate that they prefer to live in areas where their neighbors are of the same class, and they tend to have friends of similar occupational status. In this sense one may conclude that classes are indeed "social communities" (Jackman and Jackman, 1983). A similar way of examining the subjective meaning of social class is by the concept of cognitive maps, that is, "perceptions people have of class and racial inequalities in their society" (Bell and Robinson, 1980). Using this approach, Bell and Robinson studied class and racial inequalities in England and the U.S. and developed an Index of Perceived Inequality, based on respondents' answers to questions concerning comparisons of people of different social classes and different racial groups according to their equality or inequality of respect, treatment by the police and courts, jobs, education, and income. Respondents in both countries perceived that the most inequality existed in terms of respect. "In America and Britain people of higher social class are given much more respect than these of a lower social class" (Bell and Robinson, 1980). Second ranked by both groups were inequalities in treatment by the police and courts, followed by unequal opportunities for people in different social classes to get good jobs. Respondents perceived the least inequality in regard to a chance to earn a good income.

A significant aspect of this study by Bell and Robinson (1980) is its focus on perceptions of inequality in terms of opportunity and in terms of condition or treatment toward the different social classes. Respondents who perceived inequality in regard to social classes also saw it in comparisons of different racial groups. An understanding of these cognitive and evaluative maps of inequality helps in the understanding of why some individuals in communities may be discontent and seek social change, while others remain satisfied with the status quo.

THE UNDERCLASS

In recent years, social scientists and human service professionals have given considerable attention to a special group of people within the lower classes (Jencks and Peterson, 1991). These individuals and families live in poverty, some persistently, while others move in and out of poverty. Within the poverty population are people who appear to be considerably different from this population, a group of people who have been labeled the underclass. The customary criteria for determining social classes have not been viewed as sufficient for characterizing the urban underclass. The term has taken on a variety of meanings, with an important distinction being the location of underclass people outside, or under, the traditional class hierarchy. One important aspect of this location concerns the fact that these individuals are restricted by social and economic barriers from upward mobility into the traditional class structure.

People in the underclass are confined in their position by a number of societal forces, such as the educational system, the economic system, and the health and welfare system. The underclass includes people who reside, in the main, in the inner-city neighborhoods in large urban areas. A high proportion of the underclass are members of ethnic minority groups and live in segregated urban neighborhoods. As Cottingham (1982) notes, "the underclass encompasses those at the very bottom of the urban stratification system . . . they are disproportionately Black and Hispanic, and mainly reside in urban ethnically and/or racially homogeneous ghettos. . . . The underclass experiences severe income deprivation, unstable employment, low functional skills, and limited access to educational or other social services or in-kind benefits and transfers."

One of the early descriptions of underclass people was provided by Auletta (1981), who wrote about ex-offenders, ex-addicts, long-term welfare recipients, school dropouts, unemployed young people, and ex-mental patients who participated in work training programs in New York and New Jersey. Auletta noted that poverty, deviant behavior, lack of mobility, and lack of education all can be said to characterize these individuals as members of an underclass. In another early picture of the underclass, Glasgow (1980) wrote about the underclass in terms of "impoverished black Americans trapped in intergenerational poverty by chronic unemployment, underemployment, welfare dependency, racism, and other institutional barriers that prevent upward mobility." Later in the 1980s Wilson (1987) discussed the plight of the underclass in urban ghettos by adding to the perspectives of Glasgow, Auletta, and others by focusing on social change and dislocations in the inner city. These changes provide an ecological explanation for the emergence of underclass neighborhoods.

Glasgow, Auletta, Wilson, and other observers of the underclass highlight the negative effects of the existence of an underclass, both for those trapped in it, and for the community. They raise the question of social versus individual responsibility for the plight of these individuals. They conclude that community and societal forces beyond the control of the individual are largely responsible for the development of the underclass in American communities. The discussions of the underclass by these authors are only illustrative of the substantial literature on the underclass.

In their review of this literature, Devine and Wright (1993) identify four themes which have been used to describe the underclass. These include four dimensions: economic, social-psychological, behavioral, and ecological. It is clear from social science research that poor individuals and families move in and out of poverty, and that most poverty is not intergenerational (Bane and Ellwood, 1983). At the same time, a proportion of those in poverty are chronically poor. Descriptions of people entrenched in the underclass usually emphasize the discrepancy between the values and norms of this population and the rest of American society. Negative orientations toward education and employment, coupled with alienation, social isolation, and negative views of conventional society, appear to be common among people in an underclass.

In terms of behavior, underclass people are pictured as displaying "antisocial, deviant, dysfunctional, or threatening behaviors; criminal activity, drug and alcohol abuse, welfare dependency, joblessness, teenage pregnancy, and so on" (Devine and Wright, 1993). Finally, people with the economic, social-psychological, behavioral characteristics described above become concentrated in central city neighborhoods, the urban ghettos identified in terms of spatial concentration and social isolation. Taking these dimensions into account, Devine and Wright provide a useful definition of the underclass, "as persons living in urban, central city neighborhoods or communities with high and increasing rates of poverty, especially chronic poverty, high and increasing levels of social isolation, hopelessness, and anomie, and high levels of characteristically antisocial or dysfunctional behavior patterns."

Understanding the plight of the underclass is of particular importance to human service practitioners. Service workers participate in a variety of programs directed toward alleviating the problems of these individuals and in changing the conditions which retain them in this devastating state of poverty. Housing programs, job training and jobs programs, along with other social welfare programs have been developed to help underclass people escape their condition. While these programs have helped some individuals move into mainstream society, the presence of a substantial underclass within urban communities continues to be a major social and community problem.

RACE AND ETHNICITY

Race and ethnicity comprise two major concepts used in classifying people in the United States and within communities (Snipp, 1989). Classification of people according to these two dimensions usually results in identification of groups which display inequalities due to discrimination and oppression. Longres (1990) cites some of the difficulties in classifying people by race when the term signifies biological differences, especially physical characteristics and color. Authors such as Longres (1990) and Green (1982) emphasize that race is a social fact, especially in distinctions of white and nonwhite populations and in terms of people of color having minority status in a white majority society. Because of the cultural features which distinguish racial groups from each other, the concept of ethnic group has been mixed with the concept of race. As Longres (1990) has noted, race and ethnicity should be considered equally inclusive, as "Races can include people of many ethnic groups. Ethnic groups can include people of any color."

Ethnic groups have been defined in terms of criteria such as race, religion, national origin, or language, or some combination of these characteristics (Maldonado and Moore, 1985; Yankauer, 1987). Currently in the United States ethnic groups may be classified according to white ethnics and ethnic minority groups. In the first instance, there is an emphasis on groups historically differentiated in terms of a European nationality, e.g., white immigrant groups such as Polish, Italian, German, Irish. For the second group, race, minority status, and color constitute the major points of reference. The term "minority" has come to refer to people of color who are a minority in number within society and have experienced high degrees of discrimination, prejudice, and oppression (Bernal, 1990). The term "ethnic" is combined with "minority group" to refer to people of color, groups identified by the Equal Employment Commission established by the Equal Rights Act of 1964 as African American, Asian American, Native American, and Hispanic (Glazer, 1983). There is some disagreement over what names should be used to describe these groups. For example the term Black may be interchanged with African American, Latino for Hispanic (or specific Spanish-surnamed groups), Asian American for specific groups, and Native American for American Indian (Yankauer, 1987; Wright, 1990; Snipp, 1989).

White ethnic and ethnic minority groups are described in such works as the Harvard Encyclopedia of American Ethnic Groups (Thernstrom et al., 1980). Attention is given to ways in which various ethnic groups differ from one another and from the "mainstream" American culture. In these considerations, it is clear that the major categories of ethnic minority groups are not homogeneous groups in terms of ancestry. For example, there is great diversity within and between Native American tribes; between Asian groups such as Japanese, Chinese, Filipino, Vietnamese; between African American groups; and between Hispanic Americans, such as Mexican, Cuban, Puerto Rican, Central and South Americans. Often this diversity is due to national origin, social class differences, stage of acculturation and assimilation, or to other sociocultural factors. Our discussion of immigration in Chapter 3 calls attention to differences in characteristics of "older" immigrants (prior to the 1980s) and the "newer" immigrants (since that time). It is now recognized that the concepts of acculturation and assimilation seem not to be as applicable for new immigrants, and that a process of bicultural socialization may more accurately describe the experiences of new ethnic groups (Magill, 1985).

CENSUS BUREAU CLASSIFICATION

The Bureau of the Census collects information about the affiliation of individuals with racial and ethnic groups. The population of the

United States is classified in terms of racial categories of American Indian or Alaska Native, Asian or Pacific Islander, Black, White, and Other. Hispanic origin is considered as ethnicity, and persons identifying themselves as Mexican, Puerto Rican, Cuban, or Other Spanish/Hispanic origin are classified as of Hispanic origin. "The concept of race the Bureau of the Census uses reflects self-identification by respondents, that is, the individual's perception of his/her racial identity. The concept is not intended to reflect any biological or anthropological definition" (*Statistical Abstracts*, 1992). This definition is based on the idea that race identification may include both racial and national origin or sociocultural groups.

The present categories for classification of race and ethnicity continue to be problematic for some people, as indicated by the fact that a large proportion of Hispanics identify as "Other" rather than Hispanic, and by the lack of an opportunity of people with mixed parentage to classify themselves. One of the consequences of classification is that "nonwhite" status carries with it certain compensations as a result of affirmative action policies, minority contracting set-asides and antidiscrimination laws (Barringer, 1993).

According to the 1990 Census statistics, African Americans are the largest nonwhite racial group in the United States, representing 12.1 percent (29,986,000) of the total population. The American Indian, Eskimo, or Aleut population was .8 percent; Asian or Pacific Islander, 2.9 percent, and Other, 3.9 percent. Persons of Hispanic origin comprised 9.0 percent of the population, of which 5.4 percent were Mexican, 1.1 percent Puerto Rican, 0.4 percent Cuban, and 2 percent Other Hispanic.

One way of classifying individuals in the United States and within American communities is by use of census data on ancestry groups. The 1990 census includes data on reported ancestry, with the largest European groups being: German (23.3 percent), Irish (15.6 percent), English (13.1 percent), Italian (5.9 percent), and French (4.1 percent). Other groups are classified by West Indian, North Africa and Southwest Asia, sub-Saharan Africa, and North American.

SOCIAL CLASS AND ETHNIC MINORITIES

As patterns of stratification, race and ethnicity are closely related to social class. Our discussion of an underclass in American communities, particularly in large central cities, is one illustration of how class, race and ethnicity overlap. The work of the Jackmans (1983) suggests that class identity cannot be assessed without considering racial and/or ethnic identity as well. Race and social class have long been regarded as factors in determining the "life chances" of minorities in American society (Wilson, 1978). Wilson defines class in terms of one's economic position. He focuses on African Americans, recognizing that historically a mixture of class and race, of racial discrimination and oppression, and class subordination has left them disproportionately located in the lower levels of the American class structure. At the same time, Wilson contends that as a racist society becomes less racist, by virtue of changes in its policies and laws, "class takes on greater importance in determining the 'life chances' of minority individuals." Under this formulation, old barriers to mobility within the class structure are replaced by new barriers imposed by the economic conditions of the society. As a result, Wilson (1978) predicted a "progressive transition from racial inequalities to class inequalities."

Wilson's hypothesis is challenged by authors such as Boston (1988) who maintain that racism and discrimination continue to be the major forces restricting ethnic minorities to lower-class positions. However, it is clear that political and economic forces have over time enabled minorities to move into the middle class through education and employment in white-collar and high-paying blue-collar positions. Yet, further class movement of people of color, as well as the white majority population, appears to be severely restricted by adverse economic conditions. At the same time, the practice of institutional racism, however diminished by legislation and economic practices, remains a significant force in the maintenance of a large ethnic minority working class.

REVIEW

An understanding of the stratification systems in communities is pertinent to the human service professional for several reasons. First, a social profile based on social class, race, and/or ethnicity displays the geographic location of individuals within the community, a factor which has special relevance to the location, accessibility, and availability of social services. Second, the size of these population groups indicates some measure of the social needs of the community, and the resources available to meet these needs. Third, changes in the community can be documented through reference to movement between class levels, that is, the changing proportion of population groups in each of the class levels over time. Fourth, community and societal forces, such as the political economy, constitute barriers and restraints to the upward mobility of many individuals, particularly ethnic minorities, leaving such persons located mainly in the lower strata of society.

Social class, race, and ethnicity are useful ways of describing the stratification system within American communities. Objective indicators used to describe social classes include occupation, income, education, and lifestyle. Yet there is also a subjective dimension of social class. Characterized by class awareness, this dimension emphasizes the perception of status and inequality among people in American communities. Status and inequality are also related to the stratification of individuals in ethnic and racial groups. Social class and class awareness have somewhat different meanings and implications for ethnic and racial groups in American communities, especially as they are manifested in residential areas. After consideration of the nature of neighborhoods in American society in Chapter 5, we will extend our examination of class, race, and ethnicity in Chapter 6 by examining the emergence of neighborhoods in terms of these stratified groups.

SUGGESTED READINGS

Auletta, Ken (1981). "A Reporter at Large: The Underclass." *New Yorker*, November 16, 23, 30.

Sandefur, Gary D., and Marta Tienda (1988). *Divided Opportunities: Minorities, Poverty, and Social Policy*. New York: Plenum Press.

Sherraden, Michael W. (1984). "Working Over the 'Underclass.'" *Social Work* 29:4 (July-August).

Snipp, C. Matthew (1989). *American Indians: The First of This Land*. New York: Russell Sage.

Wilson, William J. (1978). *The Declining Significance of Race*. Chicago: University of Chicago Press.

Wright, Deborah (1990). "American, Not African-American." *Wall Street Journal*, October 30.

Yankauer, Alfred (1987). Hispanic/Latino—What's in a Name? *American Journal of Public Health* 77:1.

EXERCISE

As noted in Chapter 4, social class, race, and ethnicity are important bases for the stratification of residents in American communities. Describe how the influx of Asians into Flushing, New York, as related in the news report "Influx of Asians Brings Prosperity to Flushing, a Place for Newcomers," has changed the stratification of residents in this community. Describe additional ways in which the community has been transformed physically, culturally, and economically.

INFLUX OF ASIANS BRINGS PROSPERITY TO FLUSHING, A PLACE FOR NEWCOMERS

By Bernard Wysocki, Jr.

Flushing is just a few miles from Manhattan, but the 30-minute subway ride is a journey into other worlds.

In high-rise Manhattan, the economic mood is somber at best. In low-rise Flushing, a neighborhood in the less fashionable New York City borough of Queens, things are still going strong. The reason is immigrants—Asian immigrants.

Last year at least 133 new Chinese businesses sprang up in downtown Flushing—restaurants and beauty salons, banks and trading companies—bringing the total here to nearly 600 companies. And those are just the Chinese businesses. Flushing has become a mecca for immigrants from all over Asia, including Korea, Hong Kong, China, Malaysia, Thailand, Taiwan, India, and Indonesia. Even the Northeast's serious economic downturn hasn't significantly discouraged their entrepreneurial drive.

A typical optimist is Nai-Ching Sun. In the 20 years since he arrived from Taiwan, he has started 15 businesses. Some have succeeded, most have failed, but Mr. Sun keeps starting new ventures. "Chinese are risk-loving people," he says.

Flocking to Flushing

Asians have transformed the area physically, culturally, and economically, just as earlier waves of immigrants left their imprint here. The Dutch first settled Flushing in the mid-17th century, after fleeing religious persecution. The 19th and early 20th centuries brought a new wave of immigrants—German, Irish, Italian, and Jewish. Over time, Flushing became a retailing and transportation hub, serving the largely lower-middle-class neighborhoods fanning out from Main Street.

Today, entire streets of shops have signs in Korean or Chinese. On weekends, Asians from all over the New York area throng to Flushing to shop, eat, visit the dentist, or make business deals. Some entrepreneurs and shoppers alike consider Flushing an attractive alternative to Manhattan's Chinatown, which is older and more densely populated.

Some hail the activity as the rebirth of a neighborhood that had fallen on hard times. Says Myra Herce, a consultant to the Flushing Business Association: "The Asians have saved Flushing."

Bernard Wysocki, Jr., "Influx of Asians Brings Prosperity to Flushing, a Place for Newcomers," *The Wall Street Journal*, January 15, 1991. Reprinted by permission of *The Wall Street Journal*, © 1991 Dow Jones & Company, Inc. All Rights Reserved Worldwide.

The Old-Timers

Perhaps so. But there's a twist to this Asian immigrant success story. The sheer numbers of immigrants—nearly 100,000 people of Chinese and Korean lineage have moved to Flushing since the late 1970s—have brought a backlash among the "old-timers," as longtime residents, mostly white and some black, often call themselves.

Recently, culture clash has become a problem. Some residents complain they can't even read the signs on shops. In fact, Flushing's representative in New York's city council, Julia Harrison, has introduced a bill to require at least some English on all store signs.

"People feel they are being locked out of their own neighborhoods," says Mrs. Harrison, who is seen as a partisan of the old-timers. In her polyglot district of about 212,000 people—including dozens of nationalities— roughly 80,000 are of Chinese or Korean ancestry.

Some long-time shopkeepers express bitterness. Paul Kapchan will close his doors in February after more than 20 years of running the My Man clothing shop. He complains that his Asian customers often want to bargain over prices.

But more upsetting is that his landlord, who is Chinese, isn't renewing his lease, and rents along Main Street are now far beyond his means. Mr. Kapchan pays $3,000 a month for his storefront. The going rate today on such a site, he says, is more like $15,000.

Stratospheric real-estate prices are among the effects of Flushing's Asian boom. Office rents, which have softened a bit in recent months, had soared above $30 a square foot last year, making them comparable to rental rates on Wall Street. They would be incongruous in any overbuilt U.S. city.

As for real-estate sales, a storefront two stories high and 100 feet deep typically sells for $2 million or more. And although some business people have recession jitters, that hasn't stopped new and ever grander projects.

A few steps off Main Street, Yuk Chung has just opened Diamond Plaza, a big jewelry story with a purple facade. He spent several hundred thousand dollars remodeling the space. A Sheraton Hotel is under construction, designed to attract travelers arriving at nearby LaGuardia airport. The owner-developer of the $21 million, 180 room hotel (with a franchise acquired from ITT Sheraton Corp.) is a Taiwanese investment group, including members of the Wang family, which publishes a Chinese-language newspaper.

It's all a far cry from the 1970s, when Flushing was in a tailspin. Crime was increasing, while shoppers abandoned the area for Long Island malls or "the city," as Queens residents tend to call Manhattan. Many stores were boarded up.

"A Sleeping Dog"

"Flushing was just a sleeping dog," says Richard Gelman, president of National bank of New York City, based in Flushing. "It was there for the taking."

The takers mostly were Asian, and here is what they saw: a neighborhood at the end of a subway line from Manhattan. A place with a commuter railroad stop linking it with Manhattan and suburban Nassau County. Twenty-three bus lines fanning out from Main Street. Proximity not only to LaGuardia but to John F. Kennedy International Airport as well. And decent, affordable housing.

One man who saw the potential was Jentai Tsai, a Chinese student at New York University. In 1970, he opened a grocery store to cater to Japanese who lived in Flushing and had jobs in Manhattan.

Like many immigrants, Mr. Tsai tells of long hours and difficulty in getting loans to expand. A branch of the now-defunct Franklin National Bank was so close the officers could see the heavy traffic into his store, but bank officers still wouldn't lend him money. So he arranged private financing, expanded his business and, when Japanese hereabouts moved farther out to suburbs, followed them. Eventually, he set up stores in four states.

Beyond Foodstuffs

Then Mr. Tsai began thinking beyond groceries. "My dream was to open a bank," he says. After 14 years in business, he did. He raised $5 million from 120 Chinese backers and, in 1984, he opened Asia Bank N.A. in downtown Flushing. Asia Bank's forte is letters of credit for import-export businesses. "I offer one-day letter of credit," says Mr. Tsai. "The other banks, they take two weeks."

Asia Bank is one of more than 20 Asian financial institutions among many others in Flushing. Detractors slander them as money-laundering operations for illicit drugs or other illegal activities. Asian leaders hotly deny that, and law-enforcement officials say the vast majority of business activity is legitimate.

"Most Chinese businesses in Flushing are honest," says Robert Bryden, special agent in charge of the federal Drug Enforcement Agency for New York. He says that while Flushing harbors some illegal Asian drug activity, "It's only a few people causing the problem, and the criminal enterprise doesn't overpower the economic system."

Even the most cynical old-timers in flushing see things to admire. A big vacant lot has become a commercial vegetable patch. The public library is always crowded. Asian students excel in school. Many folks have come up the hard way.

Chun Soo Pyun came to the U.S. from South Korea in 1961 as a newspaper reporter. While he was on a ship crossing the Pacific, there was a coup in Seoul. The Korean military took over the newspaper he worked for, and Mr. Pyun found himself unemployed.

Once in Los Angeles, he took menial jobs, doing laundry, cleaning carpets. He moved to New York in 1970, where he once spent 72 hours straight cleaning carpets at the Statue of Liberty. He and a small crew earned $4,000 in that one long weekend. But Mr. Pyun had grander ambitions. He went into the driving school business.

He opened East West Driving School, specializing in helping Korean immigrants through New York City's bureaucratic motor-vehicle labyrinth. When imitators horned in on the driving-school business, Mr. Pyun opened an after-school academy to prepare high-school students for college entrance exams.

Today, Mr. Pyun's passion is politics. As head of the Korean American Association of Flushing, he is a leader of the Korean community throughout New York City. Mr. Pyun had his hands full in 1990, as relations between certain Korean business people and some blacks in New York turned ugly, especially in the borough of Brooklyn, where militant blacks boycotted a Korean grocery story after charging that a black woman had been roughed up by the proprietor.

Relations between blacks and Koreans in Flushing have been better. "It's completely different here," says the Rev. A. D. Tyson, pastor of the Macedonia A. M. E. church here. Still, he says, he detects jealousy among fellow blacks toward Asians in Flushing. And he complains that soaring rents have forced blacks to leave the neighborhood.

Some Asians have grown similarly weary of cultural and racial friction. Asian students talk of harassment by classmates. And the business climate isn't as sunny as it was. Competition has grown extremely fierce, notably among the open-air fruit and vegetable stands. The economic slump is hurting Asian businesses with all the rest.

"Some recent immigrants have been disappointed," says Kye Young Park, a professor at the University of California at Los Angeles. Formerly, she was at Queens College in Flushing. "The crime rate is lower in Korea, so people find [Flushing] very uncomfortable and not safe. It isn't really clean. And as minorities, Koreans are handicapped by language barriers and cultural barriers."

Those Asians who are new to Flushing also are victims of soaring prices, partly because earlier arrivals did well for themselves and drove up prices.

Housing prices in Flushing exploded in the late 1980s, rising 40% or more some years. Modest brick homes for a while were selling for nearly $400,000. John Procida, a real-estate broker, says prices now have dipped about 15%, which is a smaller decline than elsewhere in the city.

Asian buyers, agents say, have become more sophisticated and stopped overpaying. "There were stories of Koreans showing up at people's doorsteps carrying shopping bags full of cash," says Mr. Procida. He doubts such tales—though not that Asian buyers have sometimes written checks for the full cost of houses.

Will the good times keep rolling in the '90s? Some Flushing entrepreneurs believe so. Liberalized immigration laws continue to draw people and funds from Taiwan. The transfer of Hong Kong to Chinese rule in 1997 is propelling people and money to safe havens. Even some businesses in Manhattan's Chinatown have established branches here.

"Flushing will prosper for at least 10 to 15 years," predicts Mr. Sun, the insurance company entrepreneur.

One more trend: Even as they continue to work in Flushing, some Asian immigrants are moving to the suburbs. One reason is education, a major concern of many Asian parents. Some districts in Nassau and Westchester Counties in New York, and some in New Jersey, have already begun to draw Asian families out of the five boroughs of New York City.

This is in some ways the latest chapter of an old story: The first generation forms an enclave, tight-knit and suspicious of outsiders. Then the sons and daughters move toward the middle-class mainstream of suburban and corporate America.

"I'm running businesses in the Chinese community," Mr. Sun says. "But my son works at Merrill Lynch."

CHAPTER 5

Neighborhoods in American Communities

Neighborhood communities form a significant part of the social environment and an important context for social work practice. Increasingly, neighborhoods provide the location for community-based services for people with special needs, such as people with developmental disabilities, mental illness, or physical illness. Practice activities are often directed toward the strengthening of neighborhood social networks, since neighborhoods serve both instrumental and social psychological functions for their members (Choldin, 1985).

A neighborhood, first and foremost, is a geographical area which includes dwellings where people reside. As a place, or territorial area, a neighborhood may vary in size from residential units in a block to households in an area of several blocks. It is not common to use different terms to distinguish neighborhoods by size. However, it may be useful to do so. For example, the terms "nuclear" or "immediate" neighborhood may be used to refer to areas where household dwellings are in close physical proximity to one another. When the household area includes several blocks, it may be referred to as an "extended neighborhood." Somewhat larger areas of thirty blocks or more may be designated as "community neighborhoods" (Litwak, 1985).

Not all neighborhoods are exclusively residential, since they often contain nonresidential buildings such as schools, churches, stores, service buildings, police stations, fire stations, and offices.

Neighborhoods differ in scale of spatial area, size of population, architecture and appearance, and type of residential dwellings (single, multiple). Physical features of neighborhoods take on meaning when outsiders and/or residents use them to describe a neighborhood in positive or negative terms. Thus, people often identify neighborhoods in terms of their physical appearance, characterizing them as run-down, well kept, beautiful, nice, old, new, clean, or dirty. These descriptions are images people have of their own neighborhoods, as well as outsiders' views from walking or driving through a neighborhood.

In some areas, residents attempt to maintain the "looks" of neighborhoods through enforcement of municipal rules such as ordinances requiring mowing or cutting of weeds, through zoning laws with building requirements on modification and construction of buildings, and through the efforts of homeowners associations or organized voluntary groups to clean up or "paint up" the neighborhood. In other neighborhoods, especially areas described as "slums," litter, broken glass, and boarded-up dwellings leave an impression that no one cares about the physical appearance of the neighborhood.

The boundaries of a neighborhood are not easily specified. Boundaries are established by outsiders in a variety of ways, such as those designated by community social planning departments, school boards, political parties, churches, health and social service agencies, and newspapers. Once these organizational units establish boundaries, census tract data in an area can be used to describe a neighborhood in terms of size and density of the population, ethnic and/or racial composition, level of employment, age structure, and income levels.

Location is a distinguishing feature of a neighborhood. Traditionally neighborhoods are categorized as being in rural or urban areas, in central cities or suburban communities, in inner-city or transitional areas, in areas adjoining central cities, or in small towns or villages. Neighborhoods often take on a reputation and a name in keeping with their location and characteristics of the residents, such as social class and/or ethnicity.

Residents define their neighborhoods in a number of ways. Sometimes they give the neighborhood a spatial identity, which may be consistent with the geographic boundary definitions of outsiders. In suburban communities, neighborhoods are often named by subdivision or local school. Such neighborhoods usually include enough blocks of residences to be community neighborhoods. They are defined as "functional" when they provide for shelter and also for some educational, recreational, shopping, and other services. They usually include voluntary associations, such as parent-teacher organizations, homeowners groups, and church groups, which make up the formal structure of the neighborhood.

NEIGHBORHOOD AS PRIMARY GROUP

Residents often define a neighborhood as a small personal arena, or nuclear neighborhood. Such a neighborhood allows many opportunities for personal relationships, neighboring, informal helping, and exchanges of goods and services. The boundaries for a personal or nuclear neighborhood are likely to be much smaller than for functional community neighborhood areas and can usually be viewed as a primary group.

Defining a neighborhood as a primary group usually involves the use of a cognitive map. This is a subjective view of the boundaries of a neighborhood—for example, an area in which residents interact with each other, such as an area within which young children play with friends. This definition emphasizes the neighborhood as a social community with the features of a primary group. Such a neighborhood is a special kind of primary group, having some of the properties—such as face-to-face, relatively permanent, diffused, affective, and non-instrumental relationships—commonly identified with groups such as the family. The extended neighborhood may have primary group features, and such areas often include other primary groups, such as peer age groups, gangs, social club groups, athletic groups, neighborhood tavern groups, or groups that hang out at particular locations, such as parks or drug stores. These other primary groups usually draw their membership mainly from households in the neighborhood.

NEIGHBORHOOD SOCIAL INTERACTION

Neighborhood groups can be characterized by various levels and types of neighboring and social interaction. On the one hand, neighbors may serve as "good friends," providing for intimate, close, intense, and frequent social relationships. Or neighbors may be "friendly," "helpful," "good neighbors," and yet not fulfill the roles played by friends or kin. There are usually clear distinctions in social roles among neighbor, friend, and kin, although these roles may overlap. Examples of neighboring include visiting, dining together, borrowing tools or food, celebrating birthdays or holidays, block parties, exchanging services such as baby-sitting or help with household tasks, driving, and advice and information giving. Residents often establish informal "rules" or expectations about how neighbors should behave. These rules, or norms, have been found to differ in social class levels and between cultural and ethnic minority groups.

NEIGHBORHOOD FUNCTIONS

The neighborhood as a primary group can be a powerful resource for its residents, as suggested in our illustrations of activities of neighborhoods. In order to make comparisons between neighborhoods, and to estimate the value of a neighborhood as a resource, it is useful to examine the functions neighborhood communities serve for residents. Warren and Warren (1977) provide a framework which emphasizes neighborhood functions. These functions include the neighborhood as a sociability arena, an interpersonal influence center, a source of mutual aid, an organizational base, a reference group, and a status area.

People in neighborhoods have a potential set of resources and social supports (individuals and organizations) within their local environment. A number of other individuals and groups in addition to the neighborhood group—such as the members of a family or household, friends, co-workers, relatives, voluntary associations, and formal human service organizations—may also be a part of this social network. Of course, residents in local neighborhood communities vary in the extent to which they utilize these people and services.

An important aspect of neighborhoods is the "interface between perception and reality in terms of the supportive role of the neighborhood" (Warren, 1981). Inequalities are found among neighborhoods in the distribution of public services as well as the resources available from informal support systems, such as natural helpers, friends, kin, and neighbors. Individuals may perceive the neighborhood as rating from high to low in availability of resources, and the actual resources may indeed range along this continuum. In order to take advantage of neighbors as helpers, residents must be able to accurately assess the actual helping potential in the neighborhood setting, that is, perceptions need to be consistent with actual resources. Otherwise there is a danger that residents may end up under-utilizing resources or relying on resources which are not available or accessible when they are needed.

MODELS OF NEIGHBORHOOD TYPES

Neighborhood communities have social structures, although social scientists are not consistent in identifying which social dimensions aid in our understanding of these structures. Four different models for describing and analyzing neighborhood structure are presented here. All of the models present "ideal types" of neighborhoods in the sense that none of them fits a specific neighborhood in an exact way but approximates the features of a neighborhood type. These models have been selected because they can readily be used by the social worker in making assessments of a neighborhood for practice purposes.

Model 1: Warren and Warren (1977)

The first model focuses on social identity, social interaction, and linkages to the wider community. Neighborhood communities which have high identity, interaction, and linkages are labeled *integral neighborhoods*. Those with high identity and interaction but low level of linkages are known as *parochial neighborhoods*. *Diffuse neighborhoods* have high identity but low interaction and linkages. *Stepping-stone neighborhoods* are low in identity but high in social interaction and linkages. *Transitory neighborhoods* have high linkages but are low on the other two dimensions. Finally, *anomic neighborhoods* are low on all three dimensions. These six neighborhood types offer differential benefits for residents in terms of helping resources (Warren and Warren, 1977). Some of the benefits and limitations of these social contexts are as follows.

1. The *integral* neighborhood has a high capacity to identify its problems and to take action because of its internal organization and its links to the outside community. While this type of neighborhood may be easier for the higher social classes to create, it can be found not only in white-collar suburbs but in inner-city areas and blue-collar industrial communities.
2. Due to its strong group identity, through such factors as race, class, age, and physical isolation the *parochial* neighborhood has social integration, strong commitment to the locality, and a capacity to get things done when they can be accomplished without outside help. Yet, its functions for residents may be limited by a lack of linkages to the larger community.
3. The *diffuse* neighborhood has a high degree of collective capacity to act but doesn't exercise it. In this residential setting,

people feel they don't need the neighborhood for help or social interaction but, rather, are identified with their place of residence. Examples of these neighborhoods are found in some upper-class suburban housing areas and on high-rise luxury apartment dwellings.

4. *Stepping-stone* neighborhoods are areas in which people are highly mobile occupationally, socially, and residentially and, hence, positively, but not strongly, identified with their current neighborhood. They anticipate a move up in a relatively short period of time, usually connected to career and/or company moves. Of special concern would be the needs of individuals who get stuck in this type of neighborhood, who fail to move up and out. This is also not a good neighborhood for people who look to their neighbors to establish long-term friendships.

5. The *transitory* neighborhood has turnover and no mechanisms for dealing with it. People may use the broader community, or the "mass society," as a point of reference. There is little capacity for dealing with change, and at times this neighborhood appears to be anomic.

6. The *anomic* neighborhood, actually a "non-neighborhood," can be found in areas such as low-income, public-housing projects. This type of neighborhood seems to have no capacity for collective action. Large communities usually include some anomic neighborhoods.

These six neighborhood contexts are not rigid and static types. One type of neighborhood may remain as it is for years, or may evolve into another type. In some cases neighborhoods will generate problem-solving structures; in others they will lose them. This may be especially true as changes occur in the cultural/racial/ethnic groups which dominate a given neighborhood.

Model 2: Litwak (1985)

A second model for typing neighborhoods emphasizes two important dimensions of neighborhood primary groups: (1) The level of membership change or turnover and (2) the capacity to retain primary group cohesion/social integration. Using these characteristics, Litwak has created three major neighborhood types: mobile, traditional, and mass. *Mobile neighborhoods* have a high turnover of residents, but have mechanisms for quickly integrating new residents and for retaining neighborhood cohesion. The *traditional neighbor-*

hood has stability of membership and is not well suited for integrating new members. A *mass neighborhood* has high mobility of residents but little capacity for integrating new members or retaining neighborhood cohesion.

The usefulness of this typology is demonstrated by Litwak in regard to service needs of older adults. The traditional neighborhood offers these individuals the most readily available resources, as this neighborhood has some of the features of an extended family. However, when this type of neighborhood experiences a transition through an invasion of newcomers, the older adult may suffer as old-timers die or depart from the neighborhood. Older adults have the most difficulty in mass neighborhoods, especially if they are in ill health and cannot take care of the tasks of daily living. Understanding the nature of these neighborhood contexts is helpful when older adults consider making a residential move. Thus, persons with good health or minor health limitations might benefit most by moving into a mobile neighborhood, where some resources are available and where quick integration and acceptance is the norm. The mass neighborhood would not be a good move for individuals with health care needs, as it does not provide informal help from neighbors.

This model of neighborhood types, when applied to older adults, demonstrates the need for matching the resident's service needs with such features of the neighborhood as mobility of residents, the presence or absence of means of rapid social integration, and the availability of informal neighbor help and more formal services of health and welfare organizations. Health status is an important factor in considering the match between older adults and a neighborhood, especially when persons are considering a move from one residence to another.

Model 3: Fellin and Litwak (1968)

A third model of neighborhood types focuses on organizational, value, and change dimensions of neighborhood primary groups. The organizational base of neighborhoods may be identified in terms of the associational structure of informal contacts and of local formal organizations, for example, voluntary groups. Neighborhoods can be classified in terms of their level of organization and their capacity to implement their values. Values, then, comprise a second major dimension for classifying neighborhoods. Neighborhood values, such as orientation toward education and good citizenship, may be viewed on a positive-negative continuum. Neighborhoods vary in regard to whether the values of a neighborhood group are consistent with those of the general society. Combining these dimensions of organization and values leads to four types of neighborhoods, those with: (1) *positive values, organized*; (2) *positive values, unorganized*; (3) *negative values, organized*; and (4) *negative values, unorganized.*

Most "traditional" and "mobile" neighborhoods, such as middle-class suburban neighborhoods and stable working-class neighborhoods in central cities, illustrate the first neighborhood type. These neighborhoods are organized to implement positive values toward education, participation in community life, community improvement, and maintenance of law and order (Fellin and Litwak, 1968). The second neighborhood type is found in "mass" neighborhoods, such as the transitory neighborhood described by Warren and Warren (1977). The third type is represented in neighborhoods with high crime rates and many youth gangs, resembling the anomic neighborhood. The fourth type is illustrated by inner-city skid-row and rooming house neighborhood areas, as well as by many high-rise, low-income housing project neighborhoods.

Model 4: Figueira-McDonough (1991)

Figueira-McDonough uses an ecological perspective to construct a theoretical typology of communities in order to understand juvenile delinquency rates. Her typology makes use of some of the dimensions found in the previous models we have described and, while focusing on communities, is easily adapted to neighborhoods. In this model, two major dimensions guide the development of community types, population factors and organizational factors. Population factors include poverty and mobility (movement from one community to another). Organizational factors include informal networks (ties to kin, friends, informal groups), secondary formal networks (e.g., schools, recreational centers, church groups), and external links (external support, resources). In order to create "ideal" types of communities, Figueira-McDonough treats these variables as if they were dichotomous, recognizing that in real life they are continuous. In this way, four types of communities are constructed: (1) *stepping-stone community* (nonpoor and mobile; low primary networks, high secondary networks, high external links); (2) *established community* (nonpoor and stable; high primary networks, high secondary networks, low external links); (3) *disorganized community* (poor and mobile; low primary networks, low secondary networks, low external links); and (4) *parochial community* (poor and stable; high primary networks, low secondary networks, low external links). As noted above, the extent of primary and secondary networks and external links to the broader community vary among these community types.

Figueira-McDonough's stepping-stone community is similar to the stepping-stone neighborhood of Warren and Warren introduced as Model 1. The informal networks are weak, but there is high use of formal networks and strong external links. The established community is high in primary and secondary networks, low in external links, and is similar to the parochial neighborhood of Model 1. The disorganized community has difficulty in creating and maintaining primary and secondary networks, as well as external linkages, and is similar to the anomic neighborhood in Model 1. Finally, the parochial community has high primary networks, low secondary networks, and low external links, thus resembling the parochial neighborhood of Model 1.

This typology of communities emphasizes sources of resources by taking into consideration features of individual households (poverty) and of other members of the community (networks and external links). Hence this typology has particular relevance to social work practice at both the "micro" and "macro" levels, since it points to the need for assessment of the level and source of social supports available to clients. This framework can also be used to guide research on the relationship of community types to social problems. Figueria-McDonough uses the framework to predict which types of communities will have high and low rates of delinquent behavior. Thus, the disorganized community is predicted to have the highest rates of delinquency and the established community to have the lowest rates. The policy implications of these predictions suggest to Figueria-McDonough that "an effective response to the problem requires interventions that will strengthen the organization of communities . . . and that such interventions have to be tailored to the communities' characteristics and must take into account the demographic preconditions of organization."

SOCIAL WORK PRACTICE APPLICATIONS

Practice applications of the first model are illustrated in Warren and Warren's *The Neighborhood Organizers Handbook* (1977). The *Handbook* deals with how neighborhood types are related to questions of when to organize, how to identify leadership resources, how to reach out to a neighborhood, how to assess neighborhood functions, and how to select practice roles and tactics for working in a neighborhood. Another set of practice illustrations are presented in Warren's

Helping Networks: How People Cope with Problems in the Urban Community (1981). Warren uses Model 1 types of neighborhoods to assess the ways in which neighborhood contexts relate to the availability of resources within the community. Guidelines for practice interventions in the different types of neighborhoods are provided— for example, how to strengthen weak neighborhoods and how to make use of formal and informal helping networks.

The applications to practice of Model 2 have already been noted in regard to work with older adults, particularly in relation to the various neighborhood moves these individuals might make in their later years. The principal features of this model, the relationship of neighborhood membership turnover and the availability of formal and informal helping resources, can be applied to the various stages of the life cycle. For example, neighborhoods can be assessed according to these types when working with young families in need of rapid integration into a suburban neighborhood or into an inner-city neighborhood. Again, as in Model 1, this typology is useful in considering how helping resources, formal and informal, fit with the neighborhood type in order to select interventions which speed up neighborhood integration, such as creation of voluntary associations.

The neighborhood types described in Model 3 complement the typologies of Models 1 and 2. All three models include a focus on the organizational characteristics of neighborhoods, but Model 2 emphasizes the dimension of values. Recognition of the kinds of values of people in a neighborhood is helpful for both interpersonal as well as community practice. For example, as social workers engage in practice with neighborhood schools, the importance of the values of families toward education becomes apparent in working with parents in relation to problems of school children. Another example of the values dimension comes from neighborhoods which have high rates of crime and delinquency. The social worker needs to assess the values of residents toward law and order and toward tolerance of deviant behavior and their willingness to organize to implement these values.

Model 4 has some of the same features as the other models, especially in its focus on helping networks and resources. The focus of this model on poverty in relation to patterns of mutual aid makes it particularly salient for social workers. As we have already noted in our discussion of this model, practice at the community level can be enhanced through an understanding of how strong or weak primary groups and local organizations are within the neighborhood. This knowledge leads to the kinds of interventions which are most appropriate for different types of neighborhoods, such as the stepping-stone, established, disorganized, and parochial community neighborhoods. As with Model 3, this model complements the first two, and leads to similar practice applications.

NEIGHBORHOOD SOCIALIZATION PATTERNS

Once neighborhoods have been categorized in terms of major types along various dimensions of community, we may then consider additional neighborhood variations.

First, different socialization patterns in the various neighborhoods occur. Different processes emerge "in which neighbors influence one another over a period of time and shape the sense of community and values which then become the social norms of a neighborhood" (Warren & Warren, 1977). People select neighborhoods in terms of the kinds of neighbors they prefer . . . called "selective recruitment." This, combined with socialization, helps differentiate one neighborhood from another and reinforces the major categorization of a given neighborhood.

Second, neighborhood types vary in their ability to cope with change and population turnover. Thus, integral and stepping-stone neighborhoods, as mobile neighborhoods, handle turnover well in contrast to the difficulties of other types to cope with rapid population change.

Third, neighborhoods have different leadership structures in terms of local "formal" and "informal" leaders and their ability to act on behalf of the neighborhood within the group and in relation to outside groups.

Fourth, neighborhoods differ in the ways in which information is processed in terms of the complexity of neighborhood information, the content of the information, and the sources of it. These communication patterns have implications for the ways in which residents link to the larger community and utilize resources within and without the neighborhood.

SLUMS AND GHETTOS AS NEIGHBORHOODS

All large U.S. cities have "slums" and ghetto neighborhood communities. Most often these neighborhood types are not distinguished from each other. However, it is important to recognize that a ghetto may not be a slum, and a slum may not be a ghetto. Sociologists make an analytical distinction between these concepts. A ghetto is a "bounded residential area in which a defined racial or ethnic group is forced to live" (Choldin, 1985). The term *ghetto* reportedly comes from the designation of an area in Venice, Italy, where, in 1516, Jewish people were forced to live (Choldin, 1985). The most common use of the term in the U.S. today is in relation to areas where high proportions of African American or Hispanic people reside. Often the term *barrio* is used to describe a neighborhood with a high proportion of Hispanics (Reeves, 1981). The terms *ghetto* and *barrio* carry with them at least two other connotations, a poverty area and an area with a distinct culture. These residential areas are often characterized by a large number of low-income and unemployed individuals. Residents develop their own cultural patterns of social interaction, social control, and relationships to the standards of the larger community. Negative values, rejection of societal norms, and deviant behavior are attributed to the people in these areas. Increasingly, these areas have been labeled underclass communities or poverty areas (Wilson, 1987).

The reasons ghettos are often identified as slums is because of their physical environment, that is, deteriorated, run-down and undesirable housing units, evidence of filth, dirt, unsanitary conditions, including the blighted condition of the streets, alleys, parks, business buildings, and boarded-up and unoccupied structures. The atmosphere or the "feel" of the slum is created by these undesirable physical conditions, reinforced by conditions of poverty, health problems, family disorganization, high crime rates, and lack of safety.

It is instructive to reflect back to the neighborhood types developed by Warren (1981) and to consider how ghetto and slum neighborhoods fit into the Model 1 framework. Based on descriptions of ghetto and slum neighborhoods, such as parts of Harlem in New York, the South Side of Chicago, the barrio community areas of East Los Angeles (Reeves, 1981), some of these neighborhoods could be classified as "anomic" or "transitory." It appears that few ghettos or slums represent integral neighborhoods. However, some ethnic ghetto neighborhoods resemble the parochial type of neighborhood, with strong resident identification with the area, positive social interactions, and few links to the larger community. Most ghetto neighborhoods are transitory or anomic, lacking in positive identity, social interactions, or linkages to the larger community.

The common image of ghetto/slums is a negative one. The people in a ghetto or slum neighborhood are often regarded as having group or cultural characteristics, and patterns of social interaction which involve rejection of conventional societal and community norms and values and lack of moral or social order and social control. The urban skid row provides an illustration of this type of neighborhood. People living in high poverty areas of large urban cities have been described by Wilson (1987) as being socially dislocated from the mainstream community.

Another view of ghetto neighborhoods was provided by Suttles in his study of Chicago slums. Suttles (1968) found that slums, rather than being disorganized, had a social order of their own. His study of the Addams area in Chicago showed that an order emerged from the fact that most residents followed conventional norms of behavior. Even deviants developed a system of control and organization which resulted in a social order. The neighborhoods Suttles studied contained populations of African Americans, Puerto Ricans, Italians, and Mexican Americans. Suttles found that these groups used an "ordered segmentation" to guide their social relations with one another, that is, these ethnic and racial groups established informal territorial, institutional, and communication arrangements to handle conflicts.

SUBURBAN NEIGHBORHOODS

Neighborhoods in "new" suburban communities tend to be stratified by social class and segregated in terms of race. These neighborhoods still provide some of the functions of neighborhood primary groups, such as a sociability arena, an interpersonal influence center, an organizational base, a reference group, and a status area (Warren and Warren, 1977). However, the level of social interaction and mutual aid is considerably lower than that found in the "old" neighborhoods of yesteryear. Suburban neighborhoods can be classified in terms of the three dimensions of social interaction, identity, and linkages to the wider community. From this perspective, the neighborhood types of integral, diffuse, and stepping-stone are most common in the suburbs.

A social work practice response to the problems of suburban families by a child and family guidance center illustrates the use of a group-work approach in a suburban neighborhood (Malekoff, Levine, Quaglia, 1987). The North Shore Child and Family Guidance Center in New York recognized such problems and needs of families in suburban communities as disconnection, social isolation, absence of social supports, and need for parent education and self-help networks. A neighborhood-based group-work approach was used to develop a Parent's Network, which focused on the creation of small parent groups led by a social worker in a parent's home. This program demonstrates how a social agency in a suburban community can create neighborhood primary groups which focus on "the core values of mutual aid, democratic functioning, and civic responsibility" (Malekoff, Levine, Quaglia, 1987).

REVIEW

Neighborhoods are viewed as geographical areas which are "functional" for residents through the provision of services and activities in addition to shelter. Boundaries of neighborhoods may be defined to include the area in which these services and activities are located, such as an elementary school district. Neighborhoods are also defined as "personal" arenas, where the neighborhood is perceived as a small area in which the members constitute a primary group, with neighboring and personal relationships determining the boundaries. Four models of neighborhood types are introduced, followed by illustrations of the use of these models in social work practice. Attention is then given to socialization patterns of neighborhoods, as well as to the ways in which slums and ghettos have been characterized as neighborhoods. Finally, an example of a group-work program in a suburban neighborhood is introduced, illustrating how an assessment of a neighborhood can be used by social workers to respond to the needs of suburban families.

SUGGESTED READINGS

Figueira-McDonough, Josephina (1991). "Community Structure and Delinquency: A Typology." *Social Service Review* 65:1 (March).

Litwak, Eugene (1985). *Helping the Elderly*. New York: Guilford Press.

Malekoff, Andrew, Marion Levine, and Sara Quaglia (1987). "An Attempt to Create a New 'Old Neighborhood.'" *Social Work with Groups* 10:3.

Warren, Donald and Rachelle Warren (1977). *The Neighborhood Organizer's Handbook*. Notre Dame, IN: The University of Notre Dame Press.

EXERCISE

Use one of the models of neighborhood types discussed in Chapter 5 to classify the South Bronx community described in the following news story. Draw from the news report to illustrate the various socialization patterns of neighborhoods identified in Chapter 5.

A SOUTH BRONX STREET RISES THROUGH THE TOIL OF POOR HOMESTEADERS

By Ellen Graham and Joseph N. Boyce

There may be no prouder property owner in the city of New York than Jose Madrigal. Mr. Madrigal, a 43-year-old of Mexican descent, has put down deep roots in a neighborhood that until recently was written off by most people as a hellish no man's land: the South Bronx.

It's an area that has become a symbol of despair in the midst of America's plenty. In 1977, President Jimmy Carter stood amid the Dresden-like landscape and vowed to rebuild. The Bronx became a quadrennial campaign backdrop, as well as the setting for much of Tom Wolfe's apocalyptic novel *The Bonfire of the Vanities*.

The sporadic bursts of attention proved of little help to those who actually lived here. By the end of the '70s, the neighborhood had lost 70% of its population. Landlords set buildings ablaze for the insurance. "It was desolate," recalls Millie Velez, who grew up here. "Even the junkies left."

Sweat Equity

Now, however, there is change again in the South Bronx. A few of the people who stayed behind, like Mr. Madrigal, have begun to succeed where the politicians and other well-wishers failed. Poor people in need of decent housing, they banded together in 1977 and stopped the city from demolishing three empty tenements in the 900 block of Kelly Street. After working all day driving taxis or operating machines, they worked an additional eight hours in shoulder-high debris, restoring the abandoned shells that landlords had left to rot and burn. The apartments finally sold for $250 to those who had invested at least 600 hours of labor. Out of those first three buildings grew housing for 21 families.

Also created was the Banana Kelly Community Improvement Association, a grass-roots self-help organization named after the crescent-shaped block where it began. In its early days, a boxing match had to be held to raise money for tools. A dumpster was bought with $500 someone won in a beauty contest. Outside funding eventually began to trickle in as organizers learned to write proposals and to traverse the labyrinthine city bureaucracy.

Today the organization has a staff of 90 that manages 415 apartments, plus a $22 million budget that includes funds to renovate an additional 333 units. Part of the neighborhood—now largely Hispanic—has even been designated a historic landmark district, where apartments rent for up to $700 a month and stately brownstones have sold for nearly $200,000.

Something to Be Proud Of

For Mr. Madrigal and others like him, "sweat equity" arrangements, in which labor constitutes most of the down payment, have provided an otherwise unobtainable ticket to home ownership and, in many respects, to the middle class. Mr. Madrigal now proudly houses his family in a spacious five-bed-room, two-bath apartment he spent 2,800 hours renovating. "We are poor," he says, "but we have something that is ours. When you use your own blood, sweat, and tears, it's part of your soul. You stand and say, 'I did it.'"

Yet in the South Bronx today, the pride and self-determination have begun to collide with some of the grander agendas of city officials. The success of groups like Banana Kelly has shown city planners what potential lies in the vast wasteland just north of Manhattan. And in some ways, the area's new-found value poses a threat to those who have worked so hard to make it livable.

Like property owners everywhere, the homesteaders are jealously protective of their investments. They see their neighborhood as a fragile oasis of stability imperiled by the magnitude of the city's drug and housing crises. Now they are torn between extending a helping hand and pulling up the ladder before their rebuilt neighborhood is swamped by new waves of the desperately poor.

Close the Gate

"Let me tell you a true story," says Abraham Biderman, the city's commissioner of Housing, Preservation and Development. "Last year we fixed up an apartment [building] for the homeless in the Bronx. After successfully resettling the families, we began planning to fix up the building next door for more homeless people. But the families in the first building said they didn't want any more homeless in their neighborhood."

Mr. Madrigal and most of his neighbors remember their own struggles too well to turn their backs completely on those who are now in similar straits. But with the long-neglected South Bronx now a wide-open urban frontier, they are painfully aware that a delicate balance must be struck as the territory is resettled.

A central issue is the city's plan to use the thousands of still-vacant apartments it owns here to help solve its housing crisis. New York City has begun a 10-year, $5.1 billion program to create affordable housing for 250,000 homeless, low-income and middle-income families—a municipal construction project so ambitious it is equal to providing new or renovated housing for the entire population of Buffalo.

A $1 billion chunk of that funding is earmarked for the South Bronx, where 20,000 city-owned abandoned apartments are targeted for "gut rehab." Mr. Biderman boasts that "the South Bronx as a national symbol of urban blight is very quickly becoming a fading memory."

But around Kelly Street, resentment simmers over the city's plan to cluster in the South Bronx nearly 70% of the homeless families it is resettling—a policy that some term "the laundering of Manhattan." This concentration of the needy is being pushed through, local residents charge, without adequate support to help the homeless adjust. Already, they say, the influx of people is straining local services, which were cut sharply when the area lost most of its population during the '70s.

The maternity ward at Lincoln Hospital, the main municipal facility in the South Bronx, is designed for 2,500 deliveries annually but handles more than double that number. And only some 29% are "normal" births, uncomplicated by such factors as low birth weight, AIDS or drug addiction. (Nearly 500 of the infants last year were born affected by crack cocaine.)

When they first joined forces, the Kelly Street pioneers could not have envisioned a nightmare equal to the arson and abandonment then swallowing up their neighborhood. But it has come, in the form of crack. For the past three years, the highly addictive drug has been openly dealt on the south side of the area's main commercial thoroughfare, Longwood Avenue, where dealers appear to have consistent hours and clearly delineated turfs. Even some Banana Kelly buildings have become infested with dealers.

The drug has proven more than a match for police and local activists. After mustering 200 people for an antidrug rally in the neighborhood a year ago, Bertha Lewis, a neighborhood organizer until her recent move to Greensboro, N.C., and others on Banana Kelly's antidrug task force planned a second event for last November. The night before it was to take place, she says, all 30 members of the task force steering committee received telephoned threats, presumably from local dealers. Turnout for the rally was poor. Ms. Lewis thinks the demonstrators' courage in the face of this was pivotal in bringing the police Tactical Narcotics Team into the neighborhood for a 96-day sweep, during which 1,500 drug arrests were made. Now that the team has departed, however, residents fear the dealers will return. "It's just like moving dirt around," says Mr. Madrigal.

But success has another side. Banana Kelly has taken some criticism for occasionally veering from its longstanding emphasis on low-income housing. It is sponsoring construction of 80 two-family homes in the Sound View section of the Bronx that it will sell for $160,000 each. Getz Obstfeld, Banana Kelly's executive director, talks of the "balancing act" involved in stabilizing neighborhoods. "We're trying to promote a mix," he says. "There are two-earner families in the area that are renting. If we don't provide home ownership, they'll flee.

Mr. Obstfeld insists that the punishing work of homesteading, while tremendously important as a symbol of hope, is difficult to sustain. He offers this paradox: Currently, he says, Banana Kelly is trying to mobilize neighbors to renovate the Kelly Street park. "We have $30,000 to rebuild it, and minimum participation. In the old days, we had nothing to build it with, and we built it."

Fern Bars?

Banana Kelly's evolution from a movement to an organization troubles some of the earlier pioneers. It's now "a business like anything else," asserts Ms. Velez.

Some even worry that the area's new commercial potential may lead to the sort of gentrification that could force the oldtime residents out. Ms. Lewis, the organizer, doubts that the planned transformation of the South Bronx will ultimately benefit the poor. She has bitter memories of the Philadelphia slum in which she was raised, where she says the same pattern of fires, abandonment, and flight was exploited by developers who moved in and bought up land at depressed prices.

As a girl, she says, "I remember seeing a new building being built on the waterfront—I think they called it Society Towers. I said to my grandmother, 'Isn't that wonderful?' My grandmother said, 'Girl, those people got plans, and they don't include you.'"

Whether such fears are warranted or not, it is clear that the South Bronx is at a new crossroads, capable of heading in either direction. Many in the community feel powerless to decide its fate. But Mr. Madrigal believes that the pride and self-determination taking root there will ultimately allow residents to prevail. "We are so close," he says. "We could build a paradise of this neighborhood."

His son Fernando, 17, isn't sure. He says his high school is torn with strife between black, Dominican, and Puerto Rican gangs, and a friend of his was shot dead last year by a group of toughs. "It's going to be hard," he says, shaking his head doubtfully.

Mr. Madrigal takes a swig of thick Latin coffee and stares pointedly at Fernando across their dining-room table. "How many weekends we work here?" he reminds his son. "We built it ourselves. Nothing is easy, baby."

Throngs of New Pupils

The schools, too, are being pushed to the breaking point. At P.S. 62, principal Muriel Pagan says the local school district has had to absorb 239 new units of homeless housing over the summer. Many children from those families will be assigned to her school, already overburdened by overcrowding and poverty. (Only 10% of the 875 students at P.S. 62 live in homes with telephones.) Ms. Pagan has expedited repairs on the aging school building's damaged roof, which sidelined several classrooms this past year. "And if worse comes to worst, we'll have to uncap the limits on class size," she says.

Many shelter residents have already been resettled here, and tensions flare from time to time. Marta Rivera, a caseworker with the Casita Maria Settlement House on Simpson Street, lived for a time in a Banana Kelly building that took in 21 families displaced by a fire. Unemployed and crowded four to a bedroom, the homeless tenants were disruptive, she says. "There was screaming in the hallways at all hours—they'd stay up all night. It was very annoying for a person who works."

Even so, Ms. Rivera and others argue that isolating homeless families in one building or block is a mistake. The Rev. Louis Gigante, a priest whose South East Bronx Community Organization has erected 2,000 units of housing in this area, says: "We learned you can't put all poor in one place. You've got to mix it."

Under pressure from housing advocates, the city recently backed down from plans to create 100% homeless buildings under its Special Initiatives Program. Now the formula calls for half homeless and half working poor, among whom preference will be given to community residents. The housing department says many of these buildings—attractively finished with oak floors and tiled bathrooms—will offer services such as job training or day care on the premises.

Upward Mobility

The city will rely heavily on nonprofit community groups like Banana Kelly to manage this housing. Banana Kelly hopes to turn one building for the homeless at 800 Fox Street into a model, enlisting tenants in a "work prep" training program designed to get them off welfare rolls.

Nonetheless, 800 Fox Street is controversial. Gonzalo Ortiz, a 74-year-old retired city employee who has lived in the neighborhood for 40 years, says he's been assured that the homeless tenants will be screened carefully. But as he sees it, Banana Kelly "must take whoever the city tells them to take" or risk the loss of funding for its projects.

Mr. Ortiz reflects the kind of upward mobility now possible in the neighborhood. He bought the Beck Street building in which he lives 31 years ago for $10,000, and thinks it would fetch $200,000 today. A grown son and daughter live in two other buildings he owns on the block, and a grandson attends Yale University on scholarship. "Ten years ago," he says, "all the smartest people were leaving. They sold cheap, and now they are sorry."

CHAPTER 6

Emergence of Social Class and Ethnic Minority Neighborhoods

SOCIAL CLASS NEIGHBORHOODS

Neighborhoods, like the communities of which they are a part, display social differences and can be characterized according to their social class composition. Indicators of social class presented in Chapter 4—occupational status, income, education, and lifestyle—may be used singly or in some combination in order to classify neighborhoods. Community planners, the news media, and residents often label neighborhoods with terms such as working class, blue collar, white collar, middle class, or upper class, rich or poor. The status of urban neighborhoods is closely associated with these social class terms. Terms used to label lower-class neighborhoods include poor, ghetto, slum, and skid row.

The relationship between neighborhoods and social class is apparent in the following ecological perspective. "The urban neighborhood becomes a highly visible manifestation of the status structure, and individual occupational careers come to be mirrored in one's residential movements. A home is not just where you live; it is a location in a well developed status ecology and, inferentially, a telltale clue to one's location in the occupational hierarchy" (Laumann, Siegel, and Hodge, 1970).

Along these lines, Logan (1978) takes the view that "residence itself affects the chances for social rewards." When the advantages of neighborhood location and class are combined, they have a very powerful effect on the resources and liabilities of neighborhood residents. Many communities, especially suburban ones, through political actions such as zoning, taxation policies, or allocation of public resources, seek to establish and maintain these advantages of place for their neighborhoods. They act to develop and reinforce the positive features of class and status for their residents. As a consequence social differentiation of neighborhoods becomes a means of organizing inequality (Logan, 1978).

Why do people live where they live? A major factor appears to be the appeal of a place which makes them feel comfortable. Comfort may involve safety, interaction with people with similar lifestyles, or nearness to people of the same social class. It is not surprising that most neighborhoods house people of similar socioeconomic groups, as people find comfort in living with "their own kind." Thus, when a house is purchased, buyers may place equal or higher importance on "kinds of people" in the neighborhood than on the features of the house. This suggests that a combination of location, house, and people provide recognition of a neighborhood community as a highly visible status symbol.

HETEROGENEOUS AND HOMOGENEOUS NEIGHBORHOODS

Prior to the 1960s there were some striking exceptions to the picture of class-linked neighborhoods. Thus, in some residential areas largely populated by African Americans or Hispanics, residents represented different social class levels within the same neighborhood area (Wilson, 1987). For example, Warren (1975) found in his study of Detroit neighborhoods that African American ghetto areas displayed a "compression" of class levels, a blurring across class lines, and considerable heterogeneity in their populations. Residents had a diversity of values, economic differences, lifestyles, and reference-group orientations and a high degree of status inconsistency. A similar picture emerged in the study of Hispanic neighborhoods, such as Boyle Heights, California (Reeves, 1981), and in central city areas of Chicago before the out migration of middle-class whites and African Americans (Suttles, 1968; Wilson, 1987).

Other examples of neighborhoods which had heterogeneous social class levels come from studies of central-city communities with high proportions of Jewish, Catholic, Polish, Italian, or Irish populations. In these cases, some individuals who ranked higher socially than most area residents chose to reside in these neighborhoods because of family, ethnic, or religious ties. Still other examples of social class heterogeneity are found in planned communities, such as a neighborhood in Rochester, New York (Hunter, 1975); neighborhood communities in Columbia, Maryland (Hirsch, 1992), and Reston, Virginia. Likewise, neighborhoods in small towns often contained residents identified with various levels of social class.

By the 1990s, most racial and ethnic neighborhoods were no longer heterogeneous in terms of social class, especially in inner-city areas of large central cities (Rusk, 1993). Some of the changes which led to the class homogenization within ghetto poverty areas in cities such as Chicago are identified by Wilson (1987). These include societal, demographic, and neighborhood factors, such as discrimination, changes in age structure, economic changes, and concentration effects of poor people living in poverty areas. Such concentration of the poor came about as a result of the movement of working-class and middle-class people away from inner-city neighborhoods. This explanation of change in the class structure of inner-city neighborhoods is supported by Wilson's (1987) analysis of African American communities in Chicago.

SOCIAL STATUS OF NEIGHBORHOODS

Given the mobility of Americans within and between communities, is the social status of neighborhoods maintained over time? Studies of inner-city neighborhoods demonstrate the loss of status due to such changing economic circumstances of the residents as welfare dependency and the out-migration of upwardly-mobile individuals and families (Wilson, 1987). Do suburban communities experience a loss of status over time? Choldin et al. (1980) address this issue in their examination of the "suburban persistence of social status." Using income, occupational status, and education as measures of status, they found that suburban neighborhoods often do change in status over time. In a typical neighborhood life cycle, the status of an area rises over two decades, and then declines. This type of residential change by succession of social class groups differs from racial or ethnic group succession in that the change occurs over a relatively long period of time and may be a function of the age of the dwellings and the life-cycle changes of the families in the residential areas. In suburban areas neighborhood status remains reasonably stable, and changes in social status are less visible and less extensive than in lower- and underclass neighborhood communities.

Logan's (1978) work on the stratification of places suggests that communities reinforce the interests of individuals in fostering segregation by class and status. Legal restrictions, zoning in particular, are used to assure some communities of advantages of location, creating an organized and controlled pattern of inequality. Thus, home is not just where you live but also a status symbol. From this view, where you live affects your "chances for social rewards," and one would expect communities to seek to retain individuals in high status neighborhood areas or to assist in creating new status residential areas. Communities seek to maintain or enhance the social status of its neighborhoods and its residents. This is especially true under conditions of expansion and growth of communities. One can conclude, then, that suburban communities in particular retain their status through various governmental efforts, and that if and when succession occurs in terms of the social class and status of neighborhood residents, it develops very slowly. In contrast, when the succession process involves inner-city neighborhoods, with white and non-white flight of middle- and working-class people, the status of these areas goes down quickly.

ETHNIC NEIGHBORHOODS

Ethnic neighborhoods are found in the central cities of most large urban areas. They are often referred to as "communities," based on a high proportion of residents identified by a single race or nationality group. People living within and outside of these areas identify them in terms of an African American community, a Mexican American community, an Arabic community, an Italian community, a Polish community, an Irish community, and so forth. Many of these neighborhood communities are in inner-city areas where there is mixed land use, including apartments, homes, business and commercial buildings, churches, schools, and social agencies. Examples of racial and ethnic neighborhood communities are described by Suttles (1968) in terms of "locality groups" in the Addams area of Chicago, with separate neighborhoods of African Americans, Italians, Puerto Ricans, and Mexican Americans.

While Native Americans reside in central cities of metropolitan areas, their numbers are still small enough to preclude concentration into neighborhoods identified as Native American (Snipp, 1989). However, as Native Americans have relocated, there is some evidence that they seek out neighborhoods where other Native Americans already reside (Sorkin, 1978). Native Americans usually reside initially in inner-city neighborhoods and often encounter problems of housing, employment discrimination, and lack of social services. Although these neighborhoods include other ethnic minorities, especially African American and Spanish-speaking residents, Native Americans have traditionally resisted social interaction with other neighborhood residents; they are more likely to interact informally with other Native Americans—at home, in Native American centers, and in church-related programs (Sorkin, 1978).

While poor and working-class ethnic minorities mainly live in the inner cities of large metropolitan areas, where does the ethnic minority middle class live? Those with professional occupations are likely to be widely distributed throughout suburban communities. Increasingly, however, ethnic minority working-class and middle-class individuals and families have moved into central city and nearby suburban communities where there is a high concentration of minority population of similar social class (Nathan, 1991). For example, African Americans and Hispanics have been moving into these neighborhoods from poverty areas or from other communities. These neighborhoods have been identified as "zones of emergence" by Nathan (1991), not unlike the 1920s movement of the Irish in Boston beyond the center of the city.

A number of these new emerging communities stand in marked contrast to the inner-city poverty areas usually associated with ethnic minority populations. Nathan (1991) has identified some of these neighborhoods. One such area is the Buckeye-Woodland neighborhood in Cleveland, where a mostly Hungarian population has departed and approximately 20,000 African Americans now live. Another area is the Sunset Park neighborhood in Brooklyn, with a high proportion of Puerto Ricans. Other areas with increasingly high proportions of working-class and middle-class African Americans and Hispanics are found in New York City communities of Queens, Brooklyn, and the Bronx; Minneapolis Central; the Hickman Mills area of Kansas City; and Aurora, Colorado.

SPATIAL AND SOCIOPSYCHOLOGICAL COMMUNITIES

For most ethnic minority residents, the neighborhood is a spatial community as well as a sociopsychological community (Taylor, 1979). In his discussion of the development of Black ethnicity in Northern urban communities, Taylor provides a conceptual framework for analyzing the variety of ways in which these residents relate to their community. Black ethnicity is said to develop out of residential segregation patterns. For instance, as southern Blacks migrated to large northern cities under conditions of "severe racial discrimination and structured inequality" (Taylor, 1979), they settled mainly in segregated residential neighborhoods. As a result "specialized Black institutions and services, newspapers, churches, bars, cafes, developed . . . and promoted internal bonds and cohesion among older and more recent Black residents in northern cities." This form of neighborhood development is sometimes referred to as gemeinschaft or neo-gemeinschaft, indicating ethnic minority relationships that are "personal, informal, traditional, gender, and sentiment based" (Rivera and Erlich, 1981).

Strong familial and organizational ties have provided minorities with essential social and cultural resources to cope with the problems of urban society. In some cities the segregated areas take on the characteristics of self-contained communities, highly visible in such cities as New York, Chicago, Los Angeles, Philadelphia, Detroit, Cleveland, Boston, and New Haven (Kinkead, 1991; Finnegan, 1990). In these areas residential segregation fosters minority political participation, serving to reinforce ethnicity. Taylor (1979) maintains that segregation in American communities is the factor that has led to the development of the contemporary urban Black residential area as both a spatial and sociopsychological community.

Taylor's framework for understanding these communities focuses on four segments which combine residence and patterns of identification. Segment A comprises a majority of urban Blacks who reside in areas with a Black resident majority and have a positive identification with the Black community. Segment B is formed by Blacks living in integrated white communities but retaining identification with the Black community through involvements in Black organizations and social contacts with residents in Black areas. Segment C includes Blacks who live in areas with a Black majority but do not identify with or participate in the Black community. The smallest, Segment D, includes individuals who neither reside in a Black spatial community nor identify in a sociopsychological way with the Black community. While Taylor's work focuses on African Americans, his framework can be used to examine spatial and psychosocial aspects of other ethnic minority communities as well as communities identified with a white ethnic group and/or those which are associated with a religious group.

SEGREGATION IN NEIGHBORHOODS

Contrary to the popular image of America as a "melting-pot" of races and ethnic groups, most communities in the United States continue to be highly segregated in terms of white and nonwhite residents. The concepts of segregation and integration serve to describe neighborhoods and communities, with segregated neighborhoods having a high proportion of ethnic minority and/or cultural group membership (Rusk, 1993). There are various measures of residential segregation, such as the use of an index of dissimilarity developed by Taeuber and Taeuber (1965) which measures "the extent to which any two groups are separated from each other" (Farley, 1987), an exposure index which describes each group in terms of exposure to the other, and a measure of the "percentage of blacks and whites who live on racially homogeneous blocks." Harrison and Weinberg (1992) examined Black, Hispanic, Asian, and Native American groups, using 1990 Census data based on the Taeuber index and measuring for evenness, exposure, concentration, centralization, and clustering. This analysis shows segregation of ethnic minority groups. In general, African Americans were much more segregated than the other groups.

Empirical studies of housing patterns in American communities continue to leave no question about the fact that housing segregation is in large part due to discrimination and prejudice based on race or ethnicity (Tobin, 1987; *New York Times*, 1991; *Wall Street Journal*, 1992). This finding is particularly clear with regard to housing patterns of African Americans (*Wall Street Journal*, 1992). There are, of course, other reasons for the persistence of segregated housing in the United States, such as socioeconomic factors (ability to pay for the cost of housing) and a preference of nonwhites to live in racially homogeneous neighborhoods, as well as other nonracial causes. Although federal legislation such as the 1968 Fair Housing Act and court decisions have brought about some changes in the extent of discrimination in housing, the activities of several major groups involved in housing (e.g., real estate brokers, home builders, banks, savings and loan associations, and local, state, and federal governments) continue to maintain residential segregation (Darden, 1987; Karr, 1993).

WHITE FLIGHT

In a growing number of American cities, more than one-half of the population is represented by ethnic minority groups. These cities have large areas of segregated neighborhoods, whereas few suburban communities have neighborhoods with high minority membership. Changes in patterns of neighborhood residence in the United States, especially from the time of World War II to the present, provide examples of the processes of segregation and succession. In the period following World War II there was a dramatic movement of whites to suburban residential areas, often described as "white flight." This development can be explained by a combination of both racial and non-racial causes. Racially related causes for the movement of whites from the central cities to mostly segregated suburban communities include white prejudices against living in neighborhoods with ethnic minorities, increases in racial disorders within the central city, attempts to desegregate city schools, discriminatory housing practices limiting the movement of minorities to suburban areas, and increases in ethnic minorities migrating into central cities.

Non-racial causes for white flight include the following "pushes" and "pulls."

- the pent-up housing needs of white families in central cities
- the accessibility of new suburban housing with open spaces and additional rooms
- an economy which supported upward social and occupational mobility
- availability of low-interest loans from private and public sources
- new employment opportunities in suburban areas
- lower taxes
- more segregated neighborhoods in the suburbs

There were also "pushes" to the suburbs due to a growing perception of central-city problems such as rising taxes, crime, a declining quality of schools and municipal services, and a deteriorating physical environment. By all accounts many of these racial and nonracial causes continue to assure segregated neighborhood areas in the central cities. At the same time, suburban rings of central cities have always had some minority group members as residents. A select few in higher status occupational groups usually enter suburban neighborhoods in a scattered manner. In large metropolitan areas there are a few suburban neighborhoods which have had over long periods of time a high proportion of minority residents. By the 1990s, a number of suburban neighborhoods had become ethnic minority communities. At the same time, minorities in professional occupations usually move into suburban neighborhoods which are for the most part white.

SUBURBANIZATION OF AFRICAN AMERICANS

An interesting "port of entry" concept has been used by Rose (1976) to explain suburbanization of ethnic minorities. Rose studied fifteen communities which displayed movement of African Americans into suburbs. In some of these communities minorities had moved from central-city ghettos to contiguous suburban areas through a "port of entry," a housing area which connects the central city with a suburban community. As a result, "Black suburbanization simply represents another settlement phase, and not a major reordering of the way Blacks acquire residential access." Rose observed some blue-collar, lower-class, and middle-class African Americans moving through ports of entry to "inner suburbs." At the same time some middle-class and upper-middle-class African Americans were able to move from the central city or the inner suburbs into mostly white suburban areas.

The history of movement of African Americans to the suburbs has been described by Farley (1987), Farley and Frey (1994), and Tobin (ed., 1987). Types of areas which have attracted African Americans are:

1. older, densely settled suburbs that often contain, or are located close to, centers of employment (African Americans move into these white neighborhoods because they can afford the housing, which is available because whites are moving on to newer suburbs.)
2. new suburban developments built to attract African Americans, and some new, purposely integrated communities
3. low-value homes in suburban neighborhood areas and some public housing developments

Farley's (1978) characterization of integration and segregation of neighborhoods prior to the 1980s appears to hold for the 1990s, that is, the suburbanization of African Americans has not changed in patterns of racial segregation very much (Farley and Frey, 1994).

SUCCESSION

The ecological concept of succession is particularly useful in understanding changes in neighborhood residential populations. Succession is "the series of events involved in the replacement of one neighborhood population or land use by another" (Aldrich, 1975). Historically, neighborhood residential areas in central cities have changed through this process of succession—the replacement of one immigrant group by another. This type of succession, involving white European immigrants, has been regarded as a "normal and orderly process of social change in an urban community" (Aldrich, 1975). Population groups characterized by their color, such as African Americans, Hispanics, Asian Americans, and Native Americans, have increasingly been involved in the process of succession. Most dramatic in American society has been the movement of African Americans into white residential areas. In central cities, particularly, this process of succession has led to relatively "permanent" segregated housing areas, unlike the succession patterns of European immigrants.

Our understanding of succession is enhanced by the work of Aldrich (1975), who examines the process by means of a framework that can be applied to the movement of people of color into white areas.

1. the causes and initial conditions of the process
2. the process of racial change itself
3. the social and economic consequences of the process

In the first phase there is an "established" group and an "invading" group. A key condition for residential succession is that housing opportunities be available to the members of the established group. For example, when African Americans are the "invading" group, the process begins with "pioneers" breaking barriers to enter the white area. The process then moves from a normal replacement rate to a "tipping" point, when whites begin to move out rapidly. At this point, real estate people may take advantage of the situation and actively promote further change in residential composition.

The assumption is that the process continues to the point of full succession. An example of complete succession is provided in the work of Levine and Harmon (1992) on *The Death of an American Jewish Community*. During a period between 1968 and 1970 the Boston communities of Roxbury, Dorchester, and Mattapan changed from an area with 90,000 Jews to a majority of African American residents. Levine and Harmon contend that a combination of bankers and brokers, along with federal agencies, were responsible for the collapse of a Jewish community. One of the major strategies which was believed to have caused the turnover of the neighborhood was blockbusting, "the scare tactics used by commission-hungry real estate brokers to force the quick sale of homes." However dominant this pattern of complete succession may be, in many cases efforts to reverse or stop the process in order to maintain integration are successful.

A number of social consequences have been observed in neighborhood residential areas that are in the process of succession. Community-based organizations and voluntary associations associated with the established group decline or change to memberships of the invading groups. In many cases new organizational memberships emerge among the invading group. Social interaction of residents, such as neighboring, may change in these areas, but the nature of the new patterns of interaction is not well established. There is some evidence provided by Aldrich and Reiss (1976) that small businesses change from white to minority ownership. Property values often decline and eventually stabilize, but they may never rise to the extent they might have without succession.

In residential areas where African Americans move in to replace whites, the white view of the "invaders" is generally negative (Aldrich, 1975). Whites assume that there will be an increase in the density of population (conversion of single to multiple dwelling units), in the composition of households (extended family, friends), in the ways residential structures are used (as gathering places), and in the character of local institutions (more businesses owned by minorities of color). It is not uncommon that social relations between the long-time residents and the newcomers become strained.

CREATION AND MAINTENANCE OF RESIDENTIAL INTEGRATION

A number of communities have made special efforts to create and/or maintain racial diversity in their neighborhoods. Two major approaches to intervene with the process of succession and to counter the effects of housing discrimination and other forces creating residential segregation have been (1) governmental programs involving legislation and fair housing enforcement and (2) various activities of local communities. Federal, state, and local governmental fair-housing laws exist, but this has not resulted in the elimination of discrimination in housing or in the creation of residential integration. This conclusion is supported in housing studies and in various social policy statements, such as a report on "The Costs of Discrimination and Segregation: An Interdisciplinary Social Science Statement" (Tobin, 1987). A number of housing study analysts have faulted federal, state, and local governments for not achieving housing integration goals, and for creating and perpetuating segregated housing (Rabin, 1987; Lief and Goering, 1987).

A second major approach to residential integration and segregation has involved the goals and activities of local communities. Residential integration and integration maintenance have become major goals of an increasing number of local communities in the United States in the past decade. Related to these goals are various activities directed toward specific objectives stated in terms of "achieving a racial balance," "achieving integration," "integration maintenance," and "reduction of segregation." The most frequent examples involve attempts to attract African Americans into white neighborhoods and to attract whites into integrated areas to avoid resegregation. Examples of efforts toward creation of integrated communities include Oak Park, Illinois (Klibanoff, 1984); Park Forest, Illinois (Hayes, 1990); Southfield, Michigan (Jones, 1990); Shaker Heights, Ohio (Pepper, 1990); Oakland County, Michigan (Dozier, 1993; and Columbia, Maryland (Hirsch, 1993).

Crucial and challenging questions have been raised in regard to the goals and programs of these communities to promote and maintain residential integration. What is a desirable level of integration, in terms of percentages of whites/ethnic minority group and in terms of distribution of households with these characteristics? Who defines the level of desirability, the white population or the ethnic minority population, or both? Can a neighborhood or community become "too integrated"? Are programs which involve affirmative marketing through stimulation of white housing market demand or ethnic minority demand racist and discriminatory?

Saltman (1991) sought to answer some of these questions through a study of fifteen urban communities throughout the country which had engaged in neighborhood integration maintenance efforts. Neighborhoods in the study were grouped into three categories.

1. Success: live neighborhood organization, stable racially diverse neighborhood
2. Failure: dead organization, mostly Black neighborhood
3. Conditional: live organization, transitional or mostly Black neighborhood.

Based on these studies, Saltman formed the following hypotheses about the success or failure of integration-maintenance programs.

The probability of . . . achieving a stable, racially diverse neighborhood . . . is greater:
1. the greater the amenities of the target neighborhood
2. the more supportive the role of the city

3. the more comprehensive a school desegregation program
4. the more deconcentrated the location of public housing
5. the more extensive an affirmative-marketing program
6. the more effective a regional fair-housing program
7. the greater the regional housing supply for all income levels
8. the earlier the timing of the movement effort (e.g. before the target neighborhood is racially identifiable)
9. the more securely and adequately funded the neighborhood movement organization is (Saltman, 1991).

Saltman concluded that racially diverse neighborhoods are maintained only with enormous difficulty. A description of some communities where such efforts have been made supports his propositions.

COMMUNITY EXAMPLES OF DIVERSE NEIGHBORHOODS

One of the first communities to seek a "racially diverse community" was Oak Park, Illinois (Klibanoff, 1984). The local government in this community led efforts to establish an open-housing ordinance in 1968, when the percentage of African American residents was 0.2 percent. By 1984 the percentage had increased to 13 percent as a result of a written local government policy to assemble "a mixture of racial and ethnic groups throughout the village." Financial incentives were offered to apartment building owners and tenants in order to increase residential integration, along with guarantees related to sale of single housing units. Coordination of these efforts was made possible through the creation of a Housing Center. A similar approach was followed in Park Forest, Illinois, a middle-class community of approximately 24,500 residents, of which 10 percent were African American in 1978 and approximately 20 percent in 1990. This community used "affirmative marketing" as its major method for attracting African Americans to reside in the community and to attract whites to maintain integration. The program also involved "steering," through which African American home buyers were directed to housing options in other white neighborhoods, housing counseling, bans on for-sale signs, and a fair-housing review board.

In Southfield, Michigan, with a population of 75,000, the major goal of the community has been "integration maintenance" (Jones, 1990). The change in composition of the community from 9 percent African American in 1980 to 30 percent African American in 1990 created the perception among some whites that the community had become "too integrated" as a result of high demand for housing by African Americans. Thus efforts were made by the local government to create a white housing demand through a multi-racial citizens board, a Housing and Neighborhood Center, joint efforts with Oakland County, and through collaboration with the local Jewish community, which organized to retain and attract Jewish families.

A somewhat different model is illustrated in the community of Shaker Heights, Ohio, within the Cleveland Metropolitan Area (Pepper, 1990). In this community of 32,000 people, with 29 percent African American, the major goal has been integration maintenance through programs to stimulate white demand and to open up housing options for African Americans within other suburbs in order to slow down their migration into Shaker Heights. The Shaker Heights programs focused on two levels, white suburbs in the metropolitan area and white neighborhoods within Shaker Heights. As a result, efforts were made to steer African Americans to other white suburbs and to direct African Americans into neighborhoods of 85 percent or more white residents.

In these examples, local governments have taken the initiative to create and/or maintain integrated communities, mainly with respect to whites and African Americans. In communities where the presence of African Americans has reach approximately one-third of the population, programs seek to maintain integration but restrict further ethnic minority population growth, that is, to stop the process of succession and resegregation. Maintenance of property values of residents appears to be an important motivating factor in all of the programs devoted to prevention of resegregation. All programs avoid the determination of specific quotas for the representation of ethnic minority groups in a community. However, one approach to determining proportions or mixes of population has been established by a Center for Open Housing in Oakland County, Michigan (Dozier, 1993). This county established a loan program with the purpose of facilitating integration. Under the program, "pro-integrative" moves are supported, defined in terms of the ethnic minority population of the County. Thus, with the County population at 9 percent minority, 10 percent is added, creating a figure of 19 percent as a guide for eligibility for a loan. If a white family moves into a neighborhood with less than 20 percent white, the move is defined as "pro-integrative," whereas a move is "pro-integrative" when an African American family moves into a neighborhood with 19 percent or less African Americans.

Community integration goals usually relate to the proportion of white and non-white people living in an area. It is generally assumed that social interaction between different racial and ethnic groups will occur, once the population is diverse. However, some evidence is emerging to suggest that racial and ethnic balance can be attained and maintained, but that "intermingling" or social interaction may not accompany this balance. Racial integration and assimilation was one of the primary goals in the development of the planned community of Columbia, Maryland, in the 1960s (Hirsch, 1992). While residential and school integration was achieved, as of 1992 there appeared to be in this community of about 73,000 people an emergence of separate social activities and social institutions, a "withdrawing into separate worlds" by some residents. This tendency has been noticed with regard to African American and white residents, and between Jewish and gentile residents. These observations about Columbia, Maryland, suggest that an important dimension of integrated communities is the nature of social interaction and identity on the part of residents with their own racial/ethnic/religious group. The example of Columbia suggests that various types of such interaction, some integrated and some separate, are likely to be found in communities which have achieved residential integration goals.

SETTLEMENT OF NEW IMMIGRANTS

In Chapter 3 we called attention to the ethnic groups represented by new non-European immigrants. Although there seems to be no systematic way to describe the residential patterns of this widely diverse group, Hernandez (1985) has proposed a set of "community types" which can be used as a beginning framework. Hernandez suggests that immigrants are likely to enter one of these neighborhoods or move from one to another over time. He has developed this typology based on observation of residential patterns of new immigrants in Chicago and New York neighborhoods. The neighborhood areas include:

1. The first community type is still the ghetto or barrio. [It generally includes a mix of ethnic and racial groups with a predominance of a single group.]
2. The heterogeneous new immigrant district in which no single minority group predominates. [It is more cosmopolitan and has better housing and other services than the ghetto or barrio.]

3. The multiethnic, multiracial area distinguished by its instability and eventual succession by white middle class settlement in the gentrification process. [This is the kind of area to which young white urban professionals are moving.]
4. The older neighborhoods of certain satellite cities. [These are generally small cities in the metropolitan area, beyond the suburban municipalities.]
5. Scattered suburban settlements ranging from lower to upper middle class standing. . . . [In this type of community immigrant elites can mix in with other suburban residents.] (Hernandez, 1985)

There are a number of illustrations of the housing patterns of immigrants in the 1990s. For example, Levine (1990) has observed that in New York City immigrants from the Caribbean, Latin America, Asia, and Africa have "revived bleak sections of the Bronx and Brooklyn and built two new Chinatowns," rebuilt whole neighborhoods such as Kingsbridge in the Bronx, Washington Heights in Manhattan, Elmhurst in Queens, and Sunset Park in Brooklyn. New immigrants, especially from the Dominican Republic, have entered Hispanic neighborhoods, such as El Barrio, and this has caused tensions and rivalry between the Dominicans and the Puerto Rican residents (Gonzalez, 1992). Although these two groups have much in common in terms of ethnicity and language, the new Dominican community leaders seek representation in the political structure of the community, sometimes bringing about political feuding. At the same time, Puerto Ricans are concerned about losing their neighborhood identity due to the influx of new immigrants.

These examples highlight the diversity of new immigrants. The integration and segregation patterns described by Woolbright and Hartmann (1987) differ among various Asian and Latin American groups. New Asian immigrants have mainly resided in metropolitan areas, and usually in suburban areas. The one exception is the Chinese, who are as likely as African Americans to reside in segregated areas of central cities. Filipinos and Koreans are likely to be higher in social class than other Asian groups, are not likely to live in segregated areas, and are likely to live in suburban neighborhoods. Southeast Asians, such as Vietnamese, Laotians, and Cambodians, have had the most difficulty in assimilating, and those at the lower socioeconomic levels are likely to live in segregated areas. Hispanic groups vary in that Cubans are most likely to be in the suburbs, Puerto Ricans in central cities, and Mexicans in rural areas. Mexican Americans in both urban and rural areas are likely to have members in all the social classes and to be assimilated into a broad range of neighborhoods. They are more likely than African Americans to be able to enter any neighborhood they can afford. On the other hand, Puerto Ricans are likely to be lower class, in central cities, and segregated in residence. Cubans are most like whites in relation to socioeconomic status and are less likely than other Hispanics to live in segregated neighborhoods.

An interesting pattern of residential and business assimilation of new immigrants has occurred in Flushing, New York, a community which has become a mecca for Asian immigrants (Wysocki, 1991). Along with their success in business and related activities, the new Asian immigrants have moved into old neighborhoods, causing some resentment on the part of African Americans and whites. Another pattern is found in California, with new Mexican immigrants moving into barrios with poor living conditions and high rents. Due to anti-immigrant attitudes, some long-time Mexican American residents of the barrio have moved away from their old neighborhoods and into new neighborhood communities (Montana, 1986). Others remain in their old neighborhoods but believe that community problems such as crime and deterioration of residential property are a result of the entry of illegal workers into their neighborhoods (Ferguson, 1992). In many of the neighborhoods to which immigrants are moving, their housing patterns appear to be representative of the traditional process of succession, resulting in ethnic neighborhoods populated by new and different groups of people.

REVIEW

In this chapter neighborhood types have been presented in terms of social class, race, ethnicity, and patterns of identification with spatial and sociopsychological neighborhoods. As general background for understanding social class and ethnic neighborhoods, attention has been given to the ecological processes of segregation, integration, and succession. These concepts allow for the examination of changes in residential neighborhoods over time. Special attention is given to efforts to create and maintain residential integration among whites and ethnic minority groups. The settlement patterns of new immigrants, especially Asian and Latin American, are described in terms of segregated and integrated living and in regard to residence in central-city or suburban neighborhoods.

SUGGESTED READINGS

Anderson, Jervis (1981). "That Was New York: Harlem." *New Yorker*, June-July.

Farley, Reynolds and William H. Frey (1994). "Changes in the Segregation of Whites from Blacks During the 1980s: Small Steps Toward a More Integrated Society." *American Sociological Review* 59:1.

Finnegan, William (1990). "A Reporter at Large: Out There." *New Yorker*, September 10.

Hirsch, James S. (1992). "Columbia, Md., at 25, Sees Integration Goal Sliding from Its Grasp." *Wall Street Journal*, February 27.

Holden, Benjamin A. (1993). "Los Angeles 'Hood, a Blend of Races, Strives to Get Along." *Wall Street Journal*, April 8.

Kinkead, Gwen (1991). "A Reporter at Large: Chinatown." *New Yorker*, June 10, 17.

Reeves, Richard (1981). "Boyle Heights and Beyond." *New Yorker*, September 14.

Saltman, Juliet. (1991). "Maintaining Racially Diverse Neighborhoods." *Urban Affairs Quarterly* 26:3.

Tobin, G. A., ed. (1987). "Divided Neighborhoods: Changing Patterns of Racial Segregation." *Urban Affairs Annual Reviews* 32.

EXERCISE

Draw from this news report to discuss the pros and cons of efforts to maintain or change residential patterns within this metropolitan area. Identify goals regarding integration/segregation, and the kinds of interventions directed toward changes in the community and the nature of controversies over these activities.

CLEVELAND SUBURBS WORK TO ACHIEVE A RACIAL BALANCE

By Jon Pepper

White neighborhoods used to be a lot like motel swimming pools. Once a black person jumped in, white people slipped out. Dr. Winston Richie knows. He says he has taken the plunge in both and watched as the ripples from his impact made white people scatter.

Thirty-three years ago, Richie and his family initiated integration in the affluent Cleveland suburb of Shaker Heights. He built a home in the Ludlow neighborhood and watched for the white flight he hoped never would materialize.

Jon Pepper, "Common Ground: Cleveland Suburbs Work to Achieve a Racial Balance." *Detroit News*, August 19, 1990. Reprinted with permission from *The Detroit News*.

"I wanted my kids to grow up around whites so they would learn they could compete with them in college and the job market," recalls Richie, a retired Cleveland dentist. So we (the community) started on a volunteer basis a program to encourage whites to move in."

It has taken more than three decades, but Richie's efforts have evolved into a national model for maintaining integration. By stimulating white demand in Shaker Heights to counteract an expected white exodus, and at the same time opening housing options for blacks in neighboring white suburbs, the community has avoided complete racial turnover. Its average home value exceeds $149,000.

The program has slowed black in-migration to a half-percent increase per year. With the black population now at 29 percent—roughly the same as in metropolitan Cleveland—Shaker Heights officials of both races believe they have a desirable level of integration.

Moreover, Shaker Heights' vital signs are stronger than many cities that remained all white. Its housing values in the 1980s rose twice as much as its county's suburban average. Serious crimes have declined five years in a row, local police say. Schools rank either first or second in Ohio for their number of National Merit Scholarship finalists.

The success has other U.S. cities in racial transition watching closely, and occasionally mimicking the methods. Officials from at least a dozen cities— including Southfield; Oak Park, Ill.; Teaneck, N.J.; and University City, Mo.— lean on Shaker Heights for advice.

"What I admire is their approach that you have to intervene," said Nimrod Rosenthal, community relations director in Southfield, where the black population has reached 20 percent. "The secret is to maintain balance in the community, where you prevent it from going one way, and where you attract the race that is underrepresented."

Shaker Heights' program works two ways:

■ **Recruiting whites.** Because cities that are integrating typically find black housing demand rises faster than white demand, Shaker Heights seeks balance by recruiting white buyers.

Members of the Shaker Heights Community Services Department work through real estate agents, relocation firms, corporations, and colleges to find families planning to move to the Cleveland area.

Shaker Heights makes presentations to those families through brochures, newsletters, tours, and a promotional video. A few blacks are shown in the materials, but not in proportion to their population.

Donald L. DeMarco, director of Shaker Heights' program, said that's deliberate. He said the materials avoid integration themes because most whites won't buy it, surveys have shown.

"Most people think of integration as wholesale racial change: whites moving out, blacks moving in, property values don't hold up, problems occur in schools—things that actually happen," said DeMarco, who is white and has a black wife.

"That's not true here. We have honest-to-goodness integration where whites and blacks compete in the same place for housing."

White families that move into neighborhoods that are more than 45-percent black are offered financial incentives. Shaker Heights' privately financed "Fund for the Future" grants second mortgage loans of up to $6,000 at terms below market rates.

■ **Expanding housing option for blacks.** Black families interested in moving into Shaker Heights are advised to contact the East Suburban Council for Open Communities (ESCOC), which encourages them to consider six predominantly white suburbs nearby.

The office, directed by Richie, was set up by Shaker Heights, Cleveland Heights, and University Heights in 1984 partly as a defense against increasing white flight. Officials of those three neighboring suburbs wanted to show blacks there were other comparable places to live nearby.

"We are trying to expand options," Richie said. "We're not saying, 'You can't live here, you can't live there.' A lot of blacks have not even thought of living in these areas, even though they work out here. We want them to be aware of the nice houses, the good schools, low taxes."

Blacks intent on living in Shaker Heights are offered financial incentives from the "Fund for the Future" to move into three neighborhoods that are more than 85-percent white. The goal is to stabilize the black population in each of the community's nine neighborhoods between 15 and 45 percent.

Richie, DeMarco, and others say that without intervention, Shaker Heights would probably revert to segregation—this time as a predominantly black community.

"Left completely alone, integration is a temporary thing, and the ripple effect just keeps going block by block," Richie said.

"Apartheid is wrong in South Africa. Segregation ought to be wrong here."

Segregation—particularly in the deeply divided areas of Cleveland, Detroit, and Chicago—has had a notable impact on socially isolated black society, according to a 1989 study by the University of Chicago.

"Black ghetto speech has grown progressively distant from the standard English spoken by most non-Hispanic whites, and black marriage, fertility, and family patterns have diverged more sharply from the mainstream," the report said.

"Our results suggests the extremity of black residential segregation . . . may help explain the growing social and economic gap between the black underclass and the rest of American society."

Joe Darden, dean of Michigan State University's urban affairs program, said the only way to make integration work is to involve entire metropolitan areas.

"If you have areas outside (integrated cities) that are within a reasonable distance and have comparable housing, it allows an escape valve for whites and reduces chances for success," he said.

ESCOC is attempting to close that option. It is using part of a $100,000 grant from the Ford Foundation to help other suburbs set up similar programs in all parts of metropolitan Cleveland. The all-white suburb of Parma on Cleveland's west side is setting up an integration program with advice from Shaker Heights officials.

PART THREE

Social Systems Perspectives

CHAPTER 7

Voluntary Associations

A common but somewhat unusual social unit in local American communities is the voluntary association. Members of voluntary associations are involved in such activities as mutual aid, socialization, and social participation. The voluntary association is unusual in that it takes on such diverse forms and functions within communities. At times it may be a vehicle for worship, social support, social participation, political influence, self-help, or some combination of these activities. In many American communities religious denominations constitute a major form of voluntary association. Much of what is called "citizen participation" in local governmental affairs occurs through membership in voluntary associations such as "parapolitical groups," interest groups, social-movement groups, client organizations, or local neighborhood groups. Other voluntary associations provide opportunities for individuals to interact for social, service, and self-help purposes. For example, self-help organizations are voluntary groups consisting of members who have a common problem or interest, such as habit disturbance, lifestyle, physical handicap, and mental health or health concerns (Powell, 1987). These groups often have multiple purposes, such as members helping each other, community education, and advocacy.

In the 1830s, on his visit to America, Alexis de Tocqueville (1947) observed the American trait of forming and joining associations. He noted that, "The Americans of all ages, all conditions and all dispositions constantly form associations." *The Encyclopedia of Associations* includes some rather quirky group associations, such as the Hubcap Collectors Club, the National Guild of Decoupers, the Spark Club Collectors of America, the Aardvark Lovers Association, and the National Hay Association. America's "joy of joining" can be seen in community newspaper listings of myriad associations, such as Folk Dance Club, Parents Anonymous, Recovery, Alcoholics Anonymous, Go Club, and United Auto Workers. These types of voluntary organizations may be classified as follows.

- Religious (e.g., denominations of churches, synagogues, mosques, other places of worship)
- Occupation linked (e.g., unions, professional organizations)
- Social (e.g., dance clubs, card clubs, sports clubs, church social clubs)
- Political (e.g., political party groups, community advisory boards)
- Self-Help groups (e.g., AA, Recovery, etc.)
- Service (e.g., volunteer groups, Candy Stripers, hospital auxiliary, social agency groups, church groups)
- Client organizations (e.g., tenant organizations)

In order to understand how voluntary associations fit into community systems, one may examine the nature of the voluntary association as a formal organization. This involves exploring the functions an organization serves for individuals and for the community and identifying the structure and membership characteristics which differentiate one set of associations from another. One of the significant functions of voluntary associations involves the linkage such groups provide for individuals in relation to large bureaucratic organizations and to entire communities.

THE NATURE OF VOLUNTARY ASSOCIATIONS

The voluntary association, be it a parent-teachers organization, a self-help group, a political party, or a religious denomination, has an organizational form which is distinct from primary groups such as family, peer groups, and youth groups. The voluntary association has formal rules and regulations, modes of operation, membership expectations, and specialized and instrumental functions. Yet because of its size or goals, it may provide continuous face-to-face contacts, relatively permanent membership, and diffused and affective relationships among members, thus combining the qualities of primary groups with those of formal organizations. Religious organizations and self-help groups are examples of associations which have bureaucratic and primary group features.

In general, voluntary associations are defined as organized groups with the following characteristics.

1. Continuity: the association persists over some discernible period of time
2. Goals: the association is formed for specific, shared purposes
3. Motivation: membership in the association is voluntary, the result of individual choice rather than compulsion
4. Structure: the association has developed some definition of member obligations and rights, some hierarchical configuration, and some patterns of organizational activity (Rothman, 1974)

FUNCTIONS AND DIMENSIONS OF VOLUNTARY ASSOCIATIONS

Volunteer associations serve varied functions for members. Social participation is the primary function of many associations, such as those that stress expressive activities, social events, or recreation. Religious denominations perform a function of social participation through worship as well as service-oriented activities. Many types of voluntary associations allow members to engage in problem solving in regard to community issues, while other associations allow individuals to be involved in a "therapeutic quest for community" (Bellah et al., 1985). An association like a school parent-teachers association or a volunteer group within a social agency may act in a support or service capacity, serving to link its volunteers to the community. Some voluntary associations serve political functions. Political and parapolitical groups are instrumental in raising the consciousness of members regarding issues of concern, placing local issues on the political agenda of the community, producing new leaders, or creating and maintaining boundaries and political identities. Self-help groups serve some of these purposes, but the major goal is for members to help each other through participation in group meetings and other activities.

In addition to examining the major purposes of voluntary associations, other important variables to be considered include membership characteristics, organizational structure, and resources. Membership characteristics include such factors as age, gender, religion, political affiliation, residence, home ownership, income, and education. Organizational structure components include size of group, degree of formality, relationship to parent organization, membership eligibility, and length of group existence. Resources include finances, equipment, buildings, and sources of funds. The description and assessment of a local community voluntary association requires attention to these components.

VOLUNTARY ORGANIZATIONS AS A PART OF HELPING NETWORKS

The various functions served by voluntary associations, for individuals and for the community system, can be examined in relation to helping networks. Social workers define helping networks as household members, neighbors, kinship groups, friends, co-workers, voluntary associations, and formal human service organizations. Warren (1981) classifies these sources of help in four system levels, locating voluntary associations at the second level.

1. the lay informal service system
2. quasi-formal and self-help systems
3. professional service agencies
4. inter-organizational relationships

The role of voluntary associations in the helping network is most clear in self-help groups. Powell (1987) has identified five basic missions of self-help organizations: "They are to change a highly specified behavior; to modify a broad range of difficulties and coping patterns; to reform society and/or validate a lifestyle; to relieve the burden of family caregivers; and to sustain the physically disabled." Self-help groups often influence members into using formal helping sources, such as social agencies. At the same time, however, membership in some self-help groups may insulate individuals from other helping sources, such as the professional helping system. Powell (1987) suggests a mixed role for self-help groups, indicating that they may serve either as direct service resources for the professional and/or engage in helping activities which complement the professional service system. Under Powell's formulation, "self-help organizations enhance the individual's social network," and are a vital part of helping networks.

Relationships between self-help organizations and formal service agencies in the community are often complex. As Hasenfeld and Gidron (1993) have noted, these relationships are "an important issue of study because these two social organizations represent major systems of help and support to people in need." Viewing self-help groups as organizations allows for the use of both organizational and interorganizational perspectives in examining the relationships of self-help groups to social agencies. An important task is to use these perspectives to develop ways of linking the two types of organizations. One such coordination model has been developed by Hasenfeld and Gidron (1993), with a focus on various kinds of exchange relations that can occur between self-help organizations and human service organizations.

Self-help groups serve their members as "communities" of interest and identification and, as such, respond to the needs of individuals for personal identity and "sense of community." Self-help groups also are empowering, as members join together for common purposes and have control over their lives. As Riessman (1987) has noted, "Empowerment increases energy, motivation, and an ability to help that goes beyond helping oneself or receiving help," and may extend to involvement of members of self-help groups with larger community and political issues.

Volunteers often provide human services even though they are not a part of a voluntary organization. An example of this kind of voluntarism is found in residents helping the elderly in their own neighborhoods. In these situations, neighbors become a part of the helping network. Sometimes formal social agencies organize volunteers to deliver services to their clientele. A project in Chicago entitled "Elderly Neighbors" illustrates this kind of service. Project Elderly Neighbors sought to "promote the health and social well-being of persons sixty years of age and older" in an African American neighborhood. Volunteers were trained to "visit their neighbors, identify emerging social and health problems, and aid their neighbors in securing help for these problems" (Wolf, 1985). The volunteers were paid for their work, and the directors of the project soon discovered tensions due to the "professionalizing" of the volunteer work. While some aspects of the project's goals were accomplished, there were limitations imposed by some unintended consequences, that is, "the strategy transformed volunteers into workers and neighbors into clients." Thus, some of the personal benefits of having neighbors, family, and friends provide service were less likely to occur when neighbors became professionalized.

VOLUNTARY ASSOCIATIONS AS LINKS TO THE COMMUNITY

Voluntary associations link individuals to the larger community (Bellah et al., 1985). This occurs within the political process where associations with political orientations connect citizens to local and state political structures. Citizens may use voluntary associations to engage in community conflicts, especially in opposing actions of local groups and/or local government which infringe upon their interests. They also use such memberships to promote actions which will further their private interests. In this sense, many voluntary associations become politicized at times but may be neutral or nonpolitical in most of their activities.

Some voluntary associations work at the grass roots level on social welfare issues or other local issues. These interest groups, or client consumer groups, represent organized citizen participation at the local community level and enable members to combine resources and relate to large bureaucratic organizations. Increasingly these are affiliated with "roof organizations," coordinating agencies which develop resources and employ staff members. An example of this structure is found in the Michigan Area Community Organization (MACO) of Detroit, which provides linkages between a large number of local neighborhood groups and the political and economic systems of the wider community (Fears, 1989).

NEIGHBORHOOD INTEGRATION

Voluntary associations also serve to link family and neighborhood primary groups with the local community and to formal bureaucratic organizations (Litwak, 1961). They help integrate individuals into local primary groups, such as the neighborhood. This function becomes important in a community with high residential mobility, for associations strengthen the community involvement and counteract disruptions of residential change. Characteristics of voluntary associations that facilitate social integration and help individuals integrate more quickly into neighborhood primary groups include:

- A public criteria for membership, so that in many associations anyone can join and meetings are publicly known and advertised
- Opportunity for the "stranger" to initiate involvement, so that one may join without being asked by a member or approved by a board

- In local associations, membership that includes some neighbors and/or friends, thus allowing for a reinforcement of primary-group contacts outside the context of the association
- Membership that is not in conflict with other primary group activities, especially when both sexes are allowed to belong
- Issues dealt with by the association are local.
- Association meetings that permit social interaction, thus reinforcing social contacts and integrative functions (Litwak, 1961)

Obviously, not every voluntary association meets all of these conditions. But to the extent to which one does, the association promotes integration of its members into the local community.

The patterns and functions of voluntary associations may vary according to stages of neighborhood integration (Litwak, 1961). In the early stages of residence in a neighborhood, "newcomers" are likely to be busy with personal and family matters and not have time to seek membership in voluntary associations. In the second stage, when the household is somewhat settled, individuals are more likely to be able to join organizations and utilize them for further social integration. Finally, in a third stage, with longer length of residence, friendship and professional relationships may obviate the need for voluntary association memberships, with a decline in membership of "old timers." Impinging upon these stages will be other factors, such as social class and economic resources of individuals, the support or constraints on household members from employers, the ethnicity of people in the households, and the age and number of household members. While there will be variations in terms of these factors, it is clear that the voluntary associations offer numerous opportunities for individuals to develop ties to a community and to overcome the disruptions of mobility. Hence, they serve the community as mechanisms for social control and for social participation.

EXTERNALLY INDUCED ASSOCIATIONS

Formal organizations such as social agencies, schools, and churches form or actively support voluntary associations in order to have "channels of communication, sources of legitimation, vehicles of social control, and a means to organize and direct resources" (Taub et al., 1977). This is especially true when there is a pressure on formal organizations, such as governmental policy-making groups, to include local citizen participation. In other instances, organizations look for volunteers to help carry out their work. An example of this type of volunteerism is found in citizen participation in environmental agencies (Tomsho, 1993). Volunteers engage in such activities as collection of samples, monitoring of shorelines, watching for toxic dumping, monitoring the use of wetlands, and the testing of waterways.

Community social agencies, banks, hospitals, park districts, metropolitan governments, and national corporations are the types of organizations that reach out for citizen participation in their activities. These organizations "recreate community social organization" in order to have local representatives to talk to about community issues. Taub et al. (1977) investigated these ideas in a study of Chicago's South Shore and found that the "organizational and social linkages of its residents extend more frequently outside the community than within it." As a result, outside organizations spend time and resources to strengthen local voluntary associations or to create them. This leads to the emergence of voluntary associations which are not "strictly local creatures." One of the positive features of this new form of voluntary association is citizen involvement in the allocation of resources "from the wider society," which increases local resources, allows local determination of priorities for their use, and thereby extends the effectiveness of local organizations.

VOLUNTARY ASSOCIATIONS AND MINORITY MEMBERSHIP

Various explanations have been offered to explain why ethnic minorities may underparticipate or overparticipate in voluntary associations (Williams et al., 1973; McClure, 1974). Two explanations, isolation and cultural inhibition, suggest limited participation on the part of minorities. The isolation argument states that underparticipation is the result of a lack of integration into the society, a lack of skills to participate, unawareness of benefits possible through an association, and discriminations against minority membership. The cultural inhibition argument applies to individuals whose culture supports attachments to home and family, such as the Mexican American culture. In considering reasons for active participation in associations, the argument is made that people in low-status positions, such as minorities, compensate for discriminations and fulfill their needs through membership in voluntary associations. A second proposition is that people identified with an ethnic community react to pressures from the larger society by forming and joining associations to maintain their identity and to facilitate pressure-group activities in the community.

In their review of the self-help tradition of African Americans, Neighbors and his colleagues (1990) note the importance of the Black church, fraternal organizations, and Black women's groups in organizing self-help efforts and in promoting economic development and political empowerment. This review broadens the concept of self-help to include the activities of social institutions, particularly the Black church, schools, and business organizations. Thus, mutual aid and social support are important elements in the Black self-help tradition, which includes advocacy; empowerment; a tolerance for diversity in membership; racial consciousness; a broad definition of self-help, including the development of formal organizations (such as churches and schools); and a concept of the system as a legitimate target for defining problems and developing solutions. Implicit in these elements is an emphasis on "personal responsibility for advancing oneself as well as the group." This leads to the view by Neighbors et al. (1990) that "Empowerment is one of the most critical and highly valued benefits that members of the Black community can attain by participating in self-help organizations."

Empowerment, at personal, interpersonal, and political levels, is also emphasized in a review by Gutierrez et al. (1990) of self-help in the Latino community. Self-help organizations are seen as an ideal way for Latinos to gain power and control to overcome personal as well as group problems. As with African American self-help organizations, Latinos have emphasized mutual aid and have minimal levels of participation in "mainstream" self-help groups. Cultural factors have had a strong influence on these membership patterns, as "self-help is philosophically compatible with the Latino culture" (Gutierrez et al., 1990). Thus, Latinos have been involved in self-help for Latinos only, through the extended family, folk healers, religious institutions, and merchants and social clubs (Delgado and Humm-Delgado, 1982). At the same time, various barriers have limited participation in mainstream self-help groups, such as the need to deal with issues of survival, difficulties of speaking English, transportation to meeting locations, child care and family responsibilities, and demands of employment for household members (Gutierrez et al., 1990).

VOLUNTARY ASSOCIATIONS AS SOCIAL INFLUENCE ASSOCIATIONS

Some voluntary associations have particular relevance to the field of social welfare in that they advocate for their own membership or for people they care about. These social influence associations seek to influence social-policy decision makers in social agencies, courts, schools, or other organizations. For example, the membership may use its collective resources on behalf of a specific social group, such as persons with blindness, developmental disabilities, or mental illness, juveniles, older adults, members of ethnic or racial minorities, and gay men and lesbians. The Alliance for the Mentally Ill is an example of a voluntary association which has state and local chapters linked to a national organization. Members seek to advocate for mentally ill persons. A number of women's organizations, such as the National Organization for Women, are national in scope, with state and local chapters. Gay and lesbian persons are organized into social influence associations, such as the Gay and Lesbian Alliance Against Defamation, working to achieve rights for their membership and to educate the public.

A question of central importance about social influence associations is how their internal political structure affects the interest, support, and commitment of members to the organization. In a study on this question, Knoke (1981) found that "organizations with decentralized policymaking, extensive communication patterns, and high total influence among participants, generate greater commitment and lesser detachment" to the organization. This study alerts us to the range and diversity of political structures within voluntary associations. Some associations resemble work/employment organizations, with "frequent meetings, extensive rank-and-file participation, formalized committee structures, and numerous task oriented activities." On the other hand, some organizations rely heavily on staff employees or on a small circle of volunteers, while most members remain passive. This latter type of association may be labeled "minimalist." This type of association has problems when it seeks to engage the membership in social action or in issues which require a rapid response or the active involvement of the membership.

Another form of social influence or client voluntary association has emerged in the growth of tenant organizations, especially in public housing projects. Participation in these organizations is sometimes labeled "consumer" and/or "citizen" participation. It is assumed that by participation in these organizations citizens could bring about administrative reform in an agency, that is, affect management performance, overcome any negative effects of "over centralized decision-making," and make the organization "responsive to consumer preferences" (Gulati, 1982). There is also an expectation that participation will bring about increased resources/services, in quantity and quality, to residents of public housing. In comparing housing projects with tenant organizations to those without such organizations, and introducing neighborhood factors, Gulati (1982) found projects in the "worst neighborhoods" were most likely to have tenant organizations. These neighborhoods include individuals at the lowest levels of the socioeconomic order. The neighborhoods often have high crime rates and are deficient in social utilities such as police protection. As a consequence, there is a pressure for residents to join tenant organizations. This is reinforced by a perception that participation will bring about some service benefits.

WOMEN AND VOLUNTARY ASSOCIATIONS

Traditionally most mutual aid voluntary organizations have relied heavily on women for membership. With the entry of increased numbers of women into the workforce and the suburbanization of communities it was anticipated that women would be less involved in voluntary organizations. However, there is some evidence to support the continuing high membership of women in these groups, but with changing patterns of involvement. Groups traditionally known for volunteerism, such as Junior Leagues and Hadassah, show increases in membership. However, the membership has changed, with individuals entering the groups at a later age and with an increase in older adult women. Other major changes in the organizations have included short-term service projects, greater flexibility of meeting times, increased communications by phone instead of meetings, and assumption of leadership in groups once dominated by men. One of the major reasons for this continued high involvement in voluntary associations has been the interest of women to remain connected to their communities (Brooks, 1983).

Membership of women in self-help groups continues to grow, especially with groups related to the various roles of women, "as parent, worker, spouse, ill person, and well individual" (Gartner, 1985). The feminist perspective has supported self-help groups related to all of these areas, but especially to health and mental health. The overriding purpose of these groups is "to restore women's sense of autonomy over their own lives, to restore their self-reliance, and lessen their dependency on institutions that define the lives of women" (Gartner, 1985). From an empowerment perspective, self-help groups often enhance the attainment of power by women at personal, interpersonal, and political levels. While women improve their own personal lives through self-help, they are able to join together with others to bring about changes in the social conditions of communities through political power (Gutierrez, 1990).

RELIGIOUS DENOMINATIONS AS
VOLUNTARY ASSOCIATIONS

Religious denominations in a community can be viewed from a variety of perspectives. Membership in these religious groups corresponds to our definition of communities of identification and interest, and as with other types of communities members vary according to the strength of their social interaction, commitment, and identification with a particular group. Such communities have denominational labels, such as Christian (Catholic, Protestant), Jewish, and Islam. Christians often identify themselves as belonging to a church, such as the Catholic church, one of the several Protestant denominations, such as Presbyterian, Episcopal, Methodist, Congregational, and Lutheran. Members of the Jewish religion may identify themselves with a synagogue/congregation, and with one of several groups, such as Orthodox, Hasidic, Lubavitch, Traditional, Sephardic, Reform, or Conservative.

Another way of viewing religious denominations is to consider them as voluntary associations. From this perspective, local communities have a number of religious groups, identified by church, synagogue, mosque, or other organizational unit, which meet the criteria of a voluntary association. These religious groups, as voluntary associations, may also be regarded as community organizations and/or as social institutions. Since these formal community organizations are loosely affiliated with each other, if at all, we have not treated these religious groups as composing a community subsystem. At the same time, the functions of religious organizations often overlap with those of the subsystems of the community, especially social welfare, health care, and education. This is evident in the operation of religious organizations as instruments for worship, social participation, socialization, education, social control, and mutual support.

Religious organizations are a part of a community's social welfare and health care systems when they sponsor social welfare agencies, such as family and children's services, and when they provide health care services through hospitals, nursing homes, mental health treatment centers, child care institutions, missions, shelters, and food programs for homeless people. Many religious organizations create informal groups within the membership to carry out mutual aid functions, such as housing, food and clothing, home chore services, home health care visiting, transportation, and fellowship. Because of these activities, religious organizations are a significant part of a community's social support system.

One of the primary examples of church members as a source of informal social support is the religious affiliation and religious institutions of African Americans. As Taylor and Chatters (1988) have noted, "Evidence suggests that black churches are extensively involved in the provision of support to their members. Church members exchange material, emotional, and spiritual assistance with one another, as well as providing information and advice." Historically, these services and assistance have not been available from the larger community. The role of the church for African Americans is particularly significant for elderly people. The social interaction of these individuals with family, friends, and church members leads to both formal and informal social supports, such as provision of services, transportation, socio-emotional assistance, and referrals to social and health services. The research of Taylor and Chatters (1986) is an example of evidence of these social supports from church members for elderly African Americans.

Religious institutions are regarded as a natural support system in Hispanic communities, as demonstrated in the work of Delgado and Humm-Delgado (1982). Other natural systems include the extended family, folk healers, and merchants and social clubs. The Roman Catholic Church has traditionally been the religious group Hispanics affiliate with, and while this membership continues, some Hispanics have become members of Protestant groups. In all cases, churches constitute one of the major components of community supports for the various groups that make up the Hispanic community. While some members of Asian American and Native American communities belong to mainline American churches, there is a need for information on the extent of membership and what functions churches serve for these individuals.

Increasingly, religious denominations have taken on "social influence" functions similar to other voluntary associations. For instance, church groups have become involved in controversies over educational policies and school programs, seeking to influence what is taught in the schools, how public funds can be used for services to students in religious affiliated schools, and other church-state issues of education discussed in Chapter 9. Church groups often make declarations in order to influence community residents with regard to such topics as sex education, parental rights, gay and lesbian people, abortion, assisted suicide, capital punishment, and violence on television.

PRACTICE APPLICATION

Community change occurs through the efforts of members of voluntary associations. Professional social workers can play leadership roles in relation to the community action goals of these associations. Theilen and Poole (1986) have identified a number of problems which can be addressed effectively through voluntary associations, such as "the need to increase resources available to high risk populations, the need to develop self-help programs among these populations, the need to reallocate resources to programs that emphasize development and capacity, and the need for greater client influence in service delivery." The social worker's roles with voluntary associations "can support, maintain, and enhance the leadership capacities of local leaders of voluntary associations."

Theilen and Poole (1986) provide an example of social work involvement in a Community Development Support Association with regard to six leadership functions. These functions include the work of professional and volunteer leaders to: "(1) define objectives and maintain goal direction; (2) provide means for goal attainment; (3) provide and maintain group structure; (4) facilitate group action and interaction; (5) facilitate group task performance; and (6) maintain group cohesiveness and member satisfaction" (Theilen and Poole, 1986: Stogdill, 1974). Case examples of each of these functions demonstrate how social workers can assist voluntary associations in reaching their community change goals.

REVIEW

Voluntary associations serve a number of positive functions for the residents of American communities. Voluntary groups usually have the basic characteristics of formal organizations, but sometimes they can also resemble primary groups. They offer citizens opportunities to get involved in public life, to participate in social, recreational, service, and political activities, thereby providing links to the local community and the larger society. Voluntary associations form a significant part of the helping network of a community, especially when organized as religious groups, self-help groups, consumer groups, or volunteer service groups. These associations form the context for various community roles, such as the volunteer, concerned citizen, civic-minded professional, and professional activist.

Self-help groups, as a special type of voluntary association, offer opportunities for people to enhance their own personal quality of life as well as serving as an avenue for advocacy and community change. Religious denominations, through their various organizational forms, provide for citizen participation in a range of religious and community activities. When voluntary associations are involved in community change goals, they may benefit in their operations through leadership roles assumed by professional social workers. A practice example of this kind of leadership involvement with voluntary associations is provided with reference to the activities of a Community Development Support Association.

SUGGESTED READINGS

Boyce, Joseph N. (1990). "More Blacks Embrace Self-Help Programs to Fight Urban Ills." *Wall Street Journal*, July 26.

Gutierrez, Lorraine, Robert M. Ortega, and Zulema E. Suarez (1990). "Self-Help and the Latino Community." In Thomas Powell, ed. (1990). *Working with Self-Help.* Silver Spring, MD: National Association of Social Workers.

Hasenfeld, Yeheskel and Benjamin Gidron (1993). "Self-Help Groups and Human Service Organizations: An Interorganizational Perspective." *Social Service Review* 67:2.

Neighbors, Harold, Karen Elliott, and Lary Gant (1990). "Self-Help and Black Americans: A Strategy for Empowerment." In Thomas Powell, ed. (1990). *Working with Self-Help.* Silver Spring, MD: National Association of Social Workers.

Powell, Thomas, ed. (1990). *Working with Self-Help.* Silver Spring, MD.: National Association of Social Workers.

Powell, Thomas (1987). *Self-Help Organizations and Professional Practice.* Silver Spring, MD.: National Association of Social Workers.

Theilen, Gary and Dennis Poole (1986). "Educating Leadership for Effecting Community Change Through Voluntary Associations." *Journal of Social Work Education* 2:22 (Spring/Summer).

Wolf, Jacquelyn (1985). "Professionalizing Volunteer Work in a Black Neighborhood." *Social Service Review* 59:3 (September).

EXERCISE

Describe the San Francisco model of volunteerism in providing care for individuals with AIDS. Show how this model fits into a helping network framework described in the text. Discuss how this model of volunteerism differs from the more traditional voluntary association model. Identify ways in which professional social workers could contribute to the AIDS Foundation's work with volunteers.

VOLUNTEERS' DISTRESS CRIPPLES HUGE EFFORT TO PROVIDE AIDS CARE

By Marilyn Chase

Thanks to an army of volunteers, this city [San Francisco] has lavished more humane and generous care on its AIDS sufferers than any other big city in the country. Volunteers have provided the ill and dying a multitude of free services, from counseling to hot meals to housecleaning, that would cost millions of dollars a year if provided by professionals. The city wears its tradition of volunteerism like a cloak of honor. The effort has become a model, as yet unmatched, for AlDS-care programs around the land.

But its heart and soul—cadres of dedicated volunteers—are suffering from battle fatigue or burnout, or from the disease itself. "The San Francisco model is near collapse," a city task force reported to Mayor Art Agnos recently.

New recruits, many of them female, are enlisting in insufficient numbers to cope with San Francisco's increasing number of AIDS sufferers. Of the city's population of 715,000, about 8,000 are AIDS patients. By 1993, the number is expected to nearly double to 15,000. Because improved medical care has prolonged the lives of patients, their need for other services is being prolonged, too. Yet the force of volunteer care-givers is shrinking.

Emotional Trauma

"Literally hundreds of thousands of hours have been voluntarily given to support the San Francisco model of community-based care," Lee Smith, president of Levi Strauss & Co.'s international division and a member of the mayor's task force, said in recent congressional testimony. "But past and current volunteers cannot keep up with the burgeoning caseload."

Some volunteers have fallen ill from traumatic stress similar to battle fatigue. In the most extreme—if rare—cases, volunteers "have had mental breakdowns, crossed boundaries, acted inappropriately with the clients," says Eric Rofes, executive director of Shanti Project, a leading volunteer organization.

More common is burnout, Mr. Rofes says, which comes in two forms. "There's traditional burnout," he says, among "people who work and then drop, leaving their positions. Then there are people who work on [despite their burnout]. It affects them in dangerous ways."

Glynn Parmley, a 44-year-old law-firm manager, is a burnout case. Mr. Parmley, who is receiving an award this month from the San Francisco AIDS Foundation for past volunteer services, has had to quit at his doctor's order.

Marilyn Chase, "Volunteers' Distress Cripples Huge Effort to Provide AIDS Care." *Wall Street Journal,* March 12, 1990. Reprinted by permission of *The Wall Street Journal,* © 1990 Dow Jones & Company, Inc. All Rights Reserved Worldwide.

A Consuming Effort

Five years ago, Mr. Parmley began his volunteer experience answering calls on the AIDS Foundation's hotline. To help deal with the many callers who had medical questions, he began compiling medical journal reports into a thick reference book. Then he was drawn into foundation policymaking and educational and legislative campaigns. With his regular job he found himself putting in 70- and 80-hour weeks.

Home offered no respite. "My house became AIDS West," he says. Many patients gave him power of attorney to manage their finances and, he says, he found himself "making decisions for them with their doctors—and then burying them. It was too hard on me. I'd been taking care of over 50 people I'd lost. My life was work, taking care of people, and the foundation."

He developed severe pain, compounded by stress, from a pinched sciatic nerve. "I got to the point where I couldn't walk," he says. "I became very emotional, withdrawn." He quit his volunteer work a year ago, and since then has pursued hobbies and found new friends. He contemplates doing some volunteer work again. "But I don't think I'll ever return to the level of intensity I had in the past," he says. "Some of us have just spent too many years in it."

For most volunteers, stress works in subtler ways. For Bruce Werner, volunteering began as an antidote to his personal grief and led to a more generalized mourning. A 44-year-old employee of a large corporate travel agency, he began his volunteer work when his companion died of AIDS in 1984. "I was very depressed and suicidal," he says. "It was either volunteer or check out, and I didn't feel like checking out."

Guilt and Frustration

For five years. he manned a phone at the AIDS Hotline, consoling others and buoying his own spirits at the same time. "It helped me. It was a support group," he says. Then his energy began to ebb, as his guilt mounted over being healthy amid the suffering.

"You get calls from people who've just been diagnosed, and think they're going to die in a year. You get calls from people who've been thrown out of their homes. You hear a lot of hard-luck stories. . . . It was getting very hard," he says.

"Sometimes you feel guilty because you don't experience illness and death as deeply" as the clients, he adds. "And you're frustrated because you can't do more." As a result, he says, "I started calling in sick, and that isn't like me. I needed to back off a bit. The exhaustion is real."

Mr. Werner finally took a year off. He plans to rejoin the volunteer corps. "I was raised a Calvinist," he says. "We're right up there where guilt is concerned." Now he describes himself as "numb, a tough old cactus."

Ruth Brinker, founder of a volunteer program, has quit doing volunteer work herself. The elegant, silverhaired widow began Project Open Hand in 1984. Now a brisk, industrial style operation, it turns donated food into 1,500 meals a day for AIDS patients. Mrs. Brinker long ago did double duty as

Open Hand's chief executive officer and as a volunteer delivery worker, making the rounds in her car every evening after a day of administration work. "It's very satisfying," she says of the volunteer duty. "People wait for [us] at the window. We get to provide a service that's vital to existence."

But stew and solace cannot fend off death. Every week for three years, a name or two on Mrs. Brinker's client list disappeared. "It had gotten so painful, with the accumulated deaths, that I needed to divorce myself, to put some distance between me and the clients," she says. "I have watched too many people die, people that I had gotten to know well and become fond of. Even now that I don't do deliveries, when I hear someone has gone, I feel a pang."

To conserve her energy and keep the program alive, she now sticks to office work, especially the enlistment of fresh volunteers from new sources such as churches and ethnic communities. "I'm committed to staying with this program until the end of the epidemic," she says. "It's so important. We just simply must continue."

Glenn Cooper tried to avoid burnout by making a practical contribution, scrubbing and sweeping instead of counseling. The 35-year-old manager of computer services for Morrison & Foerster, a San Francisco law firm, signed on with Shanti Project's corps of practical support volunteers, doing housework.

"I thought it wouldn't be as emotionally draining as doing other kinds of support," he says. "It turned out to be not so easy. I found myself becoming quite attached to people."

Saying Goodbye

Each Saturday, he headed to the house of a client to wash the laundry and scrub toilets and sinks. He recalls a client who, at first, was embarrassed to accept such help; eventually he became confused from the neurological complications of AIDS and utterly dependent on Mr. Cooper's services. "It was as if I became his mother," Mr. Cooper says. "I'd come in and clean. Babysitting was what we called it. I'd take his temperature, give his medication. By Christmas of 1988, during the holiday festivities, he was sinking fast. I got a call to go over if I wanted to say goodbye. I said goodbye and wiped the sink for the last time. If he knew me, he didn't acknowledge it. It was as if he was asleep."

Mr. Cooper had to withdraw from the work for several months. With his next client, he tried to stay more detached. But once again, his client's death brought a sense of desolation and displacement. "I went over to help pack up," he says. "It was awkward. I wanted to grab a broom, but his roommates were having a professional come in. I needed a sense of direction. So I packed up records and sheets. There certainly was, in an emotional sense, burnout."

After another hiatus, Mr. Cooper is now weighing his options. "I was thinking about running away from the emotional attachment," he acknowledges. "But I have framed pictures of these two gentlemen by my bedside. I have decided it's worthwhile."

If it is hard for the healthy to stay on their feet, it is even harder for those with AIDS who volunteer. Larry Hjort, 42 years old, was diagnosed with

AIDS in 1986 and has been on disability from his job with a national medical organization since 1988. He recently started a second career as a trainer of emotional support volunteers at Shanti Project. He knows that if burnout doesn't limit his tenure, the virus will.

"A lot of people who used to volunteer are dead," he says bluntly. "How else can you say it? They got involved early in their diagnosis, or before they knew. Every month there's another obit for a former volunteer, and that hasn't helped. A lot of their friends get burned out. I've only done it for a year," he adds. "I don't know if I could hold up for four or five years. I doubt it."

"Brave Experiment"

The toll taken by burnout, amid a rising caseload, means that the demand for volunteer services outstrips supply right now. For the first time since its founding, Shanti Project has been unable to accommodate all the requests it gets for volunteer assistance. "We have these tremendous waiting lists," says Holly Smith, spokeswoman for Shanti, which needs to recruit 770 new volunteers this year, more than doubling its current rolls. "I'm concerned. But it [recruitment] has to succeed. The reality is, we're not going to be able to get the dollars to provide the service. That's the bottom line."

San Francisco's situation serves as a reminder to the rest of the country that volunteer care depends on a finite amount of human energy, says Robert Munk, an official of the AIDS Service Providers Association of the Bay Area, a coalition of 100 volunteer agencies. "People are living longer, so the total number of people with AIDS will continue for many years," he says. "These volunteer efforts are services that other communities are paying cash for. That's why the San Francisco model has cost less. But the day of reckoning is here: the crunch is at hand."

Given current fiscal strains, it seems improbable that sufficient financial aid will be forthcoming to pay professionals to do the work currently done gratis by volunteers here in San Francisco. But absent such cash infusions—or an outpouring of new volunteers that isn't in sight—the outlook for AIDS care programs and their patients is dreary.

Many more may be condemned to wait out their days in general hospital wards, further burdening an AIDS care system already bursting at the seams. Elsewhere the outlook for comprehensive AIDS care is at least as grim. In cities with large numbers of AIDS patients, such as New York, Chicago, Dallas, Houston, and Miami, volunteer networks are less developed than San Francisco's. These cities already rely heavily on their public hospitals and emergency rooms as caretakers of last resort, and as burnout thins their already meager ranks of volunteers the care crunch will intensify.

June Osborne, dean of the University of Michigan School of Public Health and chairman of the National Commission on AIDS, says volunteers shouldn't be asked to make up for the nation's lack of comprehensive AIDS care. She calls San Francisco's volunteer system "a historic and heroic response . . . a brave experiment, but probably doomed from the start."

CHAPTER 8

Community Social Welfare and Health Care Systems

Social welfare and health care systems are the major providers of formal mutual support in American communities. Human service professionals practice in such formal organizations within these systems as social agencies, residential treatment centers, hospitals, mental health centers, and outpatient health clinics. While the services of these organizations form a significant part of the support systems of the local community, there are a wide range of other sources of mutual support (Germain, 1991). These include informal lay helping networks such as families, kin, neighbors, friends, and voluntary associations. Some voluntary associations related to health and social welfare, such as self-help groups and religious groups, were discussed in Chapter 7. This chapter examines the ways in which formal organizations provide social welfare and health care services within the community.

HUMAN SERVICE ORGANIZATIONS

The social welfare services system in a community is complex. It includes a variety of service delivery organizations which can be characterized in a number of ways. For example, Garvin and Tropman (1992) have created a framework of eight strategic perspectives for understanding types of social service systems.

1. A *levels and methods* perspective views services in terms of the person(s) or group on whom intervention is focused, that is, individual, family and group, organization, community, or society.

2. A *sector* perspective refers to the auspices of the services, public or voluntary (private). Public services are tax supported, funded by a local, state, or the federal government or by some combination of these sources. In the private sector, social agencies are funded in a variety of ways, such as from fees, community United Way allocations from private giving, and money from bequests and fund-raising events. Private agencies have customarily been separated into sectarian (affiliated with a religious denomination), and nonsectarian.

3. A *life cycle or developmental* perspective separates services into age groups, such as children, youth, young adults, adults, and older adults.

4. A *product* perspective involves services which clients have specifically sought, such as programs related to substance abuse, weight loss, smoking, job training, and housing.

5. A *problem* perspective is similar to the product perspective in that it focuses on social problems, such as juvenile delinquency, poverty, mental illness, and homelessness.

6. An *impact* perspective emphasizes differences between direct services and indirect services and on whether the impact of the services is on individuals or on community and organizational change.

7. A *cultural, ethnic, and gender* perspective separates out social agencies which seek to serve individuals or promote causes related to a specific culture, ethnic group, or gender.

8. A *problem-solving* perspective takes into account the extent to which the services offered move from problem identification to solution. The services may be for assessment and referral only, or they may provide complete service through the problem-solving process.

An approach to classifying human service organizations which incorporates some of the perspectives offered by Garvin and Tropman (1992) is the division of social welfare into direct service organizations and community/social planning organizations. *Direct service agencies* are designed to provide individual and group services to a specified clientele, such as persons in need of marriage counseling, child welfare services, employment training, or income maintenance entitlements. The professionals in these agencies have direct contact with clients in assessing needs and providing services. *Community and Planning organizations* have as their major function the determination of social welfare needs within a community, the organization of services to meet these needs, and the allocation of resources for the delivery of services. Some voluntary associations are closely related to direct service and planning organizations in that they provide services and/or ways of communicating with consumers of services. When voluntary associations take on advocacy roles, they seek to influence the goals and operations of the formal social welfare services and planning organizations.

DIRECT SERVICE AGENCIES

Direct social service agencies are established in a community to meet the social welfare needs of residents. The major focus of these agencies is on helping individuals and groups in their social functioning. These goals may be achieved through personal counseling, assistance in acquisition of resources, and the development of problem solving capabilities. Direct service agencies are usually specialized in terms of organizational purpose (e.g., vocational rehabilitation), skills (e.g., counseling), clientele (e.g., children), auspices (e.g., government, voluntary), geography (boundaries of service) (Wilensky and Lebeaux, 1965).

Agencies such as these are usually identified in terms of fields of service, such as health and mental health, criminal and juvenile justice, income maintenance, housing, employment and workplace, and education. These fields constitute an organizational environment, or network, for the specific agencies which make up the membership in a particular service area. Agencies within a field of service relate to one another as well as to organizations in other fields of service through interorganizational exchanges. Interorganizational relationships are most apparent in agency efforts to obtain clients and develop material and personnel resources. In order to carry out these tasks, agencies are usually involved in referrals of clients, agreements on fees, reciprocal agreements on use of staff and facilities, and interagency case conferences. Various procedures may be involved in the development of these exchange arrangements, such as competition, bargaining, co-optation, cooperation, and coalition. The concept of environment is inherent in these interorganizational exchange relationships (Hasenfeld, 1983).

FIELDS OF SERVICE

A fields of service perspective is a prominent way of categorizing service agencies, as demonstrated by the extensive attention given to this framework in social work education and in texts on social welfare policies and services (Garvin and Tropman, 1993; Johnson, 1990; Brieland, Costin, Atherton, 1985). A brief description of several fields of service is presented here. However, the reader should consult textbooks on the social services for in-depth understanding of current and historical social welfare policies, programs, and service delivery systems in each of the fields. The fields of service usually include agencies from both public and voluntary sectors, and there is likely to be some overlap in services from one field to another. For example, services to families and children may occur in public and private agencies and in several fields of service.

Public Welfare and Income Maintenance

The major focus of this field of service is on provision of income benefits and services through entitlements enacted by legislation and determined by eligibility criteria. Such programs include public assistance for people of old age, blindness, families with dependent children, and persons with permanent and total disabilities (Johnson, 1990). This assistance is intended to supplement the programs provided through the Social Security System. Health benefits are provided through the Medicare and Medicaid programs of the Social Security System. For individuals not covered by the provisions of the Social Security System, "general assistance" consisting of money and services may be provided through a state or local community's system of public welfare. Public welfare programs are administered by state and local community social agencies and seek to meet the food, shelter, clothing, and medical care needs of community residents.

Services for Families and Children

This field of service includes child welfare services designed to deal with the unmet needs of children as well as more general services to entire families. These services are offered in both private and public agencies—for example, child protective services, adoptions, marriage counseling, parenting education, homemaker services. Services in the voluntary sector are offered through child and family agencies such as Catholic Family Service, Lutheran Family Service, Jewish Family Service, as well as by family agencies and child guidance clinics sponsored by the local community. Other children's services are provided outside the home, for example in foster care, day care, group homes, and residential treatment centers.

Criminal and Juvenile Justice Systems

This area of service is sometimes called the "correctional" field. It provides services for individuals involved in crime and delinquency. Services are usually divided in terms of age and gender and between services in community-based programs and services in institutions such as jails, prisons, and juvenile homes. The major components of this system are law enforcement (police), judicial (courts), and correctional (institutions) (Johnson, 1990). Social workers are most likely to be found working in services for youth, on the staff of juvenile courts, or correctional institutions.

Physical and Mental Health

Social Services related to physical health, mental health, and developmental disabilities are provided through a variety of organizations, such as hospitals, outpatient clinics, community mental health centers, family agencies, aftercare programs, day care programs, health maintenance organizations, and hospice care organizations. Further description of health care services is introduced later in this chapter under a section on the health care system.

Services in the Educational System

Preschool, elementary, and secondary schools provide settings for delivery of social services. Social workers have significant roles in carrying out the mandates of Public Law 94-142, which requires the development of educational plans and services for children with disabilities. Preschool programs such as Head Start serve as a locus for social services, especially for children from low income families. Garvin and Tropman (1993) identify a number of areas related to school social work, such as "preventing school failures, coping with disruptive behavior, reducing nonattendance, eliminating substance abuse, educating school age parents. . . ." This area of practice is further elaborated on in Chapter 9, which focuses on the educational subsystem of the community.

Occupational Social Work

Employee Assistance Programs constitute the principal form of social services in the workplace. The major foci of these programs is on absenteeism, alcoholism, substance abuse, mental disorders, employee relations, family problems, and retirement counseling.

Emerging Fields of Service

The elaboration of the "fields of service" approach to describing human service organizations provides a foundation for understanding a number of dimensions of the social welfare subsystem of the community. First, it is essential that the social worker become acquainted with the services offered by the agency of employment. Secondly, the functions and goals of this agency must be understood in relation to other organizations in the same field of service. This involves understanding the nature of these other organizations and what kinds of relationships they have with one another. Finally, the social worker may then focus on the relationship of agencies in a field of service to the organizations in other fields of service. Obviously, undertaking these steps requires time and effort on the part of the social worker, but these activities are necessary in order to fully understand how well the social welfare system is operating in a given community.

In addition to the fields of service we have described, there are other emerging fields, such as services in the housing and environmental area, in the geriatric services area, in programs for immigrants and refugees, and in continuing and higher education.

PRIVATE PRACTICE OF SOCIAL WORK

Some experienced social workers engage in practice for profit on an independent basis and are employed directly by clients. These social workers usually provide clinical services with individuals, families, and groups. While these social workers do not work under the jurisdiction of a formal human service organization, they must meet the standards of the profession. They are usually required to meet licensing or credentialing standards imposed by the laws of state and/or local government. Social workers in private practice receive referrals of clients from other professionals in the community, such as physicians, psychiatrists, psychologists, nurses, teachers, counselors, and ministers. Sometimes private practitioners contract to provide services for social and health care agencies in the community. Private social work practitioners differ from agency-based social workers in the following ways:

1. They are employed by and obligated to their clients rather than to agency employers.
2. They determine who their clients will be, instead of having agency employers assign clients to them.
3. They determine and practice their own method of treatment or intervention.
4. They use professional rather than bureaucratic norms to determine practice methods.
5. They receive no predetermined salary from agency employers but receive fees for specific services directly from clients or the clients' third-party financing agents (Barker, 1987).

EMERGENCY SERVICES

The fields of service we have reviewed all include public and private human service agencies organized to meet the needs of people in local communities. As social problems emerge, it is likely that public governmental agencies will be mandated to provide services through established social programs. However, sometimes social problems, such as hunger, homelessness, domestic violence, are viewed as emergencies by governmental agencies (Lipsky and Smith, 1989). When this happens, these agencies may decide to meet their service obligations by "purchase of services" through funding of nonprofit community private agencies. In such instances, the governmental agency contributes to the efforts to meet the emergency needs of people with social problems, but it does not make permanent commitments to those in need.

Contracting out of services for emergencies is one form of privatization, that is, the use of private social agencies to deliver services under the responsibility of the local, state, or federal government. When problems are viewed as in need of emergency services, the contracting out of services seems to have several advantages for the public agency. These advantages include more rapid response to the problem through already established programs in private organizations, positive public relations from supporting the private sector, less commitment to continued services, more options for changing service direction, and less expense due to the ongoing contributions of the private agency to serve the target population (Lipsky and Smith, 1989).

There are some potential problems to treating social problems as emergencies. This kind of response by the public sector leaves unresolved the question of how the problems will be handled on a long-term basis. There is an assumption that the problems can be handled on a short-term, "emergency" basis. For example, emergency shelters for homeless people do not solve the problem of need for affordable housing for poor people who are homeless or at risk of becoming homeless. The fact that eligibility criteria for emergency services are often subjective may end up in unfair distribution of resources and treatment for those in need. On the other hand, such programs can "accept at face value individuals' claims that they indeed qualify for benefits under particular policies" (Lipsky and Smith, 1989). Perhaps the most important issue related to emergency services concerns the length of time governmental welfare agencies are willing to fund such programs and whether or not these agencies seek long-term solutions. In the example of care of homeless people, the persistence of the problem has led state and local community governments to develop more systemic solutions and institutional commitments.

COMMUNITY ORGANIZATION AND PLANNING AGENCIES

The major purpose of organizations devoted to community and organizational change through planning "is to improve the effectiveness of a system of programs and services and to create new instrumentalities that will make a greater impact on social problems" (Perlman & Gurin, 1972). Community organization and planning agencies often overlap in their purposes and methods. They relate to both the community and its social environment, with an emphasis on the identification of needs of people and organizations and the allocation of resources to respond to these needs. These organizations generally do not provide direct client services but seek to improve services and generate resources for people through the various service agencies and voluntary organizations in the community. The particular relationships that emerge between the organizations determine in large part the allocation of resources and the use of power by community organization and planning agencies. Some examples of planning organizations are United Funds, Health and Welfare Councils, sectarian federations, and state health and mental health planning organizations. The United Fund Council illustrates some of the basic levels of social planning, as it acts for the community in such tasks as:

• setting minimum standards for affiliated agencies
• providing information and other services
• reviewing budgets and programs
• coordinating of services and programs
• organizing of new services
• determining priorities
• long range planning (Perlman & Gurin, 1972).

Community organization agencies engage in planning functions, but the nature of their work within the community includes other major activities. Some community organizations focus on issues and concerns of the total community, others on community and local neighborhood, and still others only on the local neighborhood. A major framework for differentiating community organizations was created by Rothman (1979) in relation to three models of intervention at the community level: locality development, social planning, and social action. These models, along with a fourth, social reform, are elaborated upon in most texts on community practice methods. While some community organization agencies may emphasize one or the other of these models, community practice is likely to include some mix of all of them.

The major elements of the community development model are the participation of community members in developing a capacity and consensus in identifying and solving their own problems (Kettner, Daley, Nichols, 1985; Rothman, 1979; Garvin and Tropman, 1993). Social action focuses on bringing pressure to bear on community individuals and organizations who hold power and influence in order to improve social conditions (Garvin and Tropman, 1993). Some examples of community action include the efforts of older adults to organize in obtaining and retaining benefits such as income from Social Security and health benefits from Medicare programs, civil rights groups, victims' rights groups, and gay and lesbian rights groups. Community planning as a model of community organization relies heavily on experts who carry out needs assessments and use information to bring about community change. While there may be some input from community members, this type of agency tends to focus on technical activities of evaluation in order to propose changes in community services. Finally, the social reform organization is part social planning and part social action, with the purpose of advocating for some group within society.

ORGANIZATION-ENVIRONMENT RELATIONSHIPS

Both the direct service agencies and the community organization and planning agencies of a community are involved in and influenced by the social environment, which includes an organizational environment. All organizations within the social welfare field are influenced by the general environment of a community and by the particular task environment of the social agency (Hasenfeld, 1983). General environmental factors influence the kinds of human service organizations a community can or is willing to support. The *general environment* includes factors such as economic, demographic, cultural, political-legal, and technological conditions that affect all organizations in a community. As Germain (1991) has noted, "A service organization must be familiar with the demographic characteristics of the community, including distribution patterns of age, race and ethnicity, religion, gender, family forms, and socioeconomic status," as well as the community's epidemiological data on health and illness. Knowledge of the general environment permits social service organizations to shape their programs "to fit community needs and cultural orientations to the greatest degree in order to be effective and optimally used. . . ." (Germain, 1991). An important factor in regard to utilization of services is the location of the service agency in terms of distance to be traveled by clients, access by public transportation, parking space, and accessibility for disabled people.

The *task environment* of an organization refers to a group of organizations with which a specific agency routinely and planfully interacts, exchanges resources, and collaborates with in the delivery of services. This environment may include agencies within the same field of service, but it usually involves agencies in other sectors of the community. The first step in identifying the relevant task environment of an organization is to determine the organizational domain, that is, "the claims that the organization stakes out for itself in terms of human problems or needs covered, population served, and services rendered" (Hasenfeld, 1983). Specification of the domain of an organization results in identification of the agency's task environment. Understanding the task environment means mapping the environment by taking into account a number of sectors, which include providers of fiscal resources, sources of legitimation and authority, providers of clients, providers of complementary services, consumers or recipients of an organization's products, and competing organizations (Hasenfeld, 1983).

Human service organizations must relate to all these sectors, remaining aware of how each is influenced by general environmental conditions. Of equal importance is an understanding of the "organizational network," which is crucial in the development of interorganizational change strategies that maintain and strengthen an agency or provide effective services to community residents.

VERTICAL PATTERNS OF FORMAL ORGANIZATIONS

In addition to horizontal patterns of organizations within a local community, there are organizational relationships that extend beyond the local community. These patterns have been described by Warren (1963) as vertical, that is, structured and functional relations of community social units to their extra-community systems. As we examine the vertical relationships of social agencies to extra-community units, we note how private voluntary agencies and public, tax supported agencies differ from one another. The public agencies often operate with close connections to state and federal governmental units. Local public agencies may be operated solely by county-wide governmental units but often are connected through funding sources to state and/or federal levels. In many states, for example, the state department of social service operates branch social service offices which serve counties through a county departmental structure but are connected to county government and to federal government for funding. Many community mental health agencies operate in this joint sponsorship pattern.

Many private, voluntary associations are relatively autonomous, with their own boards of directors, and are financed through voluntary giving. Yet, these voluntary associations may have vertical relationships to professional accrediting bodies at the state and/or federal level. An example of this type of vertical pattern is the local community family service agency, affiliated with the Family Service Association of America and/or Child Welfare League of America, national standard-setting organizations. Other examples of vertical patterns among private agencies are sectarian agencies, such as Lutheran, Catholic, or Jewish family services which are connected to religious organizational structures at state/federal levels.

ETHNICITY AND SERVICE DELIVERY

Thus far we have treated social agencies as organizations having formal bureaucratic characteristics which form a traditional organizational structure for the delivery of social services. However, in any given community, formal bureaucratic organizations may impose limits on the extent to which some groups utilize social services. A case in point is ethnic minority groups, for whom there is evidence of under-utilization of services in several fields of service, particularly in regard to health and mental health care.

Increasingly, ethnic groups are served by agencies which incorporate "ethnic factors" into their goals and activities. A useful framework for identifying ethnic agencies was developed by Jenkins (1980) through her study of child care agencies serving a high proportion of ethnic minority clients. She developed a means of measuring ethnic commitment in terms of three major factors: culture, consciousness, and matching. The items used to measure these factors include: (1) for culture, such factors as ethnicity of director, ethnic composition of staff and board, use of ethnic curriculum, ethnic programming, ethnic food, art, music, history, and ethnic holidays; (2) for consciousness, such factors as support of ethnic institutions, leadership on ethnic issues, relationship to ethnic power structure, and relationships to the ethnic community; and (3) for matching, such factors as policy for matching of staff with clients.

The operational definition of the "ethnic agency" is a score based on all parts of the agency ethnic-commitment instrument (Jenkins, 1980). Given the social work profession's commitment to serving special populations, Jenkins' approach to identifying and understanding ethnic minority agencies is especially useful. These ethnic agencies demonstrate that it is possible to incorporate some of the features of primary groups into formal organizations, thereby facilitating the agency's links to families and neighborhoods and increasing the utilization of services. By incorporating ethnic goals and service goals into the same organizational structure, an ethnic agency can accomplish more than the traditional social agency for certain client groups.

HEALTH CARE

Health care, including physical and mental health, constitutes an important subsystem in communities. The structure and functioning of the health care subsystem in a community can be understood by applying many of the concepts used to understand the social welfare system. Thus, the health care subsystem provides services through complex bureaucratic organizations, such as hospitals, clinics, and community mental health centers, and through the private practice of professional health service providers, such as physicians, psychiatrists, psychologists, nurses, occupational therapists, physical therapists, and social workers.

Health care organizations are dependent on community legitimation and sanction; they have both horizontal and vertical patterns of organizational relationships with their environments; and they include both direct service and planning functions. They draw heavily on private and public funding at local, state, and national levels. Health care organizations interact with other subsystems of a community, particularly those providing human services, such as social welfare and education. In examining the health care system of a community it is important that the boundaries of the relevant community be established. For example, the components and functioning of health care systems will vary in relation to their host community, that is, metropolitan, municipal, or neighborhood community. The size of the community is an important factor in the extent to which health care services, especially specialized services, are available and accessible.

Health care systems perform the function of promoting "the health of its members and work to reduce the frequency and negative effects of illness" (Garvin and Tropman, 1992). The policies, programs, and services of the health care system, along with the social welfare system, come under the general heading of mutual support, one of the five major functions of locality relevant communities. The interrelationship of the social welfare system and the health care system is apparent when health is defined as a "state of complete physical, mental, and social well-being and not merely the absence of disease or infirmity" (World Health Organization, 1948; Ware, 1989). Social well-being includes both social functioning and role functioning, areas of major concern for the social welfare system.

Generally, a community system for physical health care is distinguished from a system for mental health care, although there are strong interconnections between physical health and illness and mental health and illness (Kiesler, 1992). There is considerable overlap in the personnel who provide services in the two health care subsystems. One major component of a physical health care system includes the individual health care providers, such as physicians, dentists, nurses, social workers, public health personnel, and rehabilitation personnel. The second major component is the hospital, clinic, nursing home, in-home services, and private office. Likewise, the mental health system includes health care providers as well as settings and types of services provided, such as inpatient care in hospitals for persons needing acute care, outpatient clinics for therapy and day treatment, residential care and treatment in group homes and treatment centers, and treatment in private practice offices.

Major criticisms of the health care system include concerns about a lack of coordination and cooperation between the physical and mental health subsystems, between the private and public service sectors, and between the service units and professionals within each subsystem. In other words, in some communities the individuals and organizations within the health care system do not seem to operate as a "system" but, rather, appear to be a nonsystem. This has led to the charge that a number of consumers, patients, or clients get "lost between the cracks" in attempting to obtain health care services. There have been several responses for improving the system of health care within a community. Most of the responses are connected to the funding of health care services through various types of managed care, such as government programs of Medicare and Medicaid, private insurance and service arrangements through Health Maintenance Organizations, Preferred Provider Organizations, and review/utilization management.

Another type of response to individuals who do not benefit from appropriate health care services is found in programs directed by individual physicians. An example of this kind of response is a program for the health care of prostitutes in New York City directed by Dr. Joyce Wallace (Goldsmith, 1993). Taking note of the fact that "The prostitutes of New York have been afflicted by homelessness, physical abuse, drugs, AIDS, and the contempt of a society that chooses to ignore them," Dr. Wallace directs a program that includes a Care Van outreach program, an Off-the-Street Mobile Unit, and an alternative sentencing project at the Manhattan Criminal Court. The program includes the delivery of social services, medical care, and an education and referral service.

EXAMPLES OF COMMUNITY MENTAL HEALTH PROGRAMS

Two programs that stand out among various attempts to improve mental health care in local communities are the Community Mental Health Centers and the Community Support Programs. Under the Community Mental Health Centers Act of 1963 the federal government provided funds to local communities to establish centers in community catchment areas in order to replace institutional care with community care. In addition to provision of inpatient, out-patient, and emergency care, centers focused on the community as the social context for health by engaging in prevention, education, and consultation programs for the promotion of mental health. As a result, some needed system properties, such as coordination of services, were enhanced through the activities of the mental health centers.

A second program of the federal government directed toward local communities was the Community Support Program (Tessler and Goldman, 1982). This model of service gave special attention to the needs of severe and persistent mentally ill persons by helping to cre-ate a comprehensive system of service, a network of caring, which involved development of social supports in community settings. Under this model, local communities could receive federal money to create community support systems with a core services agency, an established target population through needs assessment, appropriate financial and administrative arrangements for service delivery, and a case management process for service. While these two programs, Community Mental Health Centers and Community Support Pro-grams, have demonstrated an achievement of some of their commu-nity goals, financial support from the federal government, as well as state and local government levels, has been inadequate for full im-plementation of the models.

Due to continued concerns about costs of health care at the federal, state, and local levels of government, and the fact that a large per-centage of Americans are without insurance for health care, health care was established as a major reform goal of President Clinton's ad-ministration in 1993. It is clear that the operation of the health care system in metropolitan and municipal communities is highly de-pendent on state and federal program funding and on the private health insurance system for coverage and financing of health care. Thus, understanding the health care system of local communities re-quires knowledge about the particular community, its health care or-ganizations and professionals, and the horizontal interorganizational arrangements for care, as well as knowledge about the general health care environment of private and public policies, organizations, and programs at state and federal levels.

PRACTICE APPLICATION

Providing social services for homeless families is often difficult due to the fragmentation of the service delivery system in a community.

One of the social agency responses to meeting the needs of homeless families has been networking. In work with homeless families at a Salvation Army lodge in St. Louis, Missouri, professional social workers identified four types of networking (Hutchinson et al., 1986). These types illustrate the ways in which a social agency may relate to residents of the community and to formal organizations. The four types of networking were: natural support systems, client-agency linkages, interprofessional linkages, and human service organization networking. In the *natural support systems* type of networking, the social worker seeks to link homeless families with other family members, friends, or acquaintances. In the *client-agency linkages* type, the social worker locates other professional services in the community which may be of assistance to the homeless family. In the *interprofessional linkages* type, the social worker develops relationships with other professionals, particularly housing experts. Finally, in *human service organization networking*, the social worker participates in the development of coalitions which focus on planning and coordination of services for homeless people. These types of networking go on while the social worker is responding to these families throughout four stages of treatment: crisis stage, stabilization stage, relocation stage, and follow-up stage. This example of the Salvation Army lodge demonstrates that "partnerships among agencies are required to meet the multiple needs of homeless families" and that "Government, corporate, and voluntary sectors must work together to share this responsibility" (Hutchinson et al., 1986).

REVIEW

Formal organizations in the social welfare and health care systems in the community contribute in large measure to the provision of mutual support for local residents. Our discussion of the types of social agencies and their relationships to organizational environments and to the general environment demonstrates how the function of mutual aid is carried out in order to meet individual and community needs. We have called attention to various ways of classifying human service agencies, such as by fields of service and by models of practice, such as direct service agencies and community organization/social planning agencies. In order to serve local residents, these agencies also engage in vertical relationships with social welfare and health care systems at local, state, and/or federal organizational levels.

An understanding of a social welfare or health care organization's social environment (task and general) is crucial for the professional involved in providing direct services to clients. Professionals in planning organizations need this understanding in order to take part in activities having to do with interorganizational relations, such as developing new programs and mediating among organizations in a community. An example of such planning is the development of ethnic agencies in order to increase and improve health and welfare services to minority populations.

The elements of the health care subsystem of a community are identified, along with illustrations of community support programs developed to improve services and service delivery to persons with mental disorders. The complexity of the health care system is highlighted by reference to the impact of federal and state health programs on the provision of health care at the local community level. Finally, a model of services to homeless families is presented to illustrate how networking is used to generate and coordinate services to this client population.

SUGGESTED READINGS

Goldsmith, Barbara (1993). "Women on the Edge." *New Yorker*, April 23.

Gutierrez, Lorraine (1990). "Working with Women of Color: An Empowerment Perspective." *Social Work* 35:2 (March).

Gutierrez, Lorraine (1992). "Macro Practice for the 21st Century: An Empowerment Perspective." *First Annual Conference on Social Work and Social Science*. Ann Arbor: University of Michigan School of Social Work (mimeo).

Hutchinson, William J., Priscilla Searight, and John Stretch (1986). "Multidimensional Networking: a Response to the Needs of Homeless Families." *Social Work* 31:6 (November/December).

Johnson, H. W. (1990). *The Social Services*, 3rd ed. Itasca, IL: F. E. Peacock Publishers.

Lipsky, Michael and Steven R. Smith (1989). "When Social Problems Are Treated as Emergencies." *Social Service Review* 63:1 (March.)

EXERCISE

Identify the special problems faced by a health care delivery system which focuses on care for ethnic minority groups.

STRUGGLE OVER HOSPITAL IN LOS ANGELES PITS MINORITY VS. MINORITY

By Joseph N. Boyce

When Martin Luther King Jr. Hospital opened for business in the Watts section of this city, it promised to help answer years of racial injustice. Here was Los Angeles's first big health center run by blacks and built right in the middle of the black community.

It was a new day dawning. But of racial harmony? Not exactly. These days King Hospital, born in the shadow of the devastating Watts riot, is a virtual combat zone itself, thick with racial tension, charges of bias—and even the occasional death threat. Read this letter that Jesse Palacios, a case manager who has worked at King for 19 years, found stuffed in his office mailbox a few months ago:

"We Heard Your The Ones Whos Been Starting All These Wet Backs To Uprise Against All Of Us Who Havebeen Here At King For A Long Time," the note said. "IfYou Continue To Try And Take Our Jobs Away Were Just Going To Have To Stopyoou, . . . If We Have To, Will Make An Expmle By Blowing Your Head Off."

A Different Neighborhood

This is the sound of the new racism in Watts. Mr. Palacios, a trim man of 40, is Hispanic. The anonymous writer, he assumes from what has been happening at King, is black. The Watts neighborhood that Mr. Palacios serves was overwhelmingly black when the hospital opened in 1972. Today, it is about 50% Hispanic. But King Hospital, built on the premise that a hospital's staff should reflect its neighborhood, hasn't kept up with the times. Just 11% of its work force of nearly 3,500 is Hispanic. The rest is black—and there's the rub. The very hospital built to answer racial injustice has now been charged by the county and federal government with its own racial discrimination.

The controversy at King Hospital represents a new fact of life in America: As the proportion of different minorities grows in the U.S., and as they become more politically powerful, they aren't always joining forces for a common political goal. At the grass-roots, they are prone to the same protect-your-own turf attitudes that have long soured black-white relations. When asked about the troubles at King, John Mack, head of the Los Angeles Urban League, knowingly sounds a theme long used by whites to exclude blacks from schools, neighborhoods, and jobs. Blacks "are entitled to have our own institutions," he argues. For others to conclude that King discriminates

Joseph N. Boyce, "Struggle over Hospital in Los Angeles Pits Minority vs. Minority," *The Wall Street Journal*, April 1, 1991. Reprinted by permission of *The Wall Street Journal*, © 1991 Dow Jones & Company, Inc. All Rights Reserved Worldwide.

against Hispanics, or that the center's leadership should be less black, "conjures up a deep emotional feeling among the brothers and sisters."

Bad Blood

Not surprisingly, it does the same with Hispanics. For nearly 10 years, Maria Acuna, a 30-year-old painter at the hospital, repeatedly tried to move up from temporary status to a permanent position. But no luck. Finally last summer, she got her wish, but by now her anger is deep-seated. Latinos get short shrift in the department, she contends, "even though they're making [blacks] permanent who have been here a year." (The hospital disputes this, noting that of the 11 permanent members of the paint department, three are Hispanic, seven are black and one is white.)

Fina Holcomb, a Hispanic who supervises Spanish-speaking interpreters at the hospital, claims the broader problem at King is favoritism. "I've seen Hispanics not given the opportunities that other people have had," she says. "Others have brought in their own family and friends, whether they can function or not. When they say it's a black hospital, damn right it's a black hospital."

That status—as a black hospital—was supposed to be a point of pride. In the months following the Watts riots in 1965, civic groups and government leaders looked for ways to prevent a similar conflagration from happening again. One of their conclusions was that the area in south Los Angeles needed better health facilities that catered more to the neighborhood. Their proposals evolved into today's Martin Luther King Jr./Charles R. Drew Medical Center, one of five Los Angeles County hospitals. The facility includes a medical school and mental health center and has grown into a complex of several modern buildings amid manicured lawns and towering palms.

The hospital "was a godsend for a lot of blacks in health care," says Ernest Smith, a longtime Watts activist. "That's how we became 90% of the employment force." Blacks have a historical mandate to run the place, he says. "The thing is self-determination."

The road has been rocky for King in recent years. A series of articles in the *Los Angeles Times* exposed serious problems in the quality of medical care at the institution. A regulatory body was even considering suspending King's accreditation, but decided to put the hospital on probation instead. Administrators and doctors there say the real problem at King is its environment: a poor neighborhood rife with crime and violence that saps resources and puts great stress on the hospital's staff.

Joanne Williams, a 40-year-old black emergency care doctor, says the hospital's patients—roughly half of whom now are Hispanic—suffer disproportionately from prenatal problems, communicable diseases and wounds from violence. "The pathology there is incredible," she says. "If it can happen, you'll see it at King."

In September 1989, as problems worsened and charges of hiring bias gathered steam, the county Department of Health Services abruptly transferred William Delgardo, the hospital's popular black administrator, to a desk job downtown. It then replaced him with another black administrator, Edward Renford, formerly chief of staff in the hospital division of the county health service.

Mr. Delgardo says he was treated unfairly by the department. King's environment put a severe strain on medical services, he argues. And as for discrimination, he says he carefully followed the county's civil service rules. Hispanics were promoted "when they qualified," he says.

Besides, claims Dr. Williams, while many of the Hispanic workers at the hospital "are sharp," a big portion of them "don't aspire to do better."

That, of course, isn't the way the Hispanic employees see it.

Raul Nunez, president of the Los Angeles County Chicano Employees Association, a labor organization, says King is an example of the widely divergent treatment different minorities get in the U.S. He has condemned King's hiring practices and, in October 1989, stood before the county board of supervisors to warn of "the escalation of conflict" between blacks and Hispanics at the medical center. The problems aren't recent ones, he says. A Los Angeles County Human Relations Commission study of affirmative action at King in 1984 found Hispanics were "severely underutilized in all job classifications" and that an "extremely serious and potentially explosive" situation existed.

Following Mr. Nunez's appearance, the county board decided to take a new look at the problems at King. It assigned Robert Arias, the county's affirmative action officer, to investigate King's hiring practices.

Two months later, Mr. Arias produced a 73-page report. Its conclusion: King's affirmative action goals weren't being met. "The hospital's system, intentional or otherwise, of relegating Hispanics to semiskilled blue-collar type jobs because of their Spanish-speaking abilities, and failing to take measures to affirmatively hire and promote them to middle- and upper-level jobs, serves to exacerbate tensions between ethnic minorities which already pervades the workplace and community at large," it said.

Separately, the U.S. Equal Employment Opportunity Commission found "reasonable cause to believe" King was violating federal fair employment laws. This conclusion was based largely on the hospital's failure to produce records of hiring and promotion practices, the EEOC said. (No Hispanic workers have filed formal discrimination charges against the hospital, though they unanimously express their claims of bias in interviews.)

About this time, race relations at the hospital were taking a turn for the worse. Fliers appeared that contended Mr. Nunez was trying to change the medical center's name. Scores of black employees turned out in protest. Mr. Nunez says he has no desire of the sort, and has sued the community groups listed on the flier as sponsors of the protest.

Mr. Arias has also paid a price for his report. "I've had my tires slashed. A person who called me made it clear that he knew my car and he was upset with what we were trying to do" at the hospital, he says. Then, late last summer, Debrya Moore, Mr. Arias's black chief deputy, charged him with "fostering racial animosity and divisiveness" between blacks and Hispanics and keeping blacks out of the investigation of bias at King. Mr. Arias denies the charges, which are still before the county civil service commission. He concedes, however, that the investigation was carried out chiefly by himself and his secretary; both are Hispanic. He adds that his chief investigator, who is black, contributed to the report, as did another staffer who is Native American.

Mr. Renford, the new administrator at King, meanwhile, got a taste of the hospital's problems his first day on the job. As he pulled up to the center, he found a group of black demonstrators protesting against his appointment and the removal of Mr. Delgardo. Mr. Renford had to enter the hospital through a side door.

He quickly went to work to recast King's leadership. Last May, he appointed a Hispanic chief operations officer for the hospital, and this year he named a Hispanic deputy director of human resources. But recruiting Hispanics to work at the inner-city hospital isn't easy, says Mr. Renford. Not all of those who are qualified want to work at King. "You have to understand that there is competition for qualified individuals—high demand but a limited resource," he says.

The new administrator has had his hands full putting down persistent rumors that each time a Hispanic is hired or promoted, a black loses out. The county's civil service guidelines protect current employees, but that doesn't reassure Clyde Johnson, president of the Black Employees Association, a county-wide organization. "What's frightening is when you have Nunez and the Chicano employees saying 'we want our fair share to come out of the black community.' My members are saying we'd like to accommodate them. We don't mind sharing the pie, but what happens to us?"

Robert Gates, the county director of health services, agrees that King is "a special case" because of "its very different origin." But he also says the medical center can't be a static memorial to some bygone day. "I think times are changing and I think that hospital has to change with the times," he says. Black employees shouldn't worry "about some wholesale shift of policy," Mr. Gates says. "We're certainly emphasizing an increased work force of Hispanics, but it is not something that is going to happen overnight."

Most of the combatants in the dispute, including Mr. Nunez, believe people at the hospital aren't to blame for all of King's problems. Some of the friction is the fault of the county's Board of Supervisors, which ignores minority institutions, they contend. Until this year, all of the board's five supervisors were white, despite the huge growth of Los Angeles's minority population. In February, a Hispanic city councilwoman became the first minority elected to the board, representing a district in east Los Angeles. Notably, both black and Hispanic groups joined in the campaign to win her the post.

"The tragedy is, in county government the representation of Latinos and African Americans is a disaster," says the Urban League's Mr. Mack. "Neither of us has really gotten very far."

Joseph Duff, president of the Los Angeles chapter of the National Association for the Advancement of Colored People, contends that county officials have "kept Martin Luther King hospital like a ghetto within the [hospital] system. It was something reserved for blacks and everybody played the game." He believes that the county doesn't care about new frictions at the hospital and is inclined to ignore the center "as long as you stay on the plantation and fight on the plantation."

Kenneth Hahn, the county supervisor who represents the Watts district, agrees that the hospital is "low on the priority list" of his fellow supervisors. Mr. Hahn played a big role in getting King built and is generally popular among Watts residents. He is quick to show visitors a photo in his office of him shaking hands with Martin Luther King in 1961. And he is quick to blame the county board for neglecting the medical center.

But Mr. Hahn is also philosophical about the root of the hospital's current travails: the conflict between competing minorities. Relations between Hispanic and black workers at King won't improve, he believes, until both groups "realize they are . . . all in one boat together." If the fight goes on, he says, the result is easy to predict. The hospital built to empower minorities will, in effect, "be torn apart."

CHAPTER 9

The Community
Education System

Local elementary and secondary schools are the primary social units responsible for educational functions in communities. These schools constitute the major formal, institutional units within the local community educational system, supplemented in important ways by families and other social institutions. The educational system in many communities includes public schools, sectarian church-related schools, and private schools. The educational system may also include preschool programs, community colleges, universities, technical schools, professional schools, and programs for continuing education of adults. Reports of Bureau of the Census, the National Center for Education Statistics, and the National Education Association can be consulted for information about school enrollment at the various levels of education, and in terms of age, gender, race, ethnicity, and school expenditures.

Local elementary and secondary community schools view education as their primary function. The concept of education can be defined in terms of educational goals, such as "(1) to transmit useful skills and information to pupils, (2) to teach values and proper conduct, and (3) to teach social conformity that corresponds to current societal styles and needs" (Allen-Meares et al., 1986). The concept of socialization is sometimes used in reference to educational goals pertaining to values and preparation for citizenship roles.

Education offered through the K–12 public schools involves interrelationships between the local community government, state government, and the federal government. Although not always recognized by local citizens, local community education is primarily a responsibility of the state. At the same time, the responsibility for actual operation of public schools is delegated to local school districts and their school boards. The school district is the locus of governance of local schools, placing school districts and school boards within the political as well as the educational system of a community. The major components of the local community educational system to be examined in this chapter include the roles of state and federal governments, school districts, school boards, schools (administrators, teachers, students), and parents and other members of the community.

ROLE OF THE STATE

State legislatures make the basic policy decisions that affect community schools, delegating some decisions to state boards and departments of education. Usually state boards of education have the legal responsibility over public elementary and secondary schools, delegating the responsibility for actual school operations to district school boards. A number of decisions about education are made at the state level. The most important of these is the generation and allocation of a major part of the public funds spent for public education. Other decisions include determination of policies about the instructional programs for elementary and secondary schools, mandatory attendance rules, course of study standards, approval of textbooks, standards for facilities, and limits on taxing powers. State agencies carry out such functions as teacher certification, planning, research and evaluation, provision of technical services, and allocation of federal funds and enforcement of federal regulations.

ROLE OF THE FEDERAL GOVERNMENT

While it is clear that education is the responsibility of states, and delivered by local communities, the federal government is involved in education in a number of ways. Examples of service and educational programs include Head Start, the National School Lunch Program, health care programs, and programs for children with special educational needs due to handicaps. The federal influence on local education frequently comes from congressional legislation and actions of federal courts and from policies and programs of the U.S. Department of Education and the Department of Health and Human Services. Some selected examples of federal legislation and federal programs dealing with education include the following.

The Elementary and Secondary Education Act of 1965

The titles of this Act provide funds for education of children of low-income families, library and instructional resources, education centers and services, research programs, and the strengthening of state departments of education. Amendments to this act in 1968 included Title VII, which focuses on provision of bilingual education.

The Educational Amendments Act (P.L. 92-318) of 1972

This act included Title IX, which prohibited sex discrimination against students and employees in programs receiving federal funds. While the act related to all school programs, attention was given by local schools to classes designed for a single gender group and to athletic programs which failed to provide opportunities for women. This act also provided for a federal grant-in-aid program for school districts involved in desegregation plans.

Title II (P.L. 94-482) of the Education Amendments of 1976

This title deals with vocational education, providing federal funds on a matching basis to state and local governments. Examples of these programs are work-study programs, cooperative programs, placement services, and support services for women.

Education for All Handicapped Children Act of 1975 (P.L. 94-142)

This act focuses on education for all handicapped children, providing federal assistance for programs which emphasized special education and related services. The Act covers eight categories of handicapped: deaf, deaf-blind, hard of hearing, mentally retarded, multi-handicapped, orthopedically impaired, other health impairment, and seriously emotionally disturbed.

Education of the Handicapped Act Amendments of 1987

This Act emphasizes preventive intervention with services to high risk children. One part of the act provides funds for programs serving children from birth through two years of age with regard to developmental delays. Closely related to these children's services is the provision of family education through school settings.

These acts represent increased involvement of the federal government in state and local educational programs. With this involvement comes increased acceptance of responsibility of the federal government, accompanied by some controls over local education through rules and reporting accountability requirements. The acts cited here are closely related to the purposes of the Civil Rights Act of 1964 in that sanctions of the civil rights can be invoked for noncompliance in areas of vocational education, education for the handicapped, and sex discrimination in the schools. These acts illustrate the fact that educational policymaking occurs at the federal level, especially when federal funds are involved.

HEAD START

Head Start is one example of an educational program created and financed through federal funds. The program was established in 1965 as one of the social programs of the War on Poverty. Its purpose continues to be to provide preschool educational activities, nutrition, and health care for low income "at risk" children. In 1990 the composition of head start children included 38 percent Black, 33 percent white, 22 percent Hispanic, 4 percent Native American, 3 percent Asian (Chira, 1990). Funding for the program has increased dramatically over the past 25 years. By 1992 there were an estimated 622,000 children enrolled in Head Start programs, funded at a level of 2.2 billion dollars per year (Dixon, 1993). Included in these programs were educational activities, medical/dental examinations, and breakfast/lunch meal programs.

A number of studies of Head Start programs have provided evidence that short-range learning and health goals are achieved. However, long-term educational success of the programs has not been established. Some social reformers have lamented the fact that many of the Head Start children continue to live in disorganized and disruptive families and neighborhoods and attend schools of poor quality. Some critics maintain that Head Start programs must be accompanied by other reforms, arguing that "there is no substitute for fixing schools and rebuilding families. No supplemental program can take the place of those two all-important institutions" (Hood, 1993). As of 1993, the Department of Health and Human Services began an extensive review of Head Start, stimulated by President Clinton's proposal for expansion from a half-day school-year program to a full-day year-around program.

STRUCTURE OF PUBLIC EDUCATION AT THE COMMUNITY LEVEL

School Districts

Local school districts are quasi-corporations to which the state delegates power for educational functions such as the implementation of state policies in the management of schools in the district. Local school districts have geographic boundaries, often conterminous with municipalities, counties, or townships. School districts carry out the state's obligations to provide public education at the local community level. There seems to be little uniformity of school districts in the United States, as districts range in size from small rural communities to some which cover large cities. Local school districts have many of the features of governmental agencies, especially since they are in large part creatures of the state government.

Intermediate school districts often are established at a level between local communities and the state. Over half of the states have intermediate units of school administration, which provide local districts with services such as planning, supportive services, special education programs, educational media services, curriculum consultation, data processing services, staff development, and vocational-technical programs and services. School attendance areas are established within the geographic boundaries of local school districts. Normally residential location determines the school students are required to attend. School boards make student attendance determinations for each school building. In recent years some school boards have introduced policies of "choice," or open enrollment, whereby parents can choose a school within the school district.

School board decisions regarding attendance areas were influenced by the 1954 Supreme Court case of *Brown et al. v. Board of Education of Topeka*, wherein the court ruled that segregation based on race existed in school districts and deprived students of equal educational opportunity. Efforts to bring about school desegregation—through busing, magnet schools, and schools with special programs—all have challenged the customary school board approaches to determining attendance areas. At the same time, as Allen-Meares (1990) has noted, "large numbers of the nation's school districts remain 'separate and un-equal,' even those that are supposed to be integrated." Other impacts on attendance boundaries come from declines in student enrollment in some areas, the closing of schools, the reorganization of school districts, and the density of the school population in a given area.

Local Boards of Education

School districts are governed by school boards. Board members are usually elected by residents of the district on a nonpartisan basis, although in some instances members are appointed by a mayor, judge, or governor. While board members are constrained by mandates from the state, members are beholden in large measure to their local constituencies. School boards have important control functions in that they hire superintendents, administrative staff, and teachers; engage in collective bargaining with teacher unions; build and maintain school buildings; and spend tax dollars from the local community and the state and federal government. School boards have a tradition and reputation of exercising local control over educational matters, always within the statutes of the state and federal government. Studies of the characteristics of board members show high representation of business and professional people, of males, and of nonminority individuals. The representation in large city school boards in the 1990s shows a considerable increase in membership of racial/ethnic minority groups, especially African Americans and Hispanics.

Teachers and Administrators

The success or failure of individual schools within a community educational system is often attributed to school personnel. Some citizens believe that school personnel exercise subtle control over education and make the major difference in whether overall educational goals are reached. When students do not perform well in standardized tests of basic skills, engage in unacceptable behaviors such as crime, drug abuse, violence, and vandalism, the blame is often placed on teachers and administrators. What is clear is that local school districts show a vast range of differences in problems and achievements and that, at least to some extent, these differences can be attributed to the quality of instruction and administration in the schools. Some of the differences are also influenced by the wealth of some districts and the impoverishment of others; by the social circumstances of the families of the students in terms of the educational backgrounds of students; and by the student's educational preparation, socialization, and expectations.

Teachers belong to professional organizations and to unions, and through these groups, they are in a position to better their own personal situations and to influence community educational systems. As teachers have become politically active through these organizations, tensions have emerged in some communities between citizens and teachers. Teachers' strikes seem to have benefited the teachers, but at the cost of alienating them from some of their community support. Teachers, as public employees, are increasingly subject to public expectations with regard to performance and accountability, expectations which do not always seem to teachers to be appropriate for members of a profession.

Students

The organization and delivery of education at the local community level is influenced by various characteristics of students. The number of students in a school district influences the educational arrangements in preschool, elementary, and secondary school programs. For example, elementary schools have traditionally been neighborhood schools, providing education to children within reasonable geographic proximity. They have tended to have smaller enrollments than middle schools or high schools. The socioeconomic status of residents in school districts and school attendance areas influences the financing of education at the elementary and secondary levels. Social-class characteristics of residents, such as education, occupational status, and income, influence the educational needs of students, with a positive correlation between middle and upper social class and academic success.

Student rights are usually established by school districts, individual schools, and the courts. Students, parents, and local organizations concerned with rights often are involved in litigation related to the schools. In regard to expulsions and suspensions, "School districts and colleges have the power to control student behavior through the use of disciplinary suspensions and expulsions" (Data Research, 1988). A controversial area of student rights has to do with the extent to which schools have the right to search students. This issue is the result of violence in the schools due to the carrying of guns by students. Numerous court cases have dealt with this matter, some upholding and others overturning such searches of students (Data Research, 1988).

Rights regarding student records were established by the Buckley Amendment (Family Educational Rights and Privacy Act of 1974), which sets the rules for parent and student rights, both for private and public schools receiving public funding. "The Amendment's major requirements are that student records be kept confidential, that parents be allowed access to their children's educational records, and that parents be allowed to challenge information kept in their children's records. Students who are eighteen years of age or older have all the rights granted to parents" (Data Research, 1988).

School districts often establish immunization requirements for prevention and control of communicable diseases. The courts have supported the rights of the school districts to establish health regulations. In general, courts have ruled that persons carrying the AIDS virus may attend school. This is in keeping with the protections of the Rehabilitation Act of 1973 concerning handicapped individuals. In addition, the Education for All Handicapped Children Act of 1975 provides rights to handicapped students—that is, the right to free appropriate public education and to related services such as developmental, corrective, psychological, recreational, medical, and counseling services and physical and occupational therapy.

The area of sex education in the public schools continues to be controversial in a number of American communities. Approximately forty states require or encourage sex education in the schools, but a report on "Risk and Responsibility: Teaching Sex Education in American Schools Today" indicates that teachers believe this education begins too late and that instructors often do not deal with topics of birth control and abortion (Hechinger, 1989). The inclusion of instruction about homosexuality continues to draw community opposition. Some major American cities—such as Los Angeles, New York, and Philadelphia—have taken leadership in developing programs which include instruction on sexual orientation. For example, Project 10 in Los Angeles was developed in 1984 as the first formal instructional program to focus on the needs of gay, lesbian, and bisexual youth (Trimer-Hartley, 1993). Since that time a number of communities, usually culturally diverse ones, have developed diversity programs which include instruction about homosexuality. However, controversies continue over instruction in the public schools about sexual orientation and about sex instruction in general. For example, one of the major objections to the Children of the Rainbow curriculum in multiculturalism in New York City involved the inclusion of content on sexual orientation and homosexuality (Hiss, 1993; Miller, 1993).

The existence of sexual harassment in the schools has received renewed attention as a result of a report of a survey on this topic by the American Association of University Women entitled "Hostile Hallways." An alarming number of students report that "they have been sexually harassed at or on their way to school, generally by other students" (Shanker, 1993). Critics of the report object to the broad definition of sexual harassment, and it appears that the high level of harassment does not necessarily lead to a "hostile learning environment." At the same time, the AAUW report identifies a significant problem for students in America's schools, one which reflects similar concerns community wide, especially within the community economic system.

SCHOOL-COMMUNITY RELATIONS

A major issue in American schools relates to the extent to which school personnel are isolated from the community (Allen-Meares et al., 1986). One approach to reducing this isolation and increasing school-community relationships and activities has been through the development of voluntary organizations. The primary example of such organizations is the Parent-Teacher Association. Parent-Teacher Associations are made up of parents related to a specific school, along with a principal, and teacher and student representatives. PTAs vary in their purposes and activities. They are often advisory in nature, providing parent input in regard to school programs and school rules and regulations. They raise money for special projects not funded by the school system. Sometimes these organizations become involved in community issues, such as school reorganization plans and millage propositions.

In addition to PTA membership and involvement of parents with teachers and students, sometimes schools form special ad hoc committees for giving advice on educational matters. This is especially true when programs under federal funds are introduced into a community due to governmental regulations. At times citizen advisory groups emerge to promote school reform, to protest school reorganization, or to lobby for or against school board issues.

Voluntary associations representing ethnic minority groups allow for citizen participation in regard to education in the local community. Some of these organizations exist at national and state levels as well as locally. Examples include chapters of the NAACP, the Urban League, CORE (Congress of Racial Equality), SCLC (Southern

Christian Leadership Conference), and PUSH (People United to Save Humanity). Voluntary associations which represent Spanish-speaking Americans are found in parts of the United States with a high representation of Hispanics. These organizations have been involved in promoting laws on bilingual education, bicultural education, education for migrants, and the rights of children of illegal aliens.

DESEGREGATION

In regard to desegregation, "the Equal Protection of the Fourteenth Amendment to the U.S. Constitution requires that public schools not be operated by the state on a racially segregated basis" (Data Research, 1988). Numerous court cases have followed the mandate of the U.S. Supreme Court in *Brown v. Board of Education* (1954). Two criteria have been employed in consideration of violation of the Supreme Court decision. "First, there must be a current condition of racial segregation, and second, this condition must have been caused or maintained by intentional state action" (Data Research, 1988). The U.S. Supreme Court has made an important distinction between de jure and de facto segregation. "The U.S. Supreme Court has firmly adhered to the view that de jure segregation, or a current condition of segregation resulting from housing patterns or other factors beyond the control of the government, does not violate the constitution" (Data Research, 1988). However, in a 1985 federal court case in Yonkers, New York, housing discrimination is linked with racial segregation in the public schools. "In this case the city government of Yonkers, New York, and the Yonkers school board were charged with intentionally creating and maintaining a racially segregated public school system, and with violating the federal Fair Housing Act by consistently locating subsidized housing in minority slum areas." Manipulations of public housing appeared to the court to have "assured racial segregation of the city's school system" (Data Research, 1988).

Usually, however, school boards have considerable discretion in choosing solutions to the segregation problem, such as closing schools, reducing staff, and busing. Busing children in order to desegregate schools emerged as an important legal and political issues in many communities (Allen-Meares et al., 1986). In a landmark case related to desegregation in Kansas City, Missouri, the U.S. Supreme Court upheld the order of a federal judge in requiring increases in taxes to pay for desegregation plans (Wermiel, 1990). In another U.S. Supreme Court case the Court ruled that school districts cannot be forced by the federal courts to integrate schools when the cause is residential patterns not under the control of the school boards (Barrett, 1992).

Innovative alternatives to busing are being tried in some communities. The Palm Beach County school system has proposed that the community's thirty-seven incorporated communities and unincorporated developments engage in marketing efforts to integrate neighborhoods. It is expected that such efforts will result in children attending neighborhood schools with a mix of majority/minority students (Celis, 1991). (A news report on this Florida community plan is included at the close of this chapter). While some desegregation programs have led to more equal educational opportunity for ethnic minority students, generally speaking, "caste-like societal and educational systems" continue to make such opportunities an unfulfilled promise (Allen-Meares, 1990). The consequences of unequal educational opportunities result in "an educational system that produces academic underachievement for people of color," which in turn "sustains class, economic and social inequities" (Williams, 1990).

CHURCH-STATE ISSUES

An important aspect of school-community relations involves litigation related to religion and the public schools by individual parents and voluntary associations such as the American Civil Liberties Union. The basis for court decisions on this topic is the "establishment clause" of the First Amendment to the U.S. Constitution that "Congress shall make no law respecting an establishment of religion," a clause which applies to school districts. A test established in the *Lemon v. Kurtzman* case (1971) is used by the courts in cases involving religion and the public schools. "The Lemon test provides that (1) a government practice or enactment must have a secular purpose, (2) its principle or primary effect must be one that neither advances nor inhibits religion, and (3) it must not foster an excessive government entanglement with religion" (Data Research, 1988).

Challenges to the activities of local schools often come about due to state statutes or local school district actions which relate to religious activities in the public schools (Epstein, 1993). For example, controversies arise over actions to allow voluntary prayer in classrooms, resulting in these activities being declared unconstitutional. The U.S. Supreme Court has ruled that clergy invited by school officials cannot deliver graduation prayers. However, the Fifth U.S. Circuit Court of

Appeals in New Orleans ruled in favor of student-led prayers, and the U.S. Supreme Court reviewed the case and left the decision standing (Hayes, 1993; Barrett, 1993). This Court decision has led a number of states to propose legislation which would allow student-led prayers at assemblies, sports events, and graduations (Hetter, 1993). Statutes which relate to curricular areas, such as Creationism, secular humanism, Darwinian theory, have been challenged in the courts, and the findings have been mixed. In regard to the use of public facilities by religious organizations, the U.S. Supreme Court ruled that excluding church-group activities violates free speech rights if the schools allow other groups access to the facilities (*Lamb's Chapel v. Center Moriches School District*). In another case involving instruction, the U.S. Supreme Court ruled that public funds could be used for services for a deaf student attending a parochial school (Barrett, 1993).

FINANCING OF PUBLIC EDUCATION

Funding for public education comes from local community, state, and federal sources. On the average, about 40 percent of local school funding is provided by the state, about 40–50 percent by local communities, and about 10 percent through federal grants for special educational purposes. States differ in the extent to which they support public education, as do the local community school districts. Local school districts usually obtain funds from residents through general property taxes based on assessed value of property. The amount of a local community millage is established by citizen vote. School reform movements, at the local as well as state levels, usually attempt to bring about "equalization" of educational resources for school districts. Comparisons between districts are often made by reference to the relationship of assessed value to per pupil in school attendance.

School districts approach the voters with two major types of funding requests, for millage renewals and increases for their operating budgets and bond proposals, usually for new schools and school renovations. State legislatures continue to debate school tax issues, especially with regard to property tax reform (Garcia, 1989). The debate centers on ways of raising more money for public schools (for example, money which goes into a statewide fund and is redistributed to school districts) and ways of closing the gap between rich and poor school districts. Proposals may involve raising a sales tax and lowering property tax for education. Local community school districts share a common problem—that is, how to create public support for financing education. A special problem for funding confronts districts with low-income neighborhoods where the tax base is low. Serving the educational needs of ethnic minority populations in inner-city areas is particularly problematic due to the lack of adequate local school funding.

A number of issues surround the financing of public education at the K–12 levels. Since most local communities pay their part of public education through the use of property taxes, a rather large disparity in funding of education has developed among rural, suburban, and urban schools. A number of states and local communities have developed alternative proposals for funding schools through sales and other taxes in combination with property taxes. In 1993 the Congressional Quarterly reported that "about 25 states are being sued for operating unconstitutional school financing systems and that supreme courts in 11 states have ruled that their systems violate state constitutions" (Rowan, 1993). An example is found in a decision of the Texas Supreme Court, which noted "glaring disparities between rich and poor school districts" and declared the state's system of financing the education of public school children unconstitutional (Green and Marcus, 1989).

In yet another example, the New Jersey Supreme Court "struck down the state's system of financing public schools, ruling that the system doesn't provide enough money for schools in poorer, urban districts" (Felsenthal, 1990). The court based its decision on the "state's constitutional guarantee of a 'thorough and efficient' education" (Felsenthal, 1990). The state of New Jersey was ordered to develop a plan for guaranteeing equal funding among school districts. One landmark court case involving funding of public education is the Supreme Court ruling in 1990 that "a federal judge may require the Kansas City school district to raise taxes to pay for desegregation" (Wermiel, 1990).

NONPUBLIC SCHOOLS

Most communities have one or more nonpublic schools, that is, elementary and or secondary schools which do not rely upon public funds for their operation. The courts have established the fact that attendance at these schools meets compulsory attendance requirements. States have the right to regulate these schools, at least in regard to basic curriculum requirements and standards, the credentials of the teachers, rules for attendance, and public health features of the facilities. States differ in regard to specific standards and the enforcement of rules and regulations.

Nonpublic-school students benefit from public funds. The courts have approved of some arrangements and have declared others unconstitutional. For example, the provision of textbooks is permissible under the First Amendment. This practice follows the doctrine of "child benefit," in that children, and not the schools, are the beneficiaries of the aid. A state may provide bus transportation to and from school for parochial school children.

Public and nonpublic schools are permitted to cooperate in providing some services to their students. One of the types of cooperation involves release-time programs. In such instances, students may be released from the public schools to take instruction from nonpublic schools (such as religious instructions), as long as the instruction is not provided at a public school location. Another example of cooperation permitted by law involves students in private schools who wish to take specialized courses, such as band, in the public school under a shared-time arrangement (*Snyder v. Charlotte Public School District*, Michigan, 1984). In general, public school personnel may not offer instruction on the grounds of nonpublic schools. Counseling and remedial services are permitted if they are given off the grounds of the nonpublic school. However, diagnostic services may be provided anywhere.

PRIVATE SCHOOLS AS COMMUNITIES

Even though nonpublic schools at the elementary and secondary levels include only about 10 percent of the total student enrollment at these levels, they play an important role in the educational system of a community. Parents choose non-public schools for their children for a variety of reasons, with a general expectation that the nonpublic school will provide a "better" or different education. There is no clear evidence that this expectation is always met, but some efforts to compare the two school systems confirm this belief. A study on this subject by Coleman, Hoffer, and Kilgore (1982) compared public and private high schools and found that "private sector schools generally produced higher achievement than did public schools for comparable students." This study has been replicated by Coleman and Hoffer (1987), with similar findings. While it remains unclear as to what factors in the two school systems contribute to the differences, Coleman et al. suggest that the nonpublic schools may do "better" due to different orientations toward education and to different types of communities the schools are associated with, that is, functional communities and value communities.

Coleman et al. (1987) identify three parent orientations to the school, "the school as agent of the larger society or the state; the school as agent of the (religious) community, and the school as agent of the individual family." It is recognized that public and private schools may be based on a mix of all three orientations, but the emphasis differs. The first orientation is associated with public schools, the second with nonpublic sectarian schools, and the third orientation with independent private schools. The second and third orientations are similar in that they both emphasize the role of the family. In the sectarian orientation, the family is a part of a community of families, with community based on religion (and/or residence) or on other factors.

From this point of view, schools are seen within a social context of different orientations and different communities, a context which influences the structure and design of the public and private school systems. Coleman et al. (1987) suggest that two major types of communities prevail in the United States. One type is called the "functional" community, a community which creates and maintains cultural norms and sanctions, and thus reinforces the goals of the family in relation to the schools. A second type of community is related to values and the extent to which values are consistent among a given group of families. What is striking is that many nonpublic sectarian schools relate to groups of families with value consistency as well as to the families constituting a "functional" community. On the other hand, independent private schools are likely to have value consistency while related to the same residential or other functional communities. Coleman et al. (1987) suggest that these communities, functional and value, provide "social capital," that is, interactions, support, and resources which contribute to higher quality education.

SCHOOL REFORM

School reform is a term used for a variety of efforts to improve the public school system. As Chira (1993) has noted, "Educators almost universally agree that the system has to change. But they disagree about whether it can be changed from within or whether they have to start fresh. . . ." In recent years school reform initiatives have been introduced at all levels of government (Finn, 1990, 1992). A major framework for school reform developed at the federal level was presented in 1983 by the National Commission on Excellence in Education under the title of "A Nation at Risk." This report indicated that there was "a rising tide of mediocrity that threatens our very future as a nation and as a people." The report recommended "more math, more science, more reading, more homework, more discipline, more school hours, more time on tasks, more 'excellence'" (Williams, 1989). A review of some of the changes in schools during the last ten years suggests that a number of improvements have been made in various states and communities. For example, almost all states strengthened graduation requirements, about one third developed stronger teacher certification programs, salaries for teachers rose about 22 percent over the rate of inflation, about 40 percent of schools lengthened the school year, most states introduced improved testing programs, four-fifths of the states have some form of teacher evaluation, and the average amount of money spent per student has risen by more than double the rate of inflation (Celis, 1993).

Notable in reviews of the changes in schools over the decade since the report "A Nation at Risk" is the lack of improvement in SAT scores, the lack of improvement in urban schools, and the inability of many states and local communities to provide adequate funding for schools. In fact, one report suggests that "By and large the reform movement has totally bypassed the cities. . . . Cities have become . . . isolated racially, culturally, and economically" (Celis, 1993). A study entitled, "Divided Within, Besieged Without: The Politics of Education in Four American School Districts," suggested that school system reforms flounder because "Most systems are top-heavy with bureaucrats, mired in regulations that discourage risk-taking, buffeted by politics and filled with special interests" (Chira, 1993).

In another commentary on public education, the former president of Yale University, Benno Schmidt, Jr. (1992) states: "The evidence that U.S. schools are not working well is depressingly familiar. One in five young Americans drops out of high school. Nearly half of all high school graduates have not mastered seventh-grade arithmetic. American 13 year-olds place near the bottom in science and math achievement in international comparisons. . . ." Schmidt concluded that the problem is not the teachers or financial resources but the system itself. As a response to these problems, Schmidt is heading up a school reform effort called the Edison project, a privately funded approach to create new models of education.

FEDERAL INITIATIVES

The call for school reform has been sounded by both Republican and Democratic presidential administrations. The major initiative under

the Bush administration was entitled, America 2000. This plan identified six major goals to be reached by the year 2000. These included:

1. All children in America will start school ready to learn.
2. The high school graduation rate will increase to 90 percent.
3. American students will leave grades four, eight and twelve having demonstrated competency in challenging subject matter, including English, mathematics, science, history and geography;
   and every school in America will ensure that all students learn
   to use their minds well, so they may be prepared for responsible
   citizenship, further learning and productive employment in our
   modern economy.
4. U.S. students will be first in the world in science and mathematics achievement.
5. Every adult American will be literate and will possess the
   knowledge and skills necessary to compete in a global economy
   and exercise the rights and responsibilities of citizenship.
6. Every school in America will be free of drugs and violence and
   will offer a disciplined environment conducive to learning
   (America 2000).

These goals have been incorporated into President Clinton's 1993
educational proposal entitled, "Goals 2000: Educate America Act."
Under this plan a board would establish national curriculum standards which would be voluntary on the part of the states (Naylor,
1993; Celis, 1993). For example, such standards would indicate major
concepts and skills for learning by various age levels. These are labeled "opportunity to learn" standards, designed to improve school
quality, and might include such things as student-teacher ratios, guarantees of teacher competency, and quality of educational facilities
(Sharpe, 1993). States would be provided federal funds if they
adhered to the federal curriculum guidelines. Unlike the Bush proposal, the Clinton plan does not include vouchers within school
choice options. Opposition to President Clinton's plan has come from
groups who oppose federal intrusion into the control of education
by the states (Chira, 1993; Manno, 1993).

MULTICULTURALISM AND CURRICULUM DEVELOPMENT

Most local community school systems throughout the United States
have given some attention to curriculum reform, which includes
teaching and learning beyond the traditional Western culture, Anglo-

American content. The recognition of cultural pluralism in American society by public school educators has led to inclusion of histories of people of color, including content on African American, Asian American, Native American, and Hispanic cultures. At the same time, critics have argued that the movement to a multicultural curricula in the public schools has led to a minimization of focus on the role of a unifying culture of Americanism (Hymowitz, 1993; Verhovek, 1991). Schlesinger (1992) has articulated this position, claiming that multicultural curricula, especially Afrocentricity, contributes to a "disuniting of America." Proponents of a multicultural curriculum claim that both approaches in education are needed, that is, focus on the unifying components of Americanism as well as on the diversity and ethnicity of population groups within the United States.

An example of controversy over the elements of a multicultural curriculum is found in the "Children of the Rainbow" curriculum of the New York City Board of Education. This curriculum is based on a 1989 resolution by the Board that "Multicultural education values cultural pluralism and rejects the view that schools should seek to melt away cultural diversity; rather, multicultural education accepts cultural diversity as a valuable resource that should be preserved and extended" (Miller, 1993). Critics have objected to a number of aspects of the Rainbow curriculum, particularly those dealing with bilingualism, feminism, homosexuality, and "family situations found in New York, including, most controversially, children being raised by gay and lesbian couples" (Hiss, 1993).

SCHOOL-CHOICE PROGRAMS

A variety of school-choice programs have been established, with a goal of improving education of elementary and high school students, especially students in impoverished inner-city areas. A number of states have legislation which permits school districts to develop school-choice programs. Under a school-choice program, parents are not restricted to sending their children to a school in a particular attendance area. Programs permit choice within a set of schools, within a school district, or within a broader area such an entire state. Most choice programs restrict the selection of a school to those within the public school system, although a few permit a choice for attendance in private schools. Since 1990 Milwaukee, Wisconsin, has had a choice program which uses public funds for low-income parents to enroll children in private nonsectarian schools. A federal suit by some Milwaukee parents seeks to extend choice to enrollment in private sectarian schools (McGroarty, 1993).

The aims of choice programs include such goals as improving the education of children in low-income areas by permitting them to leave "poor" schools and attend schools with higher quality and/or specialized education. One of the arguments in support of school choice is that such programs will promote competition among schools. This is expected to force schools with poor quality education to improve themselves. Opponents to such programs reject this argument and believe that choice plans will leave some inner-city schools with fewer students and a lowered quality of education.

Since there are such variations in school choice programs, one cannot generalize that such programs do or do not work (MacGuire, 1992; Stout, 1992). A number of programs have been evaluated and judged to improve education. Examples of programs declared to be successful are East Harlem (Fliegel, 1992), Milwaukee Parental Choice Program, which includes public funds for tuition at private schools, (Chira, 1991), programs in Minnesota that allow a choice of any school in the state (Nathan, 1993), and a magnet-school system in Kansas City, Missouri (Farney, 1992).

According to a report by the Education Commission of the States, in 1992 the states of Arkansas, Idaho, Iowa, Minnesota, Nebraska, Ohio, Utah, and Washington, had programs allowing school attendance, with some restrictions, in any district in the state. Several other states permit variations of choice within school districts or other geographical areas. Most choice programs have been the result of local community and/or state governmental policymaking. However, during President Bush's administration, federal officials began considering how the federal government might assist school-choice plans. For example, the idea was advanced that federal money might be granted to states for demonstration projects in local communities. Choice plans have become one of the major components of a broader national educational policy of "empowerment" of local communities through local control and privatization.

The theory behind choice programs has been presented by Chubb and Moe (1990) in a book entitled, *Politics, Markets, and America's Schools.* These authors propose "a new system of public education that eliminates most political and bureaucratic control over the schools and relies instead on indirect control through markets and parental choice." Such a system is expected to produce more effective schools, since "Schools compete for the support of parents and students, and parents and students are free to choose among schools.

The system is built on decentralization, competition and choice." The benefits of a choice program are believed to be twofold: the student gets a better education, and the public schools improve because they must compete for students. These programs are thought to have special benefits for poor and minority children, since the urban, inner-city schools appear to provide inferior education. It is also argued that choice programs will result in public savings, since the operating costs per student in private schools is considerably lower than in the public schools (Genetski, 1992).

Opposition to choice programs has come most forcefully from school boards, teachers' unions, and public school administrators. Among the anti-choice arguments are: school choice will upset desegregation plans, leaving inner-city schools even more heavily populated by ethnic minority students; resources will be drained from inner-city schools; there is no mechanism for assuring that schools which lose students will improve; some plans allow for state funding of private sectarian schools, out of keeping with the establishment clause of the Constitution regarding separation of church and state; and the private schools would not be accountable to the standards of the states (Putka, 1991; Chira, 1991). Despite the fact that the impact of choice programs on students and on the public school system is unknown, the movement now has a substantial base, supported by the federal government, some state legislatures, and some local communities.

EXAMPLES OF COMMUNITY-WIDE SCHOOL REFORM

With the attention given to the problems of urban school systems, it is easy to ignore the fact that some big cities have achieved rather dramatic improvements in their schools. It is useful to examine how these successes occurred. A study of big-city school systems (Hill et al., 1989) focused on ways in which six big cities—Pittsburgh, Cincinnati, Atlanta, Miami, Memphis, and San Diego—were able to improve their school systems. The major conclusion of this study was that "An urban school system can be turned around only if the entire community unites on its behalf."

The study of these big-city school systems revealed that "a city school improvement strategy must combine two complementary strands. The outside strand attracts and mobilizes political support and other resources from outside the traditional school bureaucracy, from taxpayers, businesses, and the larger community. The inside strand focuses on the content of schooling . . . curricula, academic standards, incentives and work rules for teachers, and a philosophy of school management."

The process of school reform and improvement, when successful, bears a strong resemblance to the processes described for a competent community (Cottrell, 1976). In the cities studied by Hill and colleagues,

> Community leaders and the educational establishment . . .
> * reached out to involve the larger community in educational issues
> * made information about community needs, school resources, and student performance broadly available
> * created community wide agreement and understanding about educational improvement goals
> * subordinated the traditional roles of school boards, administrators, and teachers to the broad imperatives of a system-wide improvement effort (Hill et al., 1989).

SOCIAL WORK IN THE SCHOOLS

Social work services are provided in public schools by professional social workers. The nature of these services has changed over the years, especially in the light of federal legislation related to children with special educational needs (Radin, 1989; Allen-Meares et al., 1986). Social workers are members of interdisciplinary teams organized to service children with special needs. At the same time, social workers serve other students, particularly in regard to high-risk children, family education, case management, and service evaluation (Radin, 1989). The understanding of the educational subsystem of a local community is important for all social workers, but especially for social workers practicing in the schools. Books on the social services and on school social work usually include discussions of the design and delivery of social work services in the schools (Allen-Meares et al., 1986; Winters and Eastor, 1983; Garvin and Tropman, 1992; Johnson, 1990; Brieland, Costin, and Atherton, 1985). Guidelines for practice in schools are provided by the National Association of Social Workers. These works serve to highlight the need for social workers to recognize the significance of the local community in relation to the functioning of the educational system, especially in regard to the assessment of community needs and resources (Allen-Meares et al., 1986).

REVIEW

The educational system of a community carries out major functions of learning, socialization, citizenship development, and social control. The focus of this chapter is on the structure and functioning of a community's public elementary and secondary school systems, in the context of their relationship to state and federal governments. Special issues related to school-community relations, such as desegregation, church-state relations, and school reform, are discussed. Issues related to financing of public education and to school-choice programs are introduced. The discussion of issues related to community educational systems highlights the fact that these systems serve to integrate people into the community, providing opportunities for social interaction and social identity. At the same time, the community educational system as an arena for community controversies is exemplified by reference to efforts to enhance multicultural education, to provide public school services for students in private schools, and to develop and implement school-choice programs. Finally, the reader is reminded that local community educational systems provide the context for the practice of school social work.

SUGGESTED READINGS

Allen-Meares, Paula (1990). "Educating Black Youths: The Unfulfilled Promise of Equality." *Social Work* 35:3 (May).

Coleman, J. S. and T. Hoffer (1987). *Public and Private High Schools.* New York: Basic Books.

Chubb, J. E. and T. M. Moe (1990). *Politics, Markets, and America's Schools.* Brookings Institution.

Fliegel, Seymour (1992). "Public School Choice Works . . . Look at East Harlem." *Wall Street Journal*, October 29.

Hiss, Tony (1993). "The End of the Rainbow." *New Yorker*, April 12.

Schlesinger, Arthur M. (1992). *The Disuniting of America: Reflections on a Multicultural Society.* New York: Norton and Company.

Williams, Leon F. (1990). "The Challenge of Education to Social Work: The Case for Minority Children." *Social Work* 35:3 (May).

EXERCISE

Draw from ideas in Chapter 6, as well as from Chapter 9, to discuss the ways in which initiatives regarding housing have been combined with goals related to the Florida school system described in the following new report in order to "end segregation and restore neighborhood schools."

DISTRICT FINDS WAY TO END SEGREGATION AND RESTORE NEIGHBORHOOD SCHOOLS

By William Celis, 3rd

Arguing that housing segregation was the cause of segregated schools, the Palm Beach County public school system has devised a plan to integrate housing in the county, a move that school officials hope will mean that children can again attend neighborhood schools.

The district has been under pressure from the Federal Government to improve the integration of its schools, and its plan to encourage each housing development and community within its borders to attract black and white families is the first of its kind and may become a model for other districts struggling to find an alternative to busing, education experts say.

The plan, now under review by the Education Department's Office for Civil Rights, calls on Palm Beach's 37 incorporated communities and unincorporated developments to expand marketing efforts to attract more minority residents. The details of those marketing efforts are left to the developers and communities.

"Nobody has ever done anything as comprehensive," said Gary Orfield, a professor of political science and education at the University of Chicago who was a housing official in the Carter Administration.

"New Territory"

The plan, Mr. Orfield said, is "new territory" that could provide an answer to unpopular and expensive school busing plans in effect in more than 200 communities around the nation.

Chris Pipho, director of state relations for the Education Commission of the States, a Denver-based education policy and research organization, said the plan was "worth watching."

Fifteen developers and communities in the district have agreed to participate, and developers, real estate agents, local officials and residents have generally supported the plan, although school officials said there has been an undercurrent of resistance. But, they say, the lure of neighborhood schools has proven so strong that so far it has overcome that resistance.

Voluntary Agreements

Under the plan, developers and cities sign voluntary agreements with the school district pledging to achieve a racial mix by 1995 of at least 10 percent, depending on which group is the minority race in the community.

William Celis, 3rd, "District Finds Way to End Segregation and Restore Neighborhood Schools," *New York Times*, September 4, 1991. Copyright © 1991 by the New York Times Company. Reprinted by permission.

In return, school officials would allow students to attend the school nearest their homes. The district currently buses about 50 percent of its 110,000 students; 15 percent of those are bused to achieve school desegregation.

"Housing patterns were creating a monster that we had to solve with busing," said William V. Hukill, an associate superintendent in the district overseeing the plan.

Now, Mr. Hukill said, "busing is universally unpopular, and the only way we're going to get out from under it is with help from the communities."

In 1988, several years after a Federal court ruled that the Palm Beach County school system had complied with its school desegregation orders, parents complained to the Office for Civil Rights that the school district had become lax in its desegregation efforts. The Federal authorities agreed, and last year the district agreed to improve the integration of its schools within three years or lose $30 million in Federal aid for the schools.

The Office for Civil Rights declined to comment on the new plan because it is still under review.

Mr. Hukill said he devised the new plan believing that neighborhood schools would be a strong selling point. Indeed, the promise of schools to which children have easy access has been a powerful enticement in a school district that sprawls across 2,500 square miles.

The plan has generated a variety of approaches to community desegregation. Some city and town councils are rewriting building codes to reduce development costs and, they hope, reduce housing prices to levels within reach of more people. Other communities are rezoning land for commercial and light industrial use to create more jobs at all skill levels, which would attract blacks and whites to the same community. And builders have begun aggressive marketing campaigns that include stepped-up advertising in black newspapers, reduced interest rates on mortgages for home buyers and rent subsidies for qualified tenants.

School officials say there is a two-year grace period for those who fail to meet the agreed-upon standard, allowing communities and developers to bolster their racial mix or face a resumption of busing.

Concern About Housing Laws

Many believe that the school plan raises nettlesome issues. Real estate officials say some of the desegregation approaches used by developers and communities may violate Federal fair-housing laws that ban the race-based steering of home buyers or renters to particular housing projects or communities.

"The plan creates a real question of legality," said William D. North, executive vice president of the National Association of Realtors. "What these people are doing, as far as I can tell, is embarking on a program that will have a lot of questions down the line. What happens if you sell to someone who breaks the formula?"

But local school officials say that by allowing communities and developers to use any one of a number of existing approaches to integrated housing they avoid the legal pitfalls of quotas. Integration in Palm Beach they say, can be achieved simply by opening up neighborhoods that were once closed.

Such is the case in Wellington, an unincorporated development of 28,000 people. The 10,000-acre community developed by the Core Point Corporation, is just 4 percent black. The corporation and several neighborhood associations in the development signed an agreement with the school district in February to raise that figure to at least 10 percent.

Local leaders say it will not be easy.

"What we're doing is trying to hurry a process in 5 years that would normally occur over 8, to 9 to 10 years," said Lourdes Ferris, the former chairwoman of the Wellington Education Committee, which worked out the agreement.

For starters, Wellington has altered its advertising for houses and apartments. Scenes of white men and women playing polo or tennis have given way to black and white families playing tennis, swimming and sailing.

Core Point is about to build a development that would include affordable apartments in an area that boasts homes costing $1 million or more.

Seeking Families with Children

Riviera Beach faces an even greater challenge in trying to change its housing patterns. The incorporated community of 36,000 people is 60 percent black and 40 percent white, but many of the white residents are retired and do not have school-age children to racially balance the schools. As a result, Riviera Beach children are bused to 21 schools throughout the county.

"Our task is to attract white families with children," said Gerald Adams, Riviera Beach's assistant city manager.

There is reason for optimism, he said. A $400 million hospital is scheduled to be built in Riviera Beach, and already one developer has proposed a large housing development nearby, which community leaders hope will attract enough white hospital workers to pass the 10 percent threshold. "Let's face it," Mr. Adams said. "Housing patterns are basically what caused segregation. The only recourse now is housing."

School officials point to the success of Royal Palm Beach, a town of 16,500 whose population went from less than 3 percent black in 1981 to 11 percent black this year without incentives. City officials say the increase resulted from the development of affordable housing.

Royal Palm Beach's agreement with the county calls on the village and its developers only to maintain a racial mix. But by entering into the agreement, the developers, Jess R. Santamaria and Wallace D. Sanger, insured that children in their development would attend nearby schools. At the same time, they also agreed to offer a variety of incentives to maintain a racial mix, including advertising sales for its Crestwood development, an integrated community, in black newspapers and paying mortgage origination points for qualified buyers. A point is equal to 1 percent of the mortgage balance.

The marketing campaign has helped attract buyers like Paul and Yverose Jean-Mary. Mr. and Mrs. Jean-Mary, Haitians who are both health care professionals, moved from Montclair, N.J., into a $156,000 home in Crestwood last month with four of their five children.

Explaining their decision, Mrs. Jean-Mary said simply "We found this town was the best place to live."

Royal Palm Beach officials last year wrote variances into their zoning laws to allow for the construction of smaller, more affordable homes. But Lawrence G. Zabik, a village councilman, said that despite such efforts, school integration "is not an easy quest, and there are no easy answers."

CHAPTER 10

The Community Economic System

A community's economic system includes organizations, groups, and individuals engaged in the production, distribution, and consumption of goods and services. The nature of a community economic system is related to a community of place, such as a municipality or a metropolitan area. The economy at these levels is related vertically to state, regional, and national economies, and horizontally to other local communities. Central cities in metropolitan areas are an integral part of an urban economic system. The local community economic system has interrelationships with other community subsystems, especially the political, with the term *political economy* used to designate this interdependence. Other community subsystems, such as health and social welfare and education, depend on the strength of a community's economic system to assure the fulfillment of their functions.

The economic system of a local community includes (1) numerous formal bureaucratic organizations, such as industrial companies and commercial businesses; (2) offices of professionals in private or group practice (e.g., accountants, lawyers, physicians, social workers, psychologists); (3) small, less formalized businesses, home industries, service operations; and (4) an underground economy, which includes a variety of legal and illegal remunerative activities by individuals and groups.

The functioning of a community economic system can be examined from an ecological perspective. Human ecologists view the city as a marketplace, with people living off trade and commerce. Hence, they consider the economy to be the most important element of the community, a place where people live and work (Hicks and Rees, 1993). A similar approach is taken by Marxist economists, who focus primarily on how the forces and modes of production and ownership affect social and economic problems, which result in a class struggle. The importance of the economic system is found in the early community studies, such as the Middletown study by Lynd and Lynd (1929) and the "Yankee City" studies by Warner and Lunt (1941), as these investigators looked at how social class structure is both defined and affected by the economic life of the community.

Ecological factors such as a community's size, age, geographical location, natural resources, climate, and other demographic features all relate to a community's production base, labor market, and income levels. The production base involves manufacturing, commercial, and financial functions, that is, economic productivity. The labor market can be analyzed by studying an occupational profile developed from U.S. Census data, as well as by indicators of employment and unemployment. Per capita income may be used as a measure of the viability of the community's economic system. Comparisons of income and occupation levels of specialized populations, such as ethnic minorities and women, can be used to examine the social and economic stratification of a community's population and the extent of economic inequalities.

THE ECONOMIC SYSTEM AS A SET OF WORKPLACES

Formal organizations within a community make up the bulk of employment opportunities for residents and constitute the actual locations for most work activities. Rothman (1982) highlights the fact that these workplaces may be conceptualized as functional communities. People within the workplace are likely to share a common interest or function, as is the case in a university community of students and faculty, a hospital as a therapeutic community, or a factory as a manufacturing community. The economic organization allows the individual to perform work, derive satisfaction out of a specialized occupational activity, earn income, to obtain health and welfare benefits, and establish a basis for retirement income and other benefits. In addition the workplace may tie the individual worker to the local geographic area, especially when the location of work is relatively close to the community of residence.

There are clear interdependencies between workplaces and the total community. For example, management and labor within an industrial organization have specialized needs, some of which must be met from within the community. These workplaces require land, space, facilities, a pool of employees, local services (fire, police protection), water, energy, education and health services, recreation, and cultural institutions. Most communities, even "bedroom" communities, need employment opportunities for their residents, property taxes from employed workers; taxes from the economic organizations, and an organized means of providing health and welfare benefits for its residents. Interdependencies develop in a community between the economic system and other subsystems, such as education. Many local companies give financial support to local colleges and universities as a way of insuring a pool of well qualified employees. Organizations benefit from community health and welfare agencies, which provide services that support employees in need of professional help.

EQUAL EMPLOYMENT OPPORTUNITIES

Communities vary in the extent to which workplaces provide equal opportunities for employment, pay, and advancement within the organization. Nationwide, women and ethnic minorities continue to encounter discrimination in these areas, although some companies have pioneered in their programs of affirmative action, pay equity, and promotion (Rigdon, 1993). Basic rights in these areas were established in the Civil Rights Act of 1964, which included an Equal Pay Act, monitored through the Equal Employment Opportunity Commission. Data from the Census Bureau in 1991 on median annual wages indicated that women earn 70 cents for each dollar earned by men, with minority women earning far less, 62 cents for Black women and 54 cents for Hispanic women. There are considerable differences within the work force, displayed in the following examples of women's median wages as a percentage of men's wages for the same jobs.

data-entry keyers (95 percent)
secretaries (91.6 percent)
pharmacists (90.1 percent)
engineers, architects, surveyors (85.6 percent)
computer programmers (84.1 percent)
lawyers (78 percent)

doctors (72.2 percent)
managers of marketing, advertising, public relations (68.5 percent)
machine operators etc. (67.7 percent)
financial managers (62.4 percent)
(Bureau of Labor Statistics, 1991)

A number of issues related to the workforce were examined in a 1993 survey of American workers' views about their work and personal lives (Shellenbarger, 1993). This study found that "workers of all ages said they prefer working with people of the same race, sex, gender and education." Most employees had not had an experience of working or living with people of other races and ethnic groups. Those that did have such experiences were more positive toward diversity in the workplace. Most employees agreed that members of other racial and ethnic groups had poorer chances than nonminority workers for advancement, and there was a widespread perception of discrimination against minority workers. Women were much more likely than men to rate the opportunities for career advancement as "poor" or "fair." These findings suggest a strong need for educational programs and equal opportunity policies in the workplace focused on gender and multicultural diversity.

Companies like Xerox and Avon Products have initiated programs to move ethnic minorities and women into management jobs, motivated in part by the fact that workforce growth into the year 2000 will have a strong ethnic minority presence. Companies like these seek to develop a corporate culture which promotes comfortable and productive relationships among women, ethnic minorities, and white males. Mechanisms to promote this culture include affirmative action hiring, programs for advancement of women and minorities, and special "multicultural" training programs (Solomon, 1990). Small companies have begun to provide "diversity" workshops as a way of easing tensions between workers and to make workers aware of the values and lifestyles of people from other cultures (Lee, 1993). Such companies see diversity training as a survival technique, as workplace confrontations tend to disrupt the work environment and interfere with productivity.

Multicultural workshops focus on an understanding and appreciation of differences of people from various cultures as well as differences and similarities of men and women (Hagerty, 1993). Such workshops are not without controversy, as diversity training programs sometimes backfire; that is, they are designed to promote harmony but leave race and gender divisions. This sometimes happens when workshops use negative and positive stereotypes which offend participants, when blame is given to one group in relation to another, or when a winners-losers situation arises because a program is tied to affirmative action goals (Murray, 1993).

The U.S. Labor Department has recognized that job bias and discrimination in promotions exist in subtle ways in most large U.S. corporations (Wynter and Solomon, 1989). During President Bush's administration, Labor Secretary Elizabeth Dole announced special efforts to "shatter the glass ceiling" by examining promotion practices in companies with government contracts and by threatening to cancel such contracts if companies did not cooperate (Kilborn, 1990). Despite efforts such as these, a 1993 survey of executive women found that although these individuals made major gains in pay and status, "men still outnumber women at the executive vice president level by nearly 3 to 1. An executive women's average compensation still lags behind that of men by more than one-third" (Shellenbarger, 1993). More than 90 percent of the women executives in this study reported that a glass ceiling is still intact and that "being a woman" is their greatest single career obstacle.

CAREER TRACKS

A controversial response to the lack of representation of women in management circles of large corporations personnel has been voiced by Felice Schwartz. Schwartz (1989) proposed a plan whereby corporations may overcome the fact that "the cost of employing women in management is greater than the cost of employing men." For women to succeed in management, she suggests that businesses "recognize that women are not all alike," that "like men, they are individuals with differing talents, priorities, and motivations." Based on these assumptions, she proposed that companies address their own needs and those of women by establishing two career tracks, a career-primary woman track and a career-and-family track. The later track was quickly labeled by some as a "mommy-track."

Schwartz contends that having optional career tracks introduces flexibility into the woman's work life, permits the management of maternity and work, reduces stresses, and benefits both women and companies. She suggests that flexibility in careers, along with family supports, would be desirable for both women and men. This approach is not without its critics, as demonstrated in numerous letters to the editor of the *Harvard Business Review* following publication of

the Schwartz proposal (Olofson, 1989). The debate serves to highlight the problems women face in the workplace in terms of work assignments, pay, and career advancement. Schwartz (1992) has
continued to support the idea that "Treating women as a business
imperative is the equivalent of a unique R and D product for which
there is a huge demand." In keeping with this approach to women in
the workplace, Schwartz has developed a quiz for business leaders
(*Wall Street Journal*, 1993). A 20-item questionnaire can be used to
rate companies on how they treat their women employees. "The quiz
includes such questions as: Do you trust a woman to be the chief li-
aison with one of your top 10 clients/customers? Do you support tal-
ented women who choose to limit their career paths to spend more
time with their families? Do female and male managers in your company routinely have lunch together?" Some companies have used the
findings of the questionnaire to develop sensitivity training and recruitment plans.

Issues surrounding women and careers in the workplace vs. stay-at-
home motherhood are controversial, as exemplified in the women's
movement and in the popular media. Usually the arguments center
around three positions: support for women in the workplace, in the
home, or on options of workplace and/or home. As of 1993, there
has been some indication that "stay-at-home moms are fashionable
again in many communities." These women believe that they provide better care for their children than that of "working" women, and
that they have adequate opportunities for work satisfaction through
activities and leadership in community voluntary associations.
Women with careers in the workplace often have opposite views,
leaving both types of women with pressures to be "maternally cor-
rect" (Swasy, 1993). One response to the pros and cons related to
work at home or work outside the home has been a call for "ridding
our language of the absurd term 'working mother.' All mothers work:
inside the home, outside the home, or both" (Kim, 1993).

AMERICANS WITH DISABILITIES ACT

Discrimination in hiring is one of the major problems addressed by
the Americans With Disabilities Act of 1990 (P.L. 101-336). The Congress recognized that over 43 million Americans have one or more
physical or mental disabilities and that these individuals encounter
discrimination economically, socially, vocationally, and education-
ally (P.L. 101-336). The act applies to all businesses with 25 or more

employees and has provisions which seek to eliminate discrimination in employment as well as to provide supports and accommodations which will assist disabled persons in performing their jobs (Freudenheim, 1991). The provisions of the disabilities act include:

1. Prohibit an employer from inquiring into a job applicant's disability with questions concerning such areas as medical history, prior workers' compensation/health insurance claims, work absenteeism due to illness, past treatment for alcoholism, and mental illness.
2. Require employers to make "reasonable accommodations" for disabled workers by acquiring or modifying work equipment, providing qualified readers or interpreters, adjusting work schedules, and making existing facilities such as rest rooms, telephones, and drinking fountains accessible.
3. Define a disabled person as one who has a physical or mental impairment that limits one or more life activities, has a record of such an impairment, and is regarded as having such an impairment.
4. Define a qualified disabled worker as one who can perform the "essential functions" of a job, with or without reasonable accommodation (Equal Employment Opportunity Commission; Quintanilla, 1993).

While many states have had laws with regard to discrimination with the physically disabled, this act covers job rights of both physically and mentally ill persons.

SEXUAL HARASSMENT IN THE WORKPLACE

Sexual harassment in the workplace continues to be a problematic condition of work, especially for women. Most definitions of sexual harassment emphasize that this behavior is unwanted and occurs within the context of an unequal power relationship (MacKinnon, 1979; Maypole, 1987). The Merit System Protection Board (1981) defined sexual harassment as "deliberate or repeated unsolicited verbal comments, gestures, or physical contact of a sexual nature that is considered to be unwelcome by the recipient." In the workplace, this kind of behavior "occurs when a person who is in a position to control, influence, or affect another person's job, career, or grades uses the position's authority to coerce the other person into sexual acts or relations or punishes the person if he or she refuses to comply" (Maypole and Skaine, 1983).

Sexual harassment is illegal, and recourse is available due to sex discrimination laws, Titles VII and IX of the Civil Rights Act of 1964 as well as to criminal, tort, and state employment laws. The Equal Employment Opportunity Commission (1980) guidelines on sexual harassment follow the following criteria:

- Submission to the conduct is made either an explicit or implicit condition of employment.
- Submission to or rejection of the conduct is used as the basis for an employment decision affecting the harassed employee.
- The harassment substantially interferes with an employee's work performance or creates an intimidating, hostile, or offensive work environment.

(Equal Employment Opportunity Commission, 1980)

Knowledge about sexual harassment and the legal protections against it is important for social workers in human service organizations when their clients encounter this behavior at their workplace. Social workers need to be cognizant of sexual harassment policies in relation to their own work conditions and in order to work at the community level in helping to improve work settings, especially "as social environments for women" (Maypole and Skaine, 1983).

A related form of discrimination may occur with regard to sexual orientation. Gay and lesbian employees often encounter discrimination in hiring practices if they disclose their sexual orientation to employers. Some occupational groups, such as the military, school teachers, government workers, and clergy, appear to be most negative toward hiring of gay and lesbian individuals. The Pentagon's policy guidelines related to homosexuals in the military provide a prime example of the controversies surrounding employment of gay and lesbian people. In 1993, the Pentagon, as well as the U.S. Congress, supported more restrictive policies ("Don't ask; don't tell") than those initiated by President Clinton.

Once hired, employees may choose not to disclose their sexual orientation for fear of prejudice and discrimination related to retention and advancement in employment. Williamson (1993) has identified some of the dilemmas related to disclosure and the visibility of gay and lesbian individuals in the workforce in regard to relationships with other workers, in consideration of company benefits, and in terms of the corporate culture and its interactions with clients and customers. In response to these dilemmas posed to seven experts by Williamson in a case study, the consensus was that discrimination on the basis of sexual orientation is never appropriate and that companies will benefit, not suffer, from policies and practices which are non-discriminatory. As one expert stated the issue, "Acceptable behavior, not acceptable beliefs, is the appropriate workplace standard" (Williamson, 1993).

FAMILY SUPPORT PROGRAMS

The changing workforce in American communities has resulted in increased attention to family-friendly, family-responsive company policies and programs. By 1992, approximately 46 percent of the workforce was female, over half of them women with children under three years of age, and an increasing proportion of single-parent women. The percentage of men who have employed wives rose to 67 percent, and about 20 percent of workers were responsible for care of an elderly relative (Shellenbarger, 1993). New entrants into the workforce by the year 2000 are predicted to be about 65 percent women. Family support programs developed at the initiative of private companies and governmental agencies have been responsive to some of these changes in the workforce. Corporate support for families may include programs such as child care centers, employee assistance programs, flex-time, job sharing, family leave, and eldercare services.

While there are ample examples of family support programs in the major corporations of the economic system, most corporations do not have such programs and resist them due to the costs involved. Of the programs that exist, most tend to be in large corporations which employ professionals, so that people employed in smaller companies in secondary labor markets, and low-wage jobs, do not have the benefits of family supports. For example, the working poor, women, single parents, and ethnic and racial minorities tend to be employed in organizations without family support programs (Lambert, 1993). Lambert has highlighted the fact that in the programs that do exist, "many so-called family-responsive policies function as work supports to help ensure that workers continue to give priority to work over family."

A major source of family supports has come from federal and state legislation, including "laws and regulations concerning child labor, minimum wage, safety in the workplace, payment for overtime hours, the freedom of workers to organize, and discrimination on the basis of race or gender" (Lambert, 1993). A major federal initiative is the Family and Medical Leave Act of 1993. This act was implemented in

August 1993 for workers in companies of fifty or more employees. The law allows workers to take up to twelve weeks off annually without pay to care for seriously ill or new members of their immediate family (self, children, parents, or a spouse). An important part of the act is the requirement, under most conditions, of a guarantee of the same or comparable job with equivalent pay, benefits, and working conditions, and continuation of health benefits during leave (Moilanen, 1993).

PROBLEMS IN COMMUNITY ECONOMIC SYSTEMS

It is clear that American communities vary considerably in how well their local economic systems operate. It is important to recognize that the local system is highly dependent upon other economic systems, particularly in relation to urban areas and state and national economies. An effective economic system should produce or contribute to a low level of unemployment; an adequate "division of labor," with opportunities for various occupations in the workforce; non-discrimination in hiring, promotion, and benefits; a presence of affirmative action programs directed toward employment of special populations; adequate funding for community protection (fire, police, safety); adequate tax base for public services and recreational programs; opportunities to earn adequate income above the poverty level; and provision of funding of health and welfare services for people without sufficient fiscal resources.

Evaluating a local economic system is a complex task. Yet, community studies and the deliberations of governmental bodies alert us to the extent to which economic forces have a positive or negative effect on the lives of community residents. The community acts through its economic and political organizations in the generation of money and services and the allocation of resources to community residents. The larger the community, the more difficult it is to ascertain the major features of its economic system and the causes of its problems. Special attention in recent years has been devoted to the problems of central cities in large metropolitan areas and the relationship of the economic conditions of these cities vis-a-vis suburban communities.

The economic conditions of central cities often have been characterized as an "urban crisis." Observers attribute this crisis to such factors as the decline in central city commercial-industrial growth, decline in population, the suburbanization of industry and households, competition between regions of the country for jobs and workforce, and high public investment in downtown developments (especially convention centers, and sports arenas). Any listing of these complex economic forces suggests the creation of a "fiscal plight" of the central cities, especially the inner-city areas of most large, older U.S. communities. Some of the reasons for the economic difficulties of central cities include the fact that these cities provide daily services for a large number of people, many of whom live outside the city. The fiscal ability to provide these services is lowered due to tax-base declines related to "white flight" of middle-class residents to the suburbs and increased labor costs for city utilities and services.

At the same time, suburban municipalities are not without their economic problems, particularly with regard to the delivery of public services. As federal funds to these communities have decreased, many local governments have sought relief through consolidations into larger governmental units. Some suburban communities now look to consolidation with central cities for such services as transportation, water supply, waste disposal, recreation, parks, and public health. While these local governments retain their political identity, the increased cooperation between them and central city governments signals an emerging form of economic relationships between the units of metropolitan communities (Rusk, 1993).

Among the various efforts by economic and political leaders to revitalize central city communities, three stand out. First, there is an effort to build housing that will attract middle- and upper-middle income people (new housing and rehabilitation, gentrification areas). Second, there is an effort to continue to develop the inner city as a high class "playground" of culture, dining, recreation, and entertainment to attract tourists and conventions. These efforts require a collaboration of local political leaders with economic leaders and the provision of incentives such as loan guarantees and tax abatements designed to lure new business, new housing, and new investments into the central downtown districts. Third, large central cities attempt to obtain special funds from state governments and departments of the federal government, such as Housing and Urban Development and Health and Human Services.

THE INFLUENCE OF FEDERAL AND STATE POLICIES

Central city mayors continue to seek state and federal aid for their communities. They argue that people from the entire metropolitan area use the facilities, roads, and cultural and entertainment amenities of the city, and that this requires unusually high expenditures for police and fire protection, parks, hospitals, and traffic ways. Most people who use the central city's facilities and services contribute very little to the funds needed to maintain them. Often guided by political party interests, state governments have responded in various ways to the special needs of central cities. The federal government has assumed some of the fiscal burdens of the city through revenue sharing and a variety of programs under the Department of Housing and Urban Development, including funding for street repairs, transportation, and water supply. Fiscal assistance from extra-community sources has been advocated on the premise that older urban cities have lost large numbers of people and jobs to the suburbs; have large areas with low tax bases, or no tax base (highways, urban renewal areas), have a large concentration of the poor, and have decaying physical facilities.

ENTERPRISE ZONES

Federal, state, and local governments are interested in creating new job opportunities and economic strength at the local community level. One of the ways developed to accomplish these goals is the designation of inner city areas as enterprise zones (Poole and Scarlett, 1993). Economic activities within such a zone are a response to the special problems of people in the area, such as high unemployment, high crime, and welfare dependency. Once an area has been declared an enterprise zone, special incentives for businesses are provided to assist economic development, such as tax relief for new hires and business expansion, and relaxation of regulations. The principle of the enterprise zone is that stimulation of business in these areas will generate employment opportunities for residents in the zone.

States have been the principal initiators of enterprise zone programs. Florida established the first enterprise zone legislation in 1981. As of 1993, thirty-six states and the District of Columbia had established some variation of enterprise zones, most of which were located in four states: Arkansas, Kansas, Louisiana, and Ohio (Poole and Scarlett, 1993). Based on studies by the U.S. Department of Housing and Urban Development, state enterprise zone programs in local communities have been successful in terms of capital investment and new jobs (Poole and Scarlett, 1993). Small businesses, through public-private cooperation, have been the main actors in improving the economy in enterprise zones.

Along with the activities of the states in relation to enterprise zones, the federal government has had a limited involvement in this type of economic development. This involvement increased with the passage of the Community Development Act of 1987, which included authorization for HUD to create 100 federal enterprise zones within which usual regulatory controls for businesses would be modified. More recently, a 1993 proposal by Henry Cisneros, Secretary of the Department of Housing and Urban Development in the Clinton administration, would result in an "enhanced enterprise zone" plan. The new version of enterprise zone "would let a targeted area get help, in a block grant, from a multiplicity of federal sources: HUD for housing needs, Education for its schools, Health and Human Services for clinics and family counseling, Labor for job training, Justice for public safety programs, Transportation for infrastructure needs, the Environmental Protection Agency for cleaning up its environment, and Treasure for tax abatements . . . all focused on a local design and delivered on a scale calculated to lift the neighborhood and its people into the mainstream" (*Washington Post*, 1993). This new plan for enterprise zones emphasizes neighborhood initiatives "to nurture people's sense of responsibility and self-respect."

Some of the ideas about enterprise zones espoused by HUD Secretary Cisneros were incorporated into President Clinton's budget deficit reduction legislation passed by the Congress in August 1993. Under this legislation nine "empowerment zones" are created, five in large cities, one in a medium sized city, and three in rural areas. These zones will receive tax incentives for hiring of area residents, authority to issue tax-exempt bonds to finance businesses, deductions for business property, and social service grants. There will be an additional 95 "enterprise communities," 65 urban and 30 rural, which will have special bond rules as well as federal grants. The choice to limit the number of enterprise areas was to assure that they would receive sufficient support to be evaluated for effectiveness in reaching the program's goals (McGinley, 1993).

BANKING AND THE REVITALIZATION OF NEIGHBORHOODS

Banks are a significant part of the economic system of a community. The lending patterns of banks affect the purchase and/or rehabilitation of homes and the initiation or expansion of small businesses. Although a 1977 Community Reinvestment Act places "a continuing and affirmative obligation to help meet the credit needs of the communities where they operate," evidence from numerous studies indicates that banks fail to meet this federal requirement in urban inner-city neighborhoods (Bacon, 1993; Thomas, 1991; Karr, 1993; *Wall Street Journal*, 1992). Two important developments of programs for investment in poor communities have emerged. The first is a model of commercial and community development banks initiated within urban communities. The second is a new initiative on the part of the federal government to support economic development of inner cities through the creation of community development banks.

The South Shore Bank of Chicago is the exemplar of a community bank involved in lending for purchase or rehabilitation of residential housing and for funding of small businesses (Grzywinski, 1991; Taub et al., 1977). At the time new managers took over this bank in 1973, the bank was failing and planning to leave the neighborhood. Since that time, a "development" bank was created which helped stop the decline of the neighborhood by making commercial and housing loans within the area. The bank was able to take residents' savings and invest them in the local neighborhood, thus stopping the flow of money out of the community, and improving residential housing, supporting small businesses, developing and managing business and residential property, and developing rental and cooperative housing. When the bank began its activities, this neighborhood area of approximately 80,000 people had changed from a white middle-class neighborhood to about 70 percent African American community of middle-class, working class, and poor residents. The single and multifamily housing was deteriorating, small businesses were closing or moving, and the South Shore area faced "abandonment." The South Shore Bank became a major actor in the rebuilding of the community, with the other major force being residents who became active through "ma and pa rehabbing" of residential buildings, improvements of small businesses, and creation of activist voluntary associations (Grzywinski, 1991).

The example of the South Shore Bank is one of the bank initiating the changes in banking practices which led to the involvement of community residents. Other examples include coalitions of community residents and organizations pressuring banks to make inner-city loans (Bleakley, 1992), and starting new banks (Bacon, 1993). In the first instance, community residents, African American churches, and community groups of Syracuse, New York, worked together to bring about changes in lending practices of the major bank in the city. Deliberations between community groups and the bank led to a "banking community reinvestment agreement" which involved making home loans to borrowers from poor inner-city neighborhoods and facilitating loans for small businesses (Bleakley, 1992). In the second instance, community activists in Grand Rapids, Michigan, engaged in efforts to open a start-up bank which would help minority entrepreneurs in an inner-city neighborhood get business loans. These efforts met with opposition from the mainstream banking community but gained the support of community groups, including a financial investment on the part of a local order of Dominican nuns (Bacon, 1993).

Under the administration of President Clinton, federal initiatives have been introduced with regard to lending in poor communities (Bacon, 1993). These initiatives include encouraging and facilitating commercial banks to increase their loans to residents in poor communities, as well as to help fund new community development banks. The Clinton administration has proposed the creation of a Community Banking and Credit Fund, which would provide federal money to community development financial institutions such as banks, credit unions, and loan funds. The new Fund would operate under new reinvestment rules in order to cut some bureaucratic red tape. The major goal of the Fund would be to create a network of 100 community development banks, which would be required to mix federal dollars with local community funds and to move toward operations independent of federal funding. The proposed bank in Grand Rapids, Michigan, discussed above illustrates one of the ways in which the Federal Fund could be used to stimulate "community banking," that is, to assist local community residents in establishing banks which focus on community development through lending to minority businesses, and for housing in older poor neighborhoods (Martin, 1993).

WELFARE AS A PART OF THE ECONOMIC SYSTEM

A number of social programs provide income and other benefits for local community residents. These programs are usually considered as a part of the health and social welfare subsystem of a community. At the same time, they constitute an important aspect of the local economic system. These programs provide economic benefits for people who are retired, unemployed, and/or disabled. Most such programs are financed through federal and state governments. Some programs, such as Social Security and Unemployment Insurance, are provided for through social insurance, a system under which employed individuals have contributed toward their benefits. The Social Security system also provides for in-kind benefits in health care through the Medicare program. Other programs, such as Aid to Families with Dependent Children, Supplemental Security Income, and General Assistance, are labeled public assistance, as they are financed from local, state, and federal taxes. The care of children is the major focus of the AFDC program; the care of older adults, the blind, and disabled who have not been covered by the Social Security system is the focus of the SSI program, which includes income and health care benefits (Medicaid); and the General Assistance program is provided by state and local funds for individuals not covered by federal or state programs. These public assistance programs are "means tested," and provide income and in-kind benefits (food stamps and food) based on need.

The number of individuals and families in a community receiving public assistance has an impact on other local subsystems, such as the social welfare, education, religion, and political systems. For example, additional benefits for school children, such as health and nutrition programs, come to them because of their status within the public welfare system. The social welfare and religious subsystems provide a variety of services for people living below the poverty line. Communities vary in terms of the support their local political systems provide for their underprivileged residents. In turn, a high proportion of residents in poverty has a significant impact on the tax base of the local community.

UNDERCLASS AND THE ECONOMY

Those people in a community who, over a long period of time, are not in the labor market and who persistently rely on the public welfare system for income and services have been characterized as the underclass. A large proportion of this group is made up of women with children in female-headed households. The increase in the size of this group of poor people has been called the feminization of poverty, due in part to the lack of education and training and the lack of occupational opportunities for women in American society. One of the ways proposed in regard to nonworking men and women who participate in public assistance programs has been workfare programs (Mead, 1989). Under workfare, employable individuals on welfare are required to get trained for work or work as a condition of receiving public assistance. Such programs are highly dependent on the development of occupational opportunities in communities, highlighting the close interconnections between welfare and economic subsystems.

Another group of individuals and families which has a special connection to the economic conditions of the local community is the homeless. Most urban communities have a homeless population characterized by "extreme poverty; high levels of disability resulting from poor physical and mental health; and high levels of social isolation, with weak or nonexistent ties to others" (Rossi and Wright, 1989). In a study of the homeless in Chicago, Rossi and Wright found that some homeless people engage in some work some of the time but live on less than half the poverty-level income. These authors assert that the size of the homeless population "is driven by those macro processes that affect the availability of low-skilled employment, the ability of poor families to help their less fortunate members, the market conditions affecting the supply of very low cost housing for single persons, and the coverage of income-maintenance programs for disabled and single persons." These processes include less demand for low-skilled workers, cutbacks on welfare programs, changes in coverage of disabled persons by income-maintenance programs, changes in the supply of low cost housing, and an increase in the number of persons disabled in middle adulthood. Since changes in these processes have not been forthcoming, most communities have had to respond to the homeless problem with emergency shelter and food programs, placing a strain on their fiscal resources and on their health and social service system.

Some of the changes which have occurred in urban economies have been extremely problematic for ethnic minority populations, especially for African Americans. The majority of members of ethnic minority groups have not been involved in social or spatial mobility, and some are "persistently poor ghetto dwellers characterized by substandard education and high rates of joblessness, mother-only households, welfare dependency, out-of-wedlock births, and crime" (Kasarda, 1989). One of the major changes in urban economies has been the move from "production and distribution of goods to centers of administration, finance, and information exchange," the loss of blue-collar jobs and the increase in white-collar ones. In general African Americans have suffered the most from this industrial transition, but especially young African American males who are not at the educational levels necessary for the urban economy (Kasarda, 1989).

THE ECONOMY OF THE GHETTO

Large urban cities appear to have two economies, a mainstream capitalist economy and an economy found in "pockets of poverty"

(Kemp, 1990). The economy of poverty areas of distressed neighborhoods and communities has been characterized as "America's other economy." This economy "has barriers to productive human and social activity and a virtual absence of economic incentives and rewards" (Kemp, 1990). This "other economy" has as its prototype the urban ghetto. Fusfeld (1973) and Fusfeld and Bates (1984) provide one of the most insightful pictures of the economic problems of an urban ghetto. Their analysis highlights the role the welfare economy plays in the ghetto and the relationship of the ghetto economy (the work and wages of residents) to the larger economic system of the community. The ghetto has high unemployment. While a small proportion of the residents are employed in high-wage industries, such as automobile-related jobs, the major proportion of employed residents are in low-wage industries, such as nursing homes, hospitals, hotels, small businesses, department stores, or retail food stores. Most of these jobs are nonunion and "unprotected," without benefits and job security. Many residents participate in "irregular" work, sometimes legal, sometimes illegal (Liebow, 1967).

Fusfeld (1973) contends that the welfare system helps perpetuate the poverty of ghetto residents, as it isolates them from the labor market of the larger community. At the same time it is said to stabilize the social order of the ghetto, as welfare payments serve to keep the ghetto economy in equilibrium. The mix of people in low-wage labor and/or receiving public welfare payments serves to make "the ghetto an economic subsystem which preserves the inferior position of the minorities" (Fusfeld, 1973). This is due, in part, because the ghetto economy is in some important ways "cut off from the economic forces that operate in the rest of the community." Fusfeld points out that "the outward flows of income, capital, and human resources to the rest of the economy serve to keep the ghetto in a permanently underdeveloped state." This is so because money flowing into the ghetto is largely from employment in the low-wage industries, and there is a high rate of unemployment. Along with welfare payments and transfer payments, earned income supports the internal flow of spending. These sources keep the ghetto economy somewhat isolated from the larger society, except that there is an outflow to the larger economy which is detrimental to the ghetto.

The ghetto is a residual subsystem, as social and economic barriers such as high unemployment, relatively low income, and low occupational and residential mobility prevent movement out of the ghetto. As a result, Fusfeld and Bates (1984) note, the "ghetto economy perpetuates its own poverty," with the drain of capital out of the ghetto reinforcing this poverty. The Fusfeld (1973) model of the ghetto economy is not too different from the analysis provided by Wilson (1987) and Wacquant and Wilson (1989) in regard to the ghetto poor. These social scientists argue "that the dramatic rise in inner-city joblessness and economic exclusion is a product of the continuous industrial restructuring of American capitalism" (Wilson, 1989). These authors have demonstrated that the ghetto poor, living in high poverty areas (over 40 percent of the residents below the poverty line), lack the kinds of resources, job opportunities, and economic and social capital available to residents of non-ghetto, low poverty areas.

The working poor live in poverty and non-poverty neighborhoods in a community. As noted by Wilson (1989), those living in non-poverty areas have advantages of social supports and other resources. However, they are affected in a negative way by poverty policies. It has been estimated that about one half of the adult poor work, but their wages are insufficient as measured by the federal poverty line (Bane and Ellwood, 1991). The major problems for the working poor include low pay and few or no medical benefits. Single-parent families on welfare usually are penalized by working, especially in terms of health and children's benefits. Welfare reform strategies have not been able to overcome the economic obstacles for the working poor, especially in regard to the needs of families and children. However, a National Commission on Children established by the Congress in 1987 made four goal recommendations which could be the basis for helping people on welfare move out of poverty. These goals are: "(1) Increase the economic value of work (e.g. the earned-income tax credit); (2) provide families with a children's allowance; (3) improve child support (e.g. the Family Support Act); (4) reform the health system" (Bane and Ellwood, 1991).

THE MIDDLE CLASS AND THE ECONOMY

There is a strong belief within a part of American society that national and local economies provide employment for people in the middle class, but that taxes, inflation, and other economic forces serve as barriers to upward mobility for many. There is the belief that a household needs two adults with incomes in order to maintain a middle-class lifestyle. Increasingly, however, young people with college degrees have had difficulty in obtaining jobs in middle-class occupations. Equally problematic is the experience of downward mobility for some members of the middle class. This experience is captured in the work of Newman, who states:

Hundreds of thousands of middle-class families plunge down America's social ladder every year. They lose their jobs, their income drops drastically, and they confront prolonged economic hardship, often for the first time. In the face of this downward mobility, people long accustomed to feeling secure and in control find themselves suddenly powerless and unable to direct their lives (Newman, 1988).

A variety of economic conditions at the international, national, and/or local community level, such as recessions, depressions, company reductions in workforce, bring about the loss of jobs of people with well-paid blue-collar to professional and managerial occupations. Most of these individuals find other jobs and do not skid into poverty. Still, they cannot keep up their customary middle-class status and lifestyle and "They must therefore contend not only with financial hardship but with the psychological, social, and practical consequences of 'falling from grace,' of losing their 'proper place' in the world" (Newman, 1988).

The meaning of downward mobility through economic dislocation is different for everyone, but there are some major reasons for this experience which influence how it is interpreted. Sometimes the experience is due to collective losses when companies carry out mass layoffs or dismissals or when strikes fail and employees cannot return to work. At other times the loss involves only the individual or selected individuals. In other instances downward mobility is caused by divorce, when some women are forced to enter the workforce in positions which do not support former lifestyles of self and children.

Newman (1988) illustrates downward mobility experiences of the middle class by discussing the fate of four different groups: former managers and executives, fired air traffic controllers, blue-collar workers in a plant shutdown, and divorced mothers. The experiences of these groups provide convincing evidence that their fate depends in part on the economic system of the local community. Some communities provide alternatives for work, educational and training opportunities, supportive health and social services for families and children, and community economic development programs, all of which may cushion downward mobility or assist in movement back up the occupational ladder and restoration of one's class identity and self-esteem. In short, employment is a central component in the local community economic system, and the competence of a community is measured in part by its ability to prevent downward mobility at all social-class levels and to create employment opportunities at all occupational levels.

IMMIGRANTS AND THE ECONOMY

The patterns of immigration into the United States have been of concern to the federal government as well as to local communities in regard to the effects of immigration on national and local economies. Recent immigration legislation has been formulated on the idea that the nation's economy would benefit most through the entry of high-skilled workers (Finch, 1990). Immigration policy was partly based on concerns over the impact of low-skilled immigrant workers on the employment opportunities and wages of U.S. residents. Prior to the 1990s, a high proportion of immigrants were unskilled workers. It is this group of workers which has generated a concern that immigrants compete with and take the place of native ethnic minorities in the workforce. In this regard, Reischauer (1989) reviewed studies dealing with the employment situation of African Americans and concluded that the competition from unskilled immigrants had no appreciable negative effects for native African Americans. In stating this finding, Reischauer recognizes the fact that the studies he reviewed do not take into account more recent immigration patterns in large cities like Los Angeles, Miami, New York, Houston, San Francisco, and Chicago (Wilson, 1989). At the same time, Simon's (1990, 1993) review of social science studies on immigration and the economy supports Reischauer's conclusions. Simon highlights findings such as the following, which have particular relevance for local community economies.

- Immigrants do not cause native unemployment, even among low-paid and minority groups.
- Immigrants do not "rip off" natives by over-using welfare services.
- Immigrants are typically as well-educated and occupationally skilled as natives.
- Immigrants demonstrate desirable economic traits.
- Immigrants increase the flexibility of the economy.
- Immigration reduces the uncuttable social costs of the elderly.

In some areas of the United States, most notably California, there is a concern about the effects of illegal immigrants on local economies. For example, studies of the costs to taxpayers for public services such as health, social welfare, and education for new immigrants in Los Angeles was far out of proportion to their representation in the community (Ferguson, 1992). Anti-immigrant sentiments about illegals are strong in communities like Los Angeles, with a belief that "What is really happening is that employers of this labor are taking advantage of the local taxpayers, who are covering the difference in public benefits" (Ferguson, 1992). Or, as Freeman (1991) stated, "To live here is to know that Los Angeles is becoming a vast sea of the undocumented and the illegal. Many of them work hard; some even spend their money here. Many try to send it out of the country, mostly to Mexico and Latin America."

While it is difficult to determine the number of immigrants who enter the U.S. illegally and their impact on the local economies, one estimate is a total of 3.5 million, mostly farm workers and domestic workers. Most of the domestic workers settle in New York City, New Jersey, Los Angeles, Chicago, Miami, Houston, and Washington, D.C. As an immigration lawyer noted about Washington, "They're working in the homes of our lawyers, our journalists, and our government officials" (Kilborn, 1993). Generally, despite a 1986 act to curtail illegal immigration, the Immigration and Naturalization Service is unable to control such immigration into the nation's communities.

It is clear that some immigrant groups, particularly Asians, have been successful in achieving the benefits of the local community economy (Kasarda, 1989, 1992). Dominican immigrants in New York City have displayed a capacity for entering into the economic life of the city and the surrounding areas, often accumulating funds to send back to their homeland (Rimer, 1991). Many Central and South American immigrants have become suburbanites, establishing employment and residence in New York City suburbs (Berger, 1993). Kasarda (1989) draws from studies on ethnic entrepreneurism to compare Asian immigrants and some Hispanic groups to African American native residents. Important elements which appear to contribute to the economic success of Hispanic immigrants include the fact that self-employment is supported by ethnic solidarity, kinship networks, household structures, use of family labor, thriftiness, long hours of work, reinvestment of profits, and purchasing by members of the ethnic community.

An example of Asian immigrant successes in business is Flushing, New York, a community in Queens which has attracted Asians into residential neighborhoods and into the business and professional community (Wysocki, 1991). There has been a dramatic increase in Asian owned businesses, such as restaurants, beauty salons, banks and trading companies, led by Chinese and Korean immigrants but including Asians from many countries. Nearly 100,000 Chinese and Korean immigrants have moved into Flushing neighborhoods since the late 1970s, but not without conflicts with "old-timers" who were long time residents of the area. Cultural and racial frictions have emerged, especially in regard to white and African American residents and Asian immigrants. As of 1991, there was already evidence that some members of the Asian immigrant families were engaged in social and economic mobility, moving to suburbs and "toward the middle-class mainstream of suburban and corporate America" (Wysocki, 1991).

REVIEW

The economic system of local urban and rural communities are inextricably linked to the economies of metropolitan areas, states, the nation, and the world. This system provides sustenance functions of production, consumption, and distribution of goods and services in the community. Important features in the system are the community's production base, labor market, and income opportunity structures. The community economic system includes a set of workplaces which are interdependent with the other community subsystems and with the total community. Special issues within these workplaces include equal employment, advancement opportunities, and sexual harassment.

Problems in the local economic system are most glaring in the inner-city areas of large urban municipalities. Economic policies and programs to revitalize these areas include enterprise zones and community development programs, including community banks. Social welfare programs such as social insurance and public assistance are viewed as a part of these economic programs. Two groups with special needs and demands on the local community economic and social welfare systems are the underclass and homeless people. Members of ethnic minorities fall disproportionately into the lower segments of the social class structure, due in large part to a lack of full participation in the workforce.

Members of the middle class depend heavily on the local economic system to maintain their lifestyles and status. Within this group are individuals and families who experience downward mobility, a condition which has negative effects on personal life and family lifestyles. As a consequence, it is clear that while the community economic system affects people at all social class levels, problems in the system have more devastating effects on selected groups in the community, such as ethnic minorities, women, the downwardly mobile, the underclass, and the homeless. As a result of changing federal policies on immigration, increased attention has been given to the effects of new immigrants on local, state, and national economies. While there is some evidence that immigration does not have negative consequences for native workers and does not place burdens on the welfare system, this contention continues to be challenged, especially with regard to "illegal" immigrants.

SUGGESTED READINGS

Americans with Disabilities Act of 1990

Bane, Mary Jo, and David T. Ellwood (1991). "Is American Business Working for the Poor?" *Harvard Business Review*, September-October.

Family and Medical Leave Act of 1993

Freudenheim, Milt (1991). "New Law to Bring Wider Job Rights for Mentally Ill." *New York Times*, September 23.

Grzywinski, Ronald (1991). "The New Old-Fashioned Banking." *Harvard Business Review*, May-June.

Lambert, Susan J. (1993). "Workplace Policies as Social Policy." *Social Service Review* 67:2 (June).

Maypole, Donald E. (1987). "Sexual Harassment at Work: A Review of Research and Theory." *Affilia* 2:1.

Newman, Katherine (1988). *Falling From Grace*. New York: Free Press.

Newman, Katherine (1993). *Declining Fortunes: The Withering of the American Dream*. New York: Basic Books.

Reischauer, Robert D. (1989). "Immigration and the Underclass." *Annals*, AAPSS, 501.

Schwartz, Felice N. (1989). "Management Women and the New Facts of Life." *Harvard Business Review*, January-February.

Schwartz, F. N. (1992). "Women as a Business Imperative." *Harvard Business Review*, March-April.

Williamson, Alistair D. (1993). "Is This the Right Time to Come Out?" *Harvard Business Review*, July-August.

EXERCISE

Identify the problems in the economic system which led to the development of plans for a new bank in Grand Rapids, Michigan. Discuss the features of the new bank which are expected to lead to a revitalization of inner-city neighborhoods.

INNER-CITY CAPITALISTS PUSH TO START A BANK FOR THEIR COMMUNITY

By Kenneth H. Bacon

In the basement of the New Hope Baptist Church, across the street from a public-housing project here [in Grand Rapids, Mich.], a dozen business owners are discussing how difficult it is for minority entrepreneurs to get bank loans.

Jack Black says his plans for expanding his tuxedo-rental business, Classic Formal Wear and Cleaners, are on hold because he can't get a bank loan. "I was declined because we'd only been in business two years," he says. Birthale Lambert, president of Professional Nursing Force Inc., which supplies health-care personnel, says, "I never asked for a loan because all my friends got turned down."

Frank Thomas recalls his efforts to finance a supermarket on the south side, an inner-city neighborhood dotted with abandoned buildings. "When you're talking about money, race is a dividing line," he says. As evidence, he cites a Federal Reserve finding that the home mortgage rejection rate for black applicants was about twice that for whites in 1991.

Focus on Development

To find a more sympathetic lender, Mr. Thomas, Ms. Lambert, and others are trying to start Southside Bank, a community institution that will focus on financing development in a racially mixed section that's home to 80,000 of the city's 200,000 people. The idea is simple: Recycle deposits from the area into loans to support investment there. In theory, it ought to work. Residents and businesses had bank deposits of $508 million in 1989, but institutions holding the deposits returned only about $5 million to the area in loans, according to research by officials of the planned bank.

Southside Bank is just the type of inner-city capitalism that President-elect Clinton wants to encourage. But the struggle to launch it shows how tough it's going to be to realize his pledge to establish a network of 100 community-development banks that make money while nurturing small businesses and revitalizing neighborhoods.

"For a grass-roots group of people to put together a financial institution is a huge undertaking," says Frank Lynn, president of the Coalition for Community Reinvestment, a private group that is fighting to make credit available in the inner city. Only four community-development banks exist now, and it remains an open question whether Southside will become the fifth. Investors are wary; mainstream banks have withheld support and may have discouraged some backers of the venture, Southside's officials maintain.

Clinton Plan Being Drawn

Mr. Clinton's advisers are drafting a plan for an $850 million fund to help finance community-development institutions, including banks, credit unions (of which there are about 300 now), and revolving loan funds (42 nationwide) to aid depressed areas. The money would provide technical assistance to community groups in launching lending operations and would help capitalize lenders once they got going. Every dollar of federal capital would have to be matched by $2 of private funds.

The money would be distributed over five years through a new national community-development trust, which would be sustained by repayments of loans made to help get new lenders off the ground. A Clinton adviser says the fund would probably be overseen from the White House's new National Economic Council but administered by the Treasury Department or the Department of Housing and Urban Development.

Studies showing credit problems in inner cities and higher home-mortgage rejection rates for blacks and Hispanics have made community development an increasingly pressing political and economic issue. Republicans on the House Banking Committee are studying ways to use the Community Reinvestment Act—which requires banks to lend wherever they take deposits—to increase inner-city and rural lending. And the Senate Banking Committee plans to begin hearings on the topic early next month; representatives of Southside Bank have been asked to testify.

An Area Undergoing Change

One problem the new bank is facing is the south-side neighborhood itself. It's an area in transition—but it's hard to know in what direction. New businesses and renovated houses dot the area, which has been a focal point of urban renewal efforts, including building a shopping center and using tax abatements to attract employers. But in the past few years drugs and crime have become problems. "Crack has set us back," says Chris Davenport, the city's acting community-development director.

From the beginning, regulators and potential investors have been confused about whether Southside Bank wanted to be a development agency that might make a profit, or a profit-making bank with a focus on development.

The community activists who started dreaming about Southside Bank six years ago quickly learned that they had to be bankers first and social reformers second. In early discussions about getting federal deposit insurance and a state charter, "the Michigan Financial Institutions Bureau came down on us with both feet to remind us that we're not a social-service agency." says the Rev. George Heartwell, one of Southside's founders and directors. "They looked around the table and saw that we weren't bankers."

It took Southside about a year to find a president the Federal Deposit Insurance Corp. and state officials would accept. Last year, they recruited Steven Lopez, who has 20 years of commercial banking experience in the New York area. Mr. Lopez, who is black, moves easily through the neighborhood. On a visit to El Matador Tortillas Factory, he speaks in Spanish with Miguel Navarro, the owner and a Southside board member.

A Lender That Doesn't

In promoting the bank, Mr. Lopez and his board stress that mainstream banks are better at collecting deposits from the inner city than at making loans there. Standing on the Madison Avenue site where the Southside Bank plans to open, Mr. Lopez points across the street to a branch of Old Kent Bank & Trust Co., the city's largest bank. The office will take deposits and cash checks but make no loans. (An Old Kent official says that the branch stopped making loans after reducing its staff following a robbery several years ago in which a teller was killed.)

"Businesses that are black- and Hispanic-owned deposit their money in a bank and it's loaned someplace else," Mr. Heartwell says. For local businesses "to take control of their economic destiny by owning a bank and keeping the capital in the community is an enormous" step toward "the economic empowerment of a community that has been outside the loop."

Empowerment doesn't come easily though. Mr. Lopez and his board have spent most of the last year trying to raise the $3 million in capital they need to open. So far they have only about $1 million raised from stock sales to individuals and churches, with support from city and state agencies. State officials say Southside is the first bank in memory that hasn't been able to raise its capital in the one-year start-up period. As a result, the bank must reapply to continue its efforts. "Clearly there is resistance to investing in such a venture," says Mr. Lynn of the Coalition for Community Reinvestment.

Mr. Thomas, the bank's chairman, concedes that initially the bank didn't present itself well. "At first we had a hard time selling to the community because they thought it was a social program" rather than a business venture. And because banks had historically steered clear of the area, people weren't sure what to make of this one. The steady drumbeat of bank failures around the country also raises anxieties about investing in a start-up bank.

Southside won limited backing from a local supermarket chain and the locally based Steelcase Foundation, but found other businesses cautious. Backers had expected more of an outpouring for this bootstrap effort. Grand Rapids is a conservative city known for its Dutch heritage, its office-furniture industry, and its most famous native son, former President Ford. "This is a Republican stronghold," Mr. Lopez says. "I thought they would be receptive to this type of self-help project."

Viewed as Competition

One problem is the mainstream banks. Though they've generated relatively few loans to the marginal inner-city areas, they see Southside Bank as a competitor and have rejected invitations to invest in it. And they may have cooled others to the idea; Mr. Lopez claims that Old Kent Bank told a local order of Dominican nuns that the new bank wasn't necessary, in an effort to discourage them from pledging to purchase $50,000 in stock in it. The nuns agreed to buy the stock anyway, he says.

Sister Barbara Hansen, the Grand Rapids Dominicans' counselor for finance, confirms that "Old Kent personnel expressed their view that there wasn't a need for that bank," but she says that Old Kent officials didn't offer any advice on whether they should invest in it. Richard Arasmith, Old Kent's senior vice president, community relations, says that the Dominicans wanted to discuss the banking environment in the area but that he said nothing to dissuade them from buying stock in the new bank.

However, Mr. Arasmith makes it clear that he doesn't think a new bank is necessary. He notes that Old Kent and three other banks have signed agreements with the Coalition for Community Reinvestment, pledging to increase their inner-city lending. Old Kent has agreed to increase mortgage lending in the south-side area by $10 million (a three- or fourfold increase, according to community activists) and to take various steps to make it easier for inner-city borrowers to get loans. In addition, Old Kent and NBD Bancorp have helped finance the city's urban renewal efforts.

Now that the major banks are making a commitment to lending on the south side, they don't want to give up the new business. Nor do they want to give up the deposits they've been drawing. "I don't think that there is a niche left unfilled there," Mr. Arasmith says.

Policy Debate

So to a great extent, the Grand Rapids debate is over whether to promote development by pushing existing banks to lend more in inner-city areas or to establish special community banks.

The American Bankers Association contends that existing banks, under pressure from local groups and the Community Reinvestment Act, are working harder to meet inner-city bank needs, and that the government shouldn't get involved in encouraging or subsidizing a new class of banks. "It's critical that new programs for community development banks build on the current system and not attempt to reinvent a new system from scratch," the trade association says in a position paper.

The development bank that won Mr. Clinton over to the idea is South Shore Bank in Chicago, which helped turn around a declining neighborhood by financing a revitalization plan. Mr. Clinton has noted that the bank has operated "without government involvement."

Like the Chicago bank, which operates as part of a holding company, Southside Bank hopes to set up real-estate investment and venture-capital affiliates to help it meet a full range of business and housing needs in its neighborhood.

Raising the money it needs to open won't be the end of Southside's challenges. The very problems of crime, poverty and lack of business infrastructure that make established banks reluctant to lend in the inner city will pose challenges to Southside as well. In addition, Mr. Lopez stresses that the new bank will aim for profits first and good works second. "This is a profit-making venture," he says. "Once we become operational we will be careful not to put more than 10% of our assets into any one niche."

A Positive Effect

Even if it never gets off the ground, Southside has apparently had a positive effect: spurring existing banks to pay more attention to the neighborhood. "For the first time, banks are calling and telling me what services are available," says Ms. Lambert.

"We certainly feel that we're making strides in the inner city," says Joanna Hainer, assistant vice president, community relations, at Michigan National Bank in Grand Rapids. "Our commercial-loan officers are more aware of what the needs are."

But most of the businesses getting new overtures from banks are already successful—such as Frank Thomas's Southside supermarket, which has sales of about $7 million a year, and Mike Navarro's tortilla factory. "When Southside Bank is on-line," predicts Mr. Thomas, "you're going to see a lot of competition from the majority banking system."

The change may not come soon enough for people struggling to build south-side businesses now. John and Ruby Jimmerson sold their house and put their savings into a new business, the Personally You Ltd. bakery, which opened almost a year ago. The summer wedding-cake business was good, and Thanksgiving and Christmas also were strong seasons.

"We need to upgrade our place and hire some help" to be able to bid on corporate accounts, Mr. Jimmerson says. They also want to buy an adjoining vacant parcel and turn it into a parking lot. But they can't get a loan from a bank.

Even when they had money deposited in Old Kent Bank, they couldn't get a loan there, Mr. Jimmerson said. When he was setting up the bakery, the bank said it couldn't lend because he was unemployed. When the bakery opened, he had a job, but "then they said we had to get a track record" before they would lend, Mr. Jimmerson says. He was upset when the bank sent a young, inexperienced loan officer to look at his site and review his plans. "He'd never been in this area before" and seemed uncomfortable, Mr. Jimmerson says.

But he's sure that if the Southside Bank were up and running, it would give him more serious consideration. "There's no doubt in my mind," Mr. Jimmerson says.

CHAPTER 11

The Community Political System

The political system of a community consists of formal organizations of local government, people involved in informal political processes and activities, and community leaders and organizations within the various community subsystems. As the size of the community increases the political system becomes more complex, so that small communities differ considerably from mid-sized and large municipal communities.

The local community political system carries out several significant functions (Rothman, 1974). *First,* local government provides services, such as public health, social services, protection of person and property, street maintenance, and traffic control. While most communities provide these kinds of services to some degree, they vary in the range and quality of services each provides. *Second,* local government is responsible for developing community policies in regard to public expenditures for service programs. This "communal decision-making" function relates to such matters as services, land use, economic development, and tax and budget decisions. *Third,* the local political system plays a major role in deciding who shall make decisions. Decision-making "power" is assigned to groups such as a local community zoning board, a property tax review board, a local planning commission, a mental health board. *Fourth,* the local government, along with other social units in the community, functions as an instrument of social control, using its coercive power to maintain social order. *Finally,* the political system engages in conflict management. When conflicts arise in zoning disputes or business-commercial and neighborhood group conflicts, or when individuals and interest groups vie for privileges, resources, or "rights," the local government has mechanisms for resolving such conflicts.

These community functions are carried out through various structural arrangements within a political subsystem. After briefly identifying the nature of these political structures, we use the area of criminal and juvenile justice to highlight some community issues and problems related to the service and social-control functions of political systems.

THE STRUCTURE OF A COMMUNITY POLITICAL SYSTEM

Municipal Government

The primary structure of the political system of a community is the local municipal government, its various units, and the official positions within these units. These positions usually include key elected officials, politically appointed personnel, and civil service employees. Some of these individuals are policy-makers, while others are involved in the administration of programs, such as parks and recreation, public works, legal services, library services, zoos, museums, and intermediate school districts.

The specific structure of local government varies from one community to another, especially in terms of the size of the community, from village to municipality, to county, to metropolitan area. Most municipalities are governed by either (a) a mayor and city council; (b) a city council and city manager; or (c) a council, mayor, and administrator. Depending on the amount of jurisdiction and/or influence over decision making, local governments may have strong mayors, weak councils; strong councils, weak mayors, or various other combinations of power relationships.

County Government

Municipalities come under the jurisdiction of county governments, created by state legislatures to provide specialized services through such organizations and positions as county courts, county assessor (property tax assessment), county treasurer, county clerk (records and elections), county hospitals, roads, parks, and fire and police protection (Rusk, 1993). In particular, county governments provide a range of services to unincorporated areas. County governments, especially in large urban areas, usually dominate the local community political system due to their large tax base and their service and zoning responsibilities. Examples of strong county governments include Los Angeles County, California, and Montgomery County, Maryland.

Metropolitan Government

This type of government is not common in the United States. It has been proposed as the ideal type of government for consolidating central cities with suburban communities, especially as a solution for some of the fiscal and social problems of large central cities. Metro governments have the potential for overcoming the fiscal imbalances of cities and suburbs, of reducing racial and economic segregation within these communities, and of promoting area-wide economic development (Rusk, 1993).

The problems of communication and cooperation between central cities and suburban communities continue to be unresolved (Chafets, 1990). Variations in metropolitan government as a solution to urban social problems are limited. One option is to empower county government and eliminate municipal governments within the county. A second option is to create a consolidated government, merging a central city with a single county, such as in the government arrangements of Indianapolis–Marion County, Nashville–Davidson County, and Jacksonville–Duval County. A third option involves combining counties into regional governments. New York City is the classic example of this type of government, wherein five boroughs make up New York City (Rusk, 1993).

THE CRIMINAL AND JUVENILE JUSTICE SYSTEM

Crime, delinquency, and violence are major social problems in many American communities (Chafets, 1990; Taub et al., 1984). Community governments have a primary role in providing protection and social control for community residents through law enforcement, the judicial system, and the correctional system (Johnson, 1990). Law enforcement is a responsibility of local community police departments as well as agencies at the county, state, and federal levels of government. The judicial system includes adult and juvenile courts. A third component of the justice system is corrections. At the local level, this usually includes a number of alternatives, such as incarceration in jails, community service, work release, halfway houses, probation and parole, and diversion programs.

One of the features of Long's (1958) conception of a community as an "ecology of games" is the idea of keeping score. Governmental responses to the social problem of crime and delinquency are a significant part of the "political game" of a community, and various measures are used to "keep score," that is, to assess how competent the community is in carrying out the function of social control. For example, an index of crime includes statistics on offenses of murder, rape, robbery, aggravated assault, burglary, larceny-theft, motor vehicle theft, and arson. These offenses are usually divided into violent crime and property crime. Uniform Crime Reports are provided for the country by the Federal Bureau of Investigation. National crime statistics are reported in the press for all major U.S. cities, with the result that some cities are labeled "crime capital" or "murder capital" of the nation. Reports on local community crime are compiled by state and local governments. In some communities the local press presents a monthly map showing the distribution of major crimes and attempted crimes in the various neighborhoods of the community.

There is no question of the immensity of the social problem of crime, delinquency, and violence and the fact that many local governments are unable to provide protection for their residents. A number of controversial issues surround this community problem, leading to a lack of consensus on how to prevent or respond to the problem. We will now cite a few of these issues by way of illustration.

Discrimination

There is considerable evidence that members of ethnic minority groups are treated differently—that is, negatively and more harshly—than other community members by law enforcement officials and by the courts, especially in sentencing, and in regard to correctional alternatives.

Police Behavior

The actions of the police in the handling of arrests is a controversial issue in most major American cities. This involves the treatment of individual suspects with excessive force and the use of force in responding to street violence and civil disturbance. The issue concerns the extent to which police policies and behaviors assure protection of self versus protection of the rights of crime suspects.

Family and Workplace Violence

Family violence, especially disputes which lead to deaths, and spouse abuse, such as wife-beating, has emerged as a significant problem of social order in communities (Sullivan, 1993). An important issue in this regard is the extent to which reported victimization is appropriately responded to by law enforcement officials. One response to the problem of spouse abuse has been the creation of "safe houses" in the community for women and children who are in need of protection from family violence. Another response has been court-ordered treatment programs for males who have abused family members.

Increasingly, violence occurs in the workplace. This violence ranges from homicides at work sites, to injuries, beatings, shootings, and rapes (Johnson, 1993). One response to this type of violence has been training for supervisors and management and the development of employee assistance programs which respond to the stresses of family and the workplace.

Gun Control

One of the most controversial issues related to crime and delinquency is gun control. Proponents of stricter gun-control laws assert a strong connection between laws and criminal behavior. On the other hand, some citizen groups, such as the National Rifle Association, strongly resist controls on guns. There are somewhat different laws at the various levels of government regarding possession of guns. As an example, the Brady bill, proposed by President Clinton and passed by Congress, requires a waiting period for the purchase of guns. The bill also has strong punishment provisions related to certain crimes, such as the killing of federal law enforcement officers (Birnbaum, 1993). The illegal possession of guns continues to be associated with crime in inner-city neighborhoods and with guns taken into schools by young people. Both legal and illegal use of guns are associated with home gun accidents, domestic violence, and suicides.

Youth Violence

Youth violence and other criminal behavior has become extremely problematic in many American communities. Schools have become a location of teen violence. Teen gangs are prevalent in all major U.S. cities and tend to operate in some neighborhoods and not in others. Social scientists have given considerable attention to trying to explain delinquent behavior. For example, Figueria-McDonough (1991) has hypothesized certain relationships between the structure of communities and delinquency rates. She suggests that communities with strong primary and secondary networks, that is kin, friends, and informal groups, as well as community organizations, are likely to have low delinquency rates, while "disorganized" communities without these networks are likely to have the highest rates.

Drug Dealing and Crack Houses

The sale of illegal drugs on the streets, and especially crack cocaine from houses in inner-city neighborhoods, constitutes a serious problem for law abiding residents in these communities (Anderson, 1990). Drug dealing and crack houses generate a fear of crime on the part of many residents, especially older adults. While some controversy exists over whether or not the local police are active enough in closing down crack houses, even with police involvement crack houses tend to reopen in other areas. One response to the problem has been for neighborhood block clubs to organize against the houses and report drug traffic to the police. Another approach is to require more drug testing and to provide for drug treatment facilities for all who need them.

In our identification of some of the issues related to community crime and delinquency, examples are cited of governmental and citizen response to these problems. Other examples include community policing, with police officers assigned to specific neighborhood areas, in an effort to make the police "a part of the community, not apart from the community" (Lardner, 1993). In some community policing programs, neighborhood-based police officers become involved in athletic events, attend community meetings, and visit with residents. Some successes of these programs have been reported, but some problems with this approach have also been identified. One problem arises if the police who are selected are not sympathetic to the needs, values, and concerns of the neighborhood residents (*New Yorker*, 1993). There is a belief on the part of some that recruitment of qualified and interested personnel and skills learned on the job are essential to make a community policing program work. The problem of hiring is highlighted by an official of the New York Police Department, who

> has said, with only modest exaggeration, that the N.Y.P.D. is "the only employer in the world where 'for the money' and 'it beats working' are considered perfectly acceptable answers to the question 'Why do you want this job?'" (*New Yorker*, 1993).

An example of a response to crime in local communities that has been initiated by the federal government is described in terms of

"Weed and Seed." "The basic idea of Weed and Seed is to involve the federal government with state and local governments in 'weeding out' crime from targeted neighborhoods and then in 'seeding' those communities with programs designed to aid economic and social development." As a part of these programs, police "help residents identify and resolve common problems," "move against violent street gang members," and participate in "safe haven" arrangements so that residents can safely use local neighborhood schools at night (Eastland, 1992).

CITIZEN PARTICIPATION IN LOCAL GOVERNMENT

The local government is influenced by local citizens through the voting process. Key figures in the system are elected by the "body politic." Citizens also participate in the political system by contacting public officials and seeking to influence them individually or through special-interest groups. Some citizens serve leadership roles in political parties and interest groups and engage in activities in order to influence community decision making. The role of political parties and their leaders varies in different communities, but the political party provides a major avenue for citizens to participate in the election process. Elected officials move through the political party system, and individuals seeking to influence this selection and election process ordinarily must go through this system.

Ethnic minority residents often feel left out of the political process. In some communities, African American and Hispanic residents have gained political office and influence. In other communities, one or more ethnic minority groups struggle to gain political power, as illustrated by the emergence of Hispanic groups seeking to be a part of the political "game" of the community. For example, Hispanic leaders in Detroit have created a Latino Agenda, a plan which includes goals of dealing with problems of employment and political power. This effort comes from the belief that the Hispanic community "must unite politically to survive. What can't be achieved by numbers of voters may be gained through pooling resources and mastering political, business, and media games, leaders say" (Jeffrey, 1991).

Creation of Political Districts

A long-standing controversy with regard to citizen participation in the political system has been the creation of voting districts. New districts are constructed when population shifts occur. The 1990 census data demonstrate shifts of population from central cities to suburban communities, which results in redistricting of seats in state legislatures and the U.S. House of Representatives. The migration to the suburbs leads to new political maps and to a shift in political power to people who live in these areas and to their representatives in politics (Shribman, 1991).

One of the ways in which redistricting occurs is "gerrymandering," that is, the drawing of boundaries for voting districts in such a way that white or non-white groups "vastly outnumber" the other group, assuring the majority residential group of representation in local, state, or federal government (McCaughey, 1993). The U.S. Supreme Court decided in *Shaw v. Reno* that a gerrymandered 12th Congressional District in North Carolina was unconstitutional. The Court rejected the stereotype that "members of the same racial group, regardless of their age, education, economic status, or the community in which they live think alike, share the same political interests, and will prefer the same candidates at the polls" (McCaughey, 1993). The North Carolina district had been created in order to assure representation of African Americans with a district about 160 miles long, and involving areas of 12 counties. Even in the light of the Supreme Court's decision in *Shaw v. Reno*, the "place of race in distributing electoral power" is expected to continue to be an issue in the courts (Kennedy, 1993). This is thought to be so because, as Professor Randall Kennedy (1993) notes, an important question remains unanswered, that is, "What is required to create political institutions that address the needs and aspirations of all Americans, not simply whites, who have long enjoyed racial privilege, but people of color who have long suffered racial exclusion from policy-making forums?"

Extragovernmental Political Components

The community political system is not limited to the formal structure of local government. Elected representatives in local governments make numerous decisions which affect the residents of a community. But rather than making these decisions in isolation, they are subjected to pressures and influences of individuals outside the formal governmental political system. Many other decisions that affect community residents are made within the various subsystems of the community and do not require the formal approval of local government. Many such decisions may also be made by individuals or organizations which wield "community power" but are outside the formal institutions of the community. In short, local government is a part of the community power structure. It may be a major part or it may be dominated by individuals and organizations outside the local government. Thus, in order to discover the power structure of a community, both the local government and the political system as a whole need to be examined.

COMMUNITY POWER PERSPECTIVES

In examining the power structure of a community, it is helpful to consider the conceptual differences between power and influence. Power is "the potential ability of an actor to select, change, attain the goals of a social system," with an emphasis on "potential" (Clark, 1973). In contrast, influence is the exercise of power that brings about change in a social system. A power structure is a patterned distribution of power in a social system. A decision-making structure is a patterned distribution of influence, based on decisions on specific issues. Whether we take a power or an influence perspective depends in part on whether we emphasize the identification of leadership in a community by virtue of "reputation" for power or the identification of the distribution of influence by virtue of decision-making patterns.

One perspective on community power is based on the idea that one must identify individual leaders in order to uncover a power/influence structure within a community. Leaders can be identified at all community levels: in the larger metropolitan community and in local districts; in community subsystems, such as health and welfare, religion, and education; and in voluntary groups, such as the League of Women Voters, Kiwanis clubs, welfare rights organizations, and civil rights organizations. When community leaders are found to relate to each other with regard to decision making, social activities, and membership on boards, they can be viewed as a group and, in some instances, as a "power elite." Hunter's (1953) study of the community power structure in Atlanta provides a classic example of a community elite made up of individuals from the economic system of the community.

IDENTIFYING COMMUNITY LEADERS

One can identify (and evaluate or rank) community leaders according to their position, or their reputation, or the policy decisions they have made. The positional approach directs our attention to "those persons occupying important offices, elected public officials, higher civil servants, business executives, officials of voluntary associations, heads of religious groups, leaders of labor unions and others" (Bonjean & Olson, 1966). Hunter's (1953) study of community power in Atlanta is the prime example of a reputational approach, which basically involves asking informants to name and rank the leaders in their community. In a third major approach, decisional, we seek to identify, for specific issues, the individuals who were involved in major policy decisions.

Once leaders are identified, the question still remains, do they constitute a structure of community power? While some "ideal types" of structures have emerged in the social science literature on community power, many variations of these types exist in American communities. One such variation is an "elitist" or "monolithic" power structure made up of economic elites. Leaders at lower levels carry out the policies supported and/or developed by the "power elite." In contrast, in a "pluralistic structure," power is "distributed among a number of organized community groups with domination shifting according to the issues rather than repeated domination by a single power faction across all community issues" (Perrucci & Pilisuk, 1970).

In seeking to identify leaders and power structures, four salient characteristics of leadership should be considered: legitimacy, visibility, scope of influence, and cohesiveness (Bonjean and Olson, 1964). The leadership structure is legitimate when a high proportion of leaders occupy political or associational offices. It is visible when a high proportion of leaders is recognized by the general public. The leadership structure can be described in terms of the scope of influence of individual leaders and the kinds and numbers of issues and decisions they are involved with in the community. Finally, a most interesting aspect of community power structures is the extent to which individual leaders form a cohesive group in relation to their community, business, social, and interactional activities.

Community power may reside with leaders of community-wide voluntary organizations, such as the National Association for the Advancement of Colored People, the American Civil Liberties Union, local community ministerial alliances, the League of Women Voters, the Chamber of Commerce, Parent-Teacher Associations, coalitions of neighborhood organizations. Another important source of leadership are grass roots organizations, that is, local neighborhood groups organized as block clubs, affiliates of churches, or boards of neighborhood community services agencies. Leaders within these organizations, especially ministers, priests, and rabbis, carry local power and often are involved in the broader community power structure.

COMMUNITY LEADERS: LOCAL AND COSMOPOLITAN

Robert K. Merton's classic discussion of types of influencials in a community provides an interesting and useful conceptual approach to understanding community power and influence (Merton, 1949). While both local and cosmopolitan leaders are actively involved in community affairs, they have orientations to community which are considerably different. The localite is "preoccupied with local problems," while the cosmopolitan leader has interest in the local community but is also "oriented significantly to the world outside." These basic orientations toward community, the one "parochial," the other "ecumenical," are demonstrated through a number of differences.

First, the structure of their social relations differs. The local leader is strongly identified and attached to the local community, while the cosmopolitan leader does not feel "rooted" in the community. Localites are interested in knowing as many people as possible, while the cosmopolitan is more selective, choosing to get to know the "right" kind of people. The localite belongs to voluntary associations in order to "make contacts" and extend personal relationships, while the cosmopolitan joins organizations which have activities that call on a person's knowledge and skills. The localite is an "old-timer" in the community who has influence based on a "network of personal relationships," while the cosmopolitan is likely to be a relative newcomer who comes into the community with prestige from business or professional associations.

Merton's ideas about community leaders are relevant to the social work professional's efforts to gain public support and resources for a social agency. In particular, this distinction in leadership qualities has applicability to the creation and maintenance of agency board membership. An "ideal" community board of directors would include a mix of local and cosmopolitan leaders. The localites can be expected to have social contacts which will bring public support to the agency, while the cosmopolitan leaders can provide expertise and links to the resources of the wider community, to state and federal government, and to organizations at these levels in the private sector.

COMMUNITY POWER FROM AN ORGANIZATION PERSPECTIVE

When examining the power and decision-making structures of the total community from a systems perspective, one can determine the extent to which one or more of the various subsystems is the dominant force in the community. This perspective assumes that organizations, rather than individuals, hold the key resources which form the bases of power. Arrangements between organizations provide a strong organizational claim for community power and influence.

Viewing the community as a social system made up of formal organizations within various community subsystems allows for the examination of the institutional context of community leadership. Perrucci and Pilisuk (1970) argue that "power is contained within institutional systems and that it is differentially available to individuals and groups according to their place in the larger social subsystems of which they are a part." Under this formulation resources for decision making reside in either several persons or in organizational and interorganizational networks.

Different types of community power structures are found in examining organizations and interorganizational networks. Perrucci and Pilisuk (1970) suggest that if there is no one recognized group of interorganizational leaders "community power is a shifting and amorphous thing." If interorganizational leaders are found to belong to a resource network, but "not identified as reputational leaders or as actual influencials," then the power structure can be described as pluralistic. When these interorganizational leaders have reputations as leaders, and when they participate in actual decision making, share values, and interact socially, then they represent a "power elite."

Another way of locating community power from an interorganizational perspective is to identify community decision organizations, "organizations devoted to specific kinds of decision areas, such as a redevelopment agency, a housing agency, a community action agency, a city development agency, welfare councils, health departments" (Aiken & Alford, 1970). These organizations together make up an "interorganizational field," which itself becomes a "center of power." These community decision organizations play special roles in the community, due to the fact that their "mission is to supervise the planning, coordination and delivery" of services. Aiken and Alford (1970) suggest that in areas where the major actors are organizations, the community decision organization will be central in exerting influence over decision making. This formulation is particularly useful in locating power concentrations in the areas of health and welfare, since community decision organizations in these areas exist in most communities.

ETHNIC MINORITY GROUPS, WOMEN, AND COMMUNITY POWER

Members of ethnic minority groups, economically disadvantaged people, and women have traditionally been left out of the community's political system. While involvement of people from these groups in local governmental positions has increased, underrepresentation continues and is a major barrier to community competence. Concern over the disenfranchisement of these groups in local community political structures has stimulated the development of an "empowerment" perspective within the profession of social work (Solomon, 1976). Empowerment has three major dimensions: as a goal related to personal, interpersonal, and political power; as a change process, involving consciousness-raising and increasing efficacy in achieving change; and as a method, through education, consumer input and participation in policymaking and service delivery, and the building of programs on the basis of individual and community strengths (Gutierrez, 1992).

The empowerment goal of political power involves "the ability to influence the allocation of resources in an organization or community through formal or informal means" (Gaventa, 1980). Achievement of this goal within a community often has been restricted among ethnic minority groups, women, and poor people (Gutierrez, 1990). It usually requires collective action, leadership, and coalition building. One example of empowerment is found in the activities of poverty neighborhoods which form block clubs and join the clubs together into area-wide neighborhood-community-development agencies. Another example cited earlier in this chapter involves the efforts of Hispanic community leaders to gain political power through representation in local government, to unify the various Hispanic groups within a community through the churches, health and social welfare agencies, and economic development organizations. The most visible signs of empowerment for women have been election to political positions in local, state, and national government; appointment to political positions; and membership and leadership in community boards and major community-wide voluntary organizations.

REVIEW

We have examined the key elements in the political system of a community, recognizing that this system plays a major role in making community policy and delivering community services. The major functions of the community political system are identified, along with a discussion of the criminal and juvenile justice system as an illustration of issues related to the implementation of governmental policies. The community political system is discussed in terms of major dimensions of community power and leadership, that is, personal power and leadership, individual and organizational power and influence within community subsystems, and the structure of power in the total community. Frameworks are presented to assist in the identification of community leaders, influential community organizations, interorganizational networks, and dominant community power subsystems. Finally, the concept of empowerment is introduced as a perspective of particular relevance for groups within communities who lack fair and equitable representation in the community's political system.

SUGGESTED READINGS

Boles, J. K. (1991). "American Feminism: New Issues for a Mature Movement." *Annals* 515. Sage Publications.

Chafets, Ze'ev (1990). *Devil's Night and Other True Tales of Detroit.* New York: Random House.

MacKinnon, Catharine (1989). *Toward a Feminist Theory of the State.* Cambridge: Harvard University Press.

McCaughey, Elizabeth (1993). "Court Deals a Blow to Racial Gerrymandering." *Wall Street Journal,* June 30.

Merton, Robert (1983). "Local and Cosmopolitan Influentials." In Roland Warren and Larry Lyon, eds., *New Perspectives on the American Community.* Homewood, IL: Dorsey Press.

Pildes, Richard H. and Richard G. Niemi (1993). "Expressive Harms, 'Bizarre Districts,' and Voting Rights: Evaluating Election-District Appearances after Shaw v. Reno." *Michigan Law Review* 92:3.

Rusk, David (1993). *Cities Without Suburbs.* Baltimore: Johns Hopkins University Press.

EXERCISE

Incorporate some of the ideas in Chapter 1 about defining communities of place and identification into a discussion of how changes in voting districts affect the "symbolic" definition of community.

NEW DISTRICTS REVIVE DEBATE: WHERE AND WHAT IS HARLEM?

By E. R. Shipp

For most of this century, exactitude was of little concern when defining Harlem, a name that suggests a romantic past of speakeasies and literary salons but a more dreary present of poverty and crime. That was until the New York City Districting Commission began dividing the city into 51 Council districts.

Now, politicians are scrambling to define—and defend—their parts of that historic turf.

For many people, Harlem has come to represent "wherever it was that black people lived," said Michael H. Adams, an architectural historian who is president of the Upper Manhattan Society for Progress through Preservation.

Battle of Morningside Heights

But that was not always so.

During the Revolutionary War, the Battle of Harlem Heights was fought near Broadway and 117th Street, which many people, including Columbia University officials, now call Morningside Heights.

In fact, Mr. Adams said, Harlem's southern border was once a diagonal line running roughly from the 70's on the east side to the low 100's on the west. All Manhattan north of that line was Harlem, a white upper-middle-class community favored by business executives and politicians.

Harlem became synonymous with black Manhattan in the 1920's, when thousands of blacks poured into the area. It was a time "when Harlem was in vogue," Langston Hughes wrote.

But even that Harlem, "black capital of the world," stretched only from 130th Street to 145th Street and from Fifth Avenue to Eighth Avenue.

Seemed Larger in Myth

Still, the mythical Harlem—celebrated in literature and music and symbolized by heroes like the Harlem Hellfighters of World War I and Joe Louis—always seemed much larger.

"When I think of Harlem, I think of a cultural legacy more than perhaps simply where black people are," said Peggy Shephard, a state housing official and a prospective City Council candidate from West Harlem.

Today, as the districting commission has discovered, Harlem is as Hispanic as it is black, with a growing number of whites and people of Asian background living there.

Now many blacks are coming to grips with the fact that the internationally known black metropolis is indeed only a small part of Manhattan north of Central Park and that only one of four new Council districts there seems certain to yield a black seat.

"Romantic" Harlem Evoked

The incongruity has many people considering the meaning of "Harlem."

The name usually evokes "the romantic Harlem," said William Perkins: "the Harlem of the Harlem Renaissance, the Harlem of Adam Clayton Powell, the Harlem of Abyssinian Baptist Church, but also the Harlem of Malcolm X and the Harlem of Marcus Garvey."

That is largely Central Harlem and excludes East Harlem, where Mr. Perkins, a Board of Elections official who hopes to run for the Council, grew up and still lives, and West Harlem, where Mr. Adams has lived for several years.

"The thing that's really astonishing to me," said Mr. Adams, who gives tours of Harlem, "is that if you speak to any person who's lived or visited here 30 or more years ago, they have this incredible sort of nostalgia for this place that had such a sense of community, of enrichment and vibrancy, with the power to attract people from all over the country and all over the world."

Few Think of the West Side

While even tourists have heard of East Harlem, often called Spanish Harlem or el Barrio, few people think of the west side when thinking of Harlem. Where West Harlem ends and Washington Heights begins has long been debated. And it continues to be so during redistricting.

Today, Mr. Adams said, "if you suggest to white people living in Washington Heights that they live in anything like Harlem, they would become rabid."

"Just like those 19th-century folks didn't want to be associated with the lower-class apartment dwellers in Central Harlem," he said, "so, too, these people who live in white enclaves don't want there to be a mistake that they live in this place that is perceived as being a horrible festering ghetto."

Uptown residents sometimes say, only half in jest, that where blacks live is Harlem, where Dominicans live is Washington Heights. But the groups live near each other on many blocks.

Maria A. Luna, who has lived in what she considers Washington Heights—Riverside Drive and 158th Street—for 32 years, expects a political "turf war" between blacks and Dominicans over Council seats.

"We want representation," said Miss Luna, another prospective City Council candidate. "It's not black versus Latinos or Dominicans. It's just that we don't have any representation and I think it's unfair since we are a high number of the residents in the area."

"It's Bad Harlem Now"

Definitions are not of primary concern to old-timers who know that the Harlem of their memories no longer exists. Many of them say they feel trapped in an environment that has turned hostile.

"I've seen a time when you could walk the streets at night, but you can't do that no more," said Louis Niblack, a retired cook who has lived in Harlem since 1949. "It's bad Harlem now."

But the myth of Harlem as a black mecca will not die, even though Brooklyn has more blacks and more political clout.

"Symbols have power," said the Rev. Dr. Preston Washington, pastor of the Memorial Baptist Church in Central Harlem, who grew up in East Harlem but now lives in Westchester County.

"Some symbols are dead, but some symbols have life and can re-energize people. Harlem is one of those things."

PART FOUR

Community Process

CHAPTER 12

Community Conflict

At one time or another all communities have conflicts, controversies, and tensions. Examples of such controversies include protest by community residents of a local government's decision to place a homeless shelter in their neighborhood (Hunt, 1991); legal action by residents against a local government to remove adult entertainment places (Holly, 1993; Lam, 1993); conflicts between groups within Hispanic communities (Montana, 1986); and conflicts between African Americans and Jewish residents (Breindel, 1993).

These examples suggest a number of dimensions of community conflict. First, controversies arise when groups seek to change the equilibrium of the community. Often when one or more ad hoc groups, voluntary associations, or racial/ethnic groups seek to change the community system, the changes are resisted by formal organizations within the community. Controversy also occurs when formal community organizations seek to bring about changes, such as when social agencies seek to establish group homes or shelters for homeless people. Community controversies, then, may arise through efforts of residents or formal organizations to bring about change and/or to protest some decision or action within the community.

A second dimension of community conflict involves its scope, that is, how widespread the conflict is, how many people are involved, and how many people the conflict affects. School strikes may involve large numbers of families in a school district and be viewed as community-wide in scope. On the other hand, a dispute over the location of a small night-time shelter for homeless people might be viewed as narrow in scope. Some labor-management industrial strikes have an impact on the total community and are broad in scope; others may be confined to a relatively small number of people. A public bus transportation strike is widespread in scope; a nurses strike in a single hospital of a large city may have a narrow scope unless professional associations and other hospitals join in the controversy.

A third dimension of community conflict involves whether or not it is conventional or rancorous (Gamson, 1966). Conventional conflicts are handled within established political rules and procedures and represent normal differences of opinion about various issues. Rancorous conflicts are those wherein acceptable and legitimate norms for settling differences are not followed and a high level of hostility and/or violence occurs during the controversy. For example, physical attacks are made on individuals in picket lines, buildings are burned, or open meetings are disrupted. While we have used the terms *conflict, controversy,* and *tensions* interchangeably, these words suggest different degrees of rancor.

THE PROCESS OF COMMUNITY CONFLICT

The dimensions of conflict initiation, scope, and convention/rancor provide a context for examining the actual process of community controversies. Within this context, Coleman's (1957) work on the dynamics of community controversy contributes to our understanding of these situations. Coleman maintains that "the most striking fact about the development and growth of community controversies is the similarity they exhibit despite diverse underlying sources and different kinds of precipitating incidents. Once the controversies have begun, they resemble each other remarkably." Coleman presents a framework for understanding changes in the issues of a controversy and in the structure of organizations and associations in the community. Issues appear to change according to the following stages.

1. Initial single issue.
2. Disrupts equilibrium of community relations.
3. Allows previously suppressed issues against opponent to appear.
4. More and more of opponent's beliefs enter into the disagreement.
5. The opponent appears totally bad.

6. Charges against opponent as a person.
7. Dispute becomes independent of initial disagreement.

These stages are helpful in understanding the dynamics of community controversy. News media accounts of local controversies provide useful case studies to which Coleman's principles can be applied. However, to fully assess the meaning of a conflict, one usually must be present in the particular community where the conflict occurs.

During community conflicts, elements of the social organization of the community change. Coleman (1957) identifies these changes as: (1) a polarization of social relations, (2) a formation of partisan organizations, (3) the emergence of new leaders, (4) a mobilization of ongoing community organizations, and (5) an increase in word-of-mouth communication. All of these changes do not always occur in the community during a controversy, but one may use these categories as a framework for explaining the dynamics of community controversies.

POSITIVE FUNCTIONS OF COMMUNITY CONFLICT

Community conflict is a form of social conflict, "a struggle over values and claims to scarce status, power and resources in which the aims of the opponents are to neutralize, insure or eliminate their rivals" (Coser, 1956). The functions of social conflict can be applied to social groups and social relations within a community. Rather than viewing social conflict as a totally negative phenomenon, it is useful to consider some of its positive functions, which can be applied to transactions among social groups in a community:

1. Conflict serves to establish and maintain the identity and boundary lines of societies and groups.
2. Conflict provides an opportunity for group members to "vent hostility" and "express dissent" and thereby maintain relationships between groups.
3. While there may be hostility and tensions in conflict relationships between groups, this is not necessarily so.
4. Conflicts arise in many instances between groups which are interdependent—such as union-management, school-family—and resolutions of conflicts serve to stabilize group relationships as long as the conflicts do not threaten basic consensus.

5. Conflict with another group increases the cohesion of a group.
6. Conflict allows a group to assess the power and influence of another group and thus serves as a balancing mechanism to maintain the overall system.
7. Conflicts provide a unifying function by bringing people and groups together into coalitions and temporary associations.

These propositions emphasize the positive functions of social conflicts (Coser, 1956). They may not hold for all groups in community conflicts, but they give us a framework for assessing and understanding specific conflicts.

COMMUNITY CONFLICTS AND THE COMMUNITY SYSTEM

Social system and ecological system perspectives on communities both employ the concept of conflict. From the ecological point of view, conflict is a process which governs the allocation of resources and leads to dominant and subdominant social units within community and society. Conflict is considered to be a natural phenomenon, to be accepted, not eliminated. In contrast, a social system perspective views conflict as a disruption of the equilibrium of the system, one which should be controlled and prevented. System maintenance (Parsons, 1951) requires the minimization of social conflict. Conflict activities are considered to be essentially negative, since they disturb the social order. For example, social conflict in the form of class conflict is seen as disturbing the stability of a community.

Are there variations in patterns of conflict and resolution from one community to another? We would expect some communities to vary in their toleration for conflicts, in the institutionalization of conflict activities, and in the ways in which conflicts are terminated. Some communities will tolerate conflicts such as school strikes for only a limited time before going to the courts for settlement. Other communities tolerate conflict activities for much longer periods. Some communities may even tolerate the use of violence to move toward settlement of group conflicts.

Patterns of community conflict are illustrated in the cases presented here. These represent only some of the various types of community controversies, such as ethnic minority relations, community based homes, shelters, and treatment centers, and urban redevelopment. The reader can find such cases in the daily press and in television programs. For example, the case of urban violence in Los Angeles following the Rodney King court decision could be analyzed as an illustration of multiethnic "riots," as the major participants were from several ethnic groups—Latino, Korean, African American, and others (Goldberg, 1993). This case was the focus of a documentary, "L.A. is Burning: Five Reports from a Divided City" (PBS). In each of our examples, we have given attention to the process features of the conflict. However, the reader may wish to consider the role social workers might play during and after such community conflicts.

Community-Based Treatment Centers

The movement of patients and residents of public institutions into the community has engendered community controversies in many American communities. Conflicts of this kind are expressed in terms of "community opposition" to facilities, homes, or other housing arrangements which vary from the usual dwellings and household uses in residential neighborhoods. Group homes and treatment centers often house unrelated individuals who have been deinstitutionalized. Opposition at the neighborhood level is often associated with fears of decline in property values, concern for safety of residents, or negative consequences of abnormal behavior of the new residents. This type of opposition has been labeled as a "not in my back yard" process (Gilbert, 1993).

Community conflicts over proposals to establish community-based residential care centers often result in preventing these centers from being developed in local neighborhoods. If a center is established in spite of local opposition, it may be difficult for it to function in the aftermath of conflict conditions. This is especially true if one of the purposes of locating individuals in the centers is the reintegration of the patients into the local community, a goal difficult to achieve if the opposition to the center has been strong. Gilbert (1993) has suggested that some of the negative reaction to the establishment of group homes, shelters, and treatment centers comes from deficiencies on the part of the social agencies. She recommends that social service agencies need to plan more carefully, reach out to neighborhood residents and organizations, and understand more fully the impact of the agency facility on the neighborhood. In this way, social workers not only serve their clients, but also meet the needs of the neighborhood and community.

Davidson's (1981, 1982) work on community-based treatment centers provides some useful insights into local community conflict and resistance to the location of treatment centers in local neighborhoods. Davidson suggests that resistance to these centers will be low in neighborhoods in which "deviant" behavior is tolerated, in those neighborhoods with residents who do not regard the neighborhood as sufficiently valuable to defend it against intrusions, and in those neighborhoods that lack the resources necessary for effective political mobilization. Such "transitional" neighborhoods are likely to be in inner cities, not in the suburbs.

Some neighborhoods seem to have the capacity, through formal and informal resources, to mount "effective campaigns to influence local officials with respect to neighborhood issues" (Davidson, 1981). Community opposition through such campaigns is regarded as a significant barrier to the "survival and effective functioning of community-based treatment centers" (Davidson, 1981). Even under the best of circumstances, these centers operate in a "potentially turbulent" environment, especially if the clients' behavior is of concern to the local neighborhood residents.

A case example of a controversy over the establishment of a group home is located at the close of this chapter (George, 1992). When a program run by the Sisters of the Good Shephard to help women escape prostitution needed a new home for up to ten women and their children, the Dominican Sisters offered a former rectory on their 34-acre campus, which had been used to house aspiring nuns. Community opposition developed by some residents of a 750 home neighborhood surrounding the Dominican Sisters campus. Residents opposed to the program contended that "the women will attract pimps and drug pushers and threaten safety," "jeopardize property values," and "pave the way for more institutions in the neighborhood." The social worker with the program indicated that "many of the residents' fears stem from inaccurate perceptions of prostitutes as oversexed women who choose their lifestyle and make a lot of money." At the same time, some residents did not oppose the location of the program in their neighborhood. However, one of the petition signers against the home said, "I want the women to be able to get out of prostitution and break the cycle, but I don't want it in my neighborhood" (George, 1992).

In this example, the controversy occurred when a formal organization sought to establish a social service program in a residential neighborhood. The controversy was moderately narrow in scope, affecting a rather large upscale neighborhood, and conventional methods of resolving the conflict were employed, such as petitions to the local government and the use of zoning laws. Elements of social organization of the neighborhood were already in place, with the existence of a neighborhood association and leaders who could represent the neighborhood to the local government.

Urban Redevelopment

The relocation of people to new residential and business sites in urban redevelopment projects provides another example of community conflict. A case in point is the Poletown Project in Detroit, where the city of Detroit, the General Motors company, and other involved parties cooperated to redevelop 465 acres for a new Cadillac auto plant. A 319-acre portion of the site in the city of Detroit "included 1,176 residential, commercial and industrial structures, as well as major community institutions. The demolition of these and the displacement of the people owning and using them were at the heart of the Poletown controversy. . . ." (Warner et al., 1982).

A total of approximately 3,800 persons were displaced. The city of Detroit promised to provide relocation assistance and financial compensation to those displaced for the larger community's welfare— that is, for the industrial employment and revenue base for the city of Detroit. The city of Hamtramck was the location of another part of the 465-acre project. Two major community institutions, the Catholic Archdiocese of Detroit and St. Joseph's Hospital, did not oppose the project. However, while some residents welcomed the opportunity to move, a number opposed the plan for redevelopment. Prominent among the resisters were older Polish residents, especially those attached to Catholic churches in the area. Many of these residents had already been involved in revitalization efforts for the neighborhood and were joined in their opposition to the project by young political activists and outside groups, such as Ralph Nader's people, and inside leadership from the parish pastor. After much talk, protest, and an unsuccessful court challenge, demolition proceeded, and the General Motors Cadillac factory was built (Auerbach, 1985).

Controversies Over Adult Entertainment

Residents of some neighborhoods in large cities are in constant battle in a fight against certain types of adult entertainment. These controversies occur when a concentration of businesses such as topless bars, massage parlors, and adult book stores develops near a residential neighborhood (Holly, 1993; Lam, 1993). Residents often organize to influence the local government in revoking business licenses, in limiting the issue of new licenses, and in prosecuting violations of local laws related to adult entertainment. The most usual complaint is that these establishments bring with them prostitution and crime. Residents usually seek to intervene by bringing lawsuits against the establishments or in seeking to change city zoning ordinances. These controversies tend to be narrow in scope, and the patterns for resolution are usually conventional. Successful opposition to adult entertainment establishments usually occurs only when the neighborhood is highly organized through involvement of residents as leaders and members of neighborhood associations, church groups, and school groups.

Keeping Out the Homeless

The question of where to house homeless people has created controversy in a number of American communities. One such example is Santa Monica, California, where the community of 87,000 people "is fiercely at war with itself over the swelling homeless population of between 1500 and 2000 that dominates some city parks and sidewalks, harasses pedestrians for money and commits crimes ranging from public urination to murder" (Lubman, 1992). While the community provides for a number of services for homeless people, such as shelter and food, a principal controversy has been over the use of public places, especially parks, parking structures, beaches, and playgrounds. The principal groups seeking restrictions on the homeless have been an anti-crime Citizens' Protection Alliance of local citizens and a Santa Monicans for Renters' Rights group. These groups have sought to influence the city council in passing ordinances which will place controls on use of public places for the homeless.

The City of Miami, Florida, provides a second example of controversy over the behavior of homeless persons in local communities. A federal judge ordered the City of Miami to "create 'safe zones' where the homeless can eat, sleep, bathe and cook without fear of arrest" (Rohter, 1992). A number of groups, such as public officials, lawyers, advocates for the homeless, have been in conflict over the conditions under which the homeless can be arrested. Many cities have ordinances controlling vagrancy, begging, park curfews, etc., which are used against the homeless. The safe zones to be created in Miami are essentially "arrest free" zones where an estimated 6000 homeless persons "can eat and sleep and exist in a healthy, safe environment" (Rohter, 1992).

Controversies Over Barricades

Crime is a major social problem in American communities, especially in urban areas and in inner-city neighborhoods. Efforts to combat crime through local neighborhood organizations such as block clubs, neighborhood associations, and neighborhood watch programs rarely generate any controversy. However, controversies have developed when neighborhoods organize to prevent crime by prevailing upon a city to construct street barriers dividing one neighborhood community from another. Sometimes the barriers are in the form of gates into a neighborhood, at other times they are physical barriers which keep all traffic out. Examples of the "Do Fence Me In" approach to crime prevention can be found in many large cities, such as Los Angeles, Chicago, Miami, Detroit, and in some suburban communities such as Oak Park, Illinois, and Shaker Heights, Ohio (Etzioni, 1992; Holly, 1993; Wilkerson, 1993).

A case example of a controversy between neighbors over the erection of street barriers is found in neighborhoods of Detroit and Grosse Pointe Park, Michigan (Holly, 1993; Mathews, 1993). Residents in the Grosse Pointe Park neighborhood petitioned the city council to construct barriers at selected streets which adjoin the dividing line between the two communities. In a nearby area, street barriers were erected to prevent traffic from moving on these three streets from one major artery to another, both leading into the inner-city and downtown area of Detroit. The controversy has been characterized as racial, since the community erecting the barriers is almost entirely white and affluent, and the neighboring community is mostly African American and working class. Residents of the Detroit neighborhood see the barriers as "offensive," as symbolic of negative attitudes toward African Americans. In this controversy, the Grosse Pointe Park community gained the support of the local government and succeeded in getting the barriers constructed.

In another example of a controversy over street barricades, Mayor Richard Daley has proposed that some streets in Chicago be blocked off in neighborhoods in order to restrict the movement of criminals in these communities. This plan was viewed as an effort to "cul de sac" the entire city of Chicago (Wilkerson, 1993). The opposition to the plan came from "poor black wards" of the city, whose residents saw the effort as "dangerous," "oppressive," and a way to further segregate the races. As of mid-1994, the plan had not been implemented due to the controversy and to financing problems related to construction of the barrier gates.

African American and Jewish Relations

Tensions among African American and Jewish residents are apparent in many American communities (Breindel, 1993; Gates, 1993; West,

1993). These tensions are disturbing to many members of both communities, and community groups have organized in an effort to resolve some of these tensions and to avoid conflicts. A number of issues appear to be the foundation for controversies between these two groups. West (1993) has identified two major issues that often divide these two groups. One is "the question of what constitutes the most effective means for black progress"—that is, affirmative action and social programs. Another is "the meaning and practice of Zionism as embodied in Israel," or the "moral content of Jewish and Black identities." These issues represent some of the underlying tensions between Jewish and African American residents. There are also examples of more overt conflicts, such as racial unrest and disturbances in Brooklyn's Crown Heights neighborhood in 1991 (Roberts, 1993).

The complexity of the example of community conflict in Crown Heights between Jewish and African American communities is apparent in a report of the State of New York's criminal justice director and in the drama, *Fires in the Mirror* (PBS). The incident that touched off the conflict was an automobile accident on August 19, 1991, when "a black child was fatally injured when a car driven by a member of the Hasidic community accidentally struck him" (Breindel, 1993). Shortly afterwards, a young Jewish man, a visiting scholar from Australia, was chased and stabbed by a group of African American youths. In the aftermath of four days of violence, some 80 Jewish people and about 100 police were physically injured in what was called in the press an "anti-Semitic riot," and in the state report, "the most extensive racial unrest faced by the city in more than 20 years" (Breindel, 1993).

The investigation into this disturbance revealed a number of features of this community conflict. This disturbance illustrates a community conflict that involved two identificational communities interacting in a geographical community and the response to the conflict by the political system. The patterns of the conflict were rancorous, with personal injuries and destruction of businesses. The scope of the conflict appears to be narrow due to the occurrences in one neighborhood area, but it was widespread in relation to its impact on members of both Jewish and African American communities. The New York State report was critical of the process of the conflict, indicating that the mayor and the police failed to respond in a timely and appropriate manner to the incidents and to the events thereafter. News accounts of the disturbance suggest that there was a new polarization of social relations between the Jewish and African American communities.

Rivalries Among Hispanics

With the arrival of numbers of immigrants from the Dominican Republic, the New York City Hispanic population has changed dramatically (Gonzalez, 1992). As these new immigrants have moved into El Barrio, the Hispanic neighborhoods, competition with other Hispanic groups, particularly Puerto Ricans, has increased. This situation has developed into community controversies between the major Hispanic groups, the more established Puerto Ricans, and the new Mexicans, Dominicans, and other Spanish-speaking groups. Often the controversies involve the search for political power and representation and the efforts on the part of these groups to make economic progress through entrepreneurship and to secure fair treatment in receiving social services and education.

Another example of intra-ethnic group controversy is found in some California communities, where long-time Mexican American residents clash with new Mexican immigrants, particularly undocumented workers (Montana, 1986). In these communities, "working-class, Mexican-Americans, many of whom prefer to be called Chicanos, blame undocumented workers for lower salaries or the loss of jobs, the overcrowding of schools and health clinics, and the deterioration of neighborhoods. Many Chicanos, fearful of a loss of status in the wider community, don't want to be confused with the newcomers" (Montana, 1986). Tensions which divide the new immigrants from the long-time Mexican American residents come from concerns over the use of social service agencies by the new arrivals, the high home rental prices charged by long-timers renting to newcomers, the costs for health care for the new immigrants, and problems in the public schools for those who speak only Spanish.

REVIEW

This chapter identifies the various dimensions of community conflicts, the elements involved in most controversies at the community level, and some of the functions such controversies serve for the groups involved. What is apparent in community controversies is the fact that both sides believe they make legitimate claims. In some cases the efforts of small community groups serve to modify the actions of formal organizations, but rarely do they succeed in "defeating" the larger institutional forces. In contrast, the creation of "safe zones" for homeless people in Miami, Florida, by order of a federal judge is an example of a decision in support of the position of advocacy groups over that of the local government.

One of the principal areas of community controversy related to the social welfare system has been related to the movement of institutionalized individuals, mentally ill persons, people from the criminal justice system, and children and youth with developmental disabilities into local community neighborhoods (Fellin, 1993). Efforts to achieve goals of social integration for these citizens have been met with barriers such as protective zoning ordinances, neighborhood group opposition, and social rejection by neighbors. While informal resistance to community care of individuals who cannot care for themselves continues through a "not in my back yard" attitude on the part of neighbors, the courts have often ruled in favor of community residential care under certain conditions, such as number of residents in a home and appropriate supervision of residents.

In American society, intergroup relations form the basis for many community controversies. Conflicts arise between ethnic minority groups and between ethnic minority groups and ethnic religious groups, such as African Americans and Koreans, Jewish and African Americans, and rivalries between Hispanics. At the same time, as illustrated in our discussion of segregated and integrated neighborhoods in Chapter 6, the white majority population is often in conflict with ethnic minority populations over issues related to residence. As noted in our case examples, intergroup conflicts often become rancorous and disturb the social order of the community. During these conflicts, social workers may play important roles in working with clients in the neighborhoods where disturbances occur as well as working with neighborhood community organizations to prevent violence and to create positive community conditions.

SUGGESTED READINGS

Auerbach, Joseph (1985). "The Poletown Dilemma." *Harvard Business Review* 63:3 (May-June).

Coleman, James (1983). "The Dynamics of Community Conflict." In R. Warren and L. Lyons, eds., *New*

Perspectives on the American Community. Homewood, IL.: Dorsey Press.

Gilbert, Dianne (1993). "Not in My Backyard." *Social Work* 38:1 (January).

EXERCISE

Use the ideas about multiple communities, personal community, and social integration (see Chapter 13) to discuss the controversy over the location of a community-based program for former prostitutes. What roles might social workers play in relation to the reaction of the residents of the neighborhood to the location of the Rose Haven home?

HOUSE DIVIDES GRAND RAPIDS NEIGHBORS

By Maryanne George

Mary remembers the day in April when she and her three children walked through the door at Rose Haven, a home for former prostitutes run by nuns on the city's southeast side.

"I was dirty, I was hungry, I needed someone to be there for me," said Mary, 39, a prostitute for 15 years and former crack cocaine addict who spoke on the condition her real name not be used. "I was getting away from a boyfriend who was also my drug supplier, but I didn't know where to go. If there had been a place like this earlier, I would have gotten out long ago.

Mary, Rose Haven's first resident, moved into her own home with her children in October and works as a cook in a retirement home.

"Life is wonderful," Mary said this week. "If it wasn't for the program I couldn't say that."

But for the Sisters of the Good Shepherd, who started Rose Haven in March and have helped 36 women like Mary escape prostitution, life has gotten difficult.

The owner of the modest two-story house has sold it and the nuns must leave by Dec. 15, said Sister Dolores Kalina, the program's director. An offer by the Grand Rapids Dominican Sisters to move Rose Haven to a former rectory on their Marywood campus has residents in the peaceful, upscale neighborhood it border up in arms.

Today the Grand Rapids Board of Zoning Appeals is expected to decide whether the Dominicans need to seek a zoning variance for the program. The Dominicans are appealing a ruling by the Grand Rapids Planning Commission requiring the variance.

Sister Carmelita Murphy, prioress of the Grand Rapids Dominicans, said it saddens her that some neighbors no longer speak because of conflicting views about Rose Haven.

Maryanne George, "House Divides Grand Rapids Neighbors." *Detroit Free Press*, December 3, 1992. Reprinted with permission.

The nuns say that housing former prostitutes is essentially the same as housing the seven aspiring nuns who now occupy the two-story, red brick rectory. Rose Haven would house a maximum of 10 women and their children.

The aspiring nuns would be moved from the rectory.

Sister Jarrett DeWyse of the Dominican General council said the two groups are indeed similar when "you talk about a residence built around a shared value system and goals. These women are here to make a life together and a life for themselves."

But some residents of the 750-home Michigan-Oaks neighborhood surrounding the 34-acre campus say the women will attract pimps and drug pushers and threaten safety.

Others say the program is illegal under current zoning and will jeopardize property values and pave the way for more institutions in the neighborhood, where well-kept homes range in price from $60,000 to $300,000.

Zoning in the neighborhood permits only four unrelated people in one house. The nuns are exempt because they lived on the campus before the zoning code was established.

The controversy has pitted some residents of Grand Rapids—a city that many say prides itself on charitable works—against women and their children who desperately need help. It has also caused much soul-searching among neighbors and nuns.

The Michigan-Oaks Neighborhood Association board in July passed a resolution opposing the program as a zoning violation. This fall 500 residents signed a petition opposing Rose Haven and about 40 put up lawn signs reading "Marywood, just say no."

Joseph Dole, MONA president, said, "This is a good program, but it is not permitted in this district."

Murphy said the Dominicans, who were concerned for their own safety as well as the neighbors', carefully investigated Rose Haven.

They found the program had no trouble with crime, drug dealers, or pimps, she said. Women agree to strict rules regarding visitors, curfews, and household tasks. They must break ties to people in their past and complete substance abuse counseling, if necessary.

Suzanne Peters, the social worker for Rose Haven, said many of the residents' fears stem from inaccurate perceptions of prostitutes as oversexed women who choose their lifestyle and make a lot of money.

Peters said studies by similar programs find that 95 percent of prostitutes were sexually abused as children. Many run away from home to escape the abuse. Seventy-five percent began working as prostitutes as teenagers.

"We see them come to us with nothing on their backs but bruises," Peters said. "Their self-concept is that they are objects of sexual pleasure for men. These women are sexually abused for money.

"They want safety, love, dignity, and a home for themselves and their children, the same thing all men and women want."

Diana Sieger, a neighborhood resident who supports locating Rose Haven at the rectory, said the MONA board does not represent all the residents. Sieger is concerned that the conflict is dividing the neighborhood.

Shelley Volkert, who lives less than a block from the rectory, signed the petition opposing the program.

"I've been back and forth on the issue and I'm conflicted," she said. "I want the women to be able to get out of prostitution and break the cycle, but I don't want it in my neighborhood."

CHAPTER 13

Social Integration in Communities

The concept of social integration guides the assessment of the extent to which people are attached to and participate in the social institutions of a community (Padilla, 1990). The concept also applies to the way in which the parts of the various community subsystems operate, and how these systems fit together in the community as a whole. The concept of social integration has a number of meanings and is measured in various ways. Landecker's (1951) classic discussion of social integration distinguishes four subtypes: "cultural, or consistency among the standards of a culture; normative, or conformity of conduct in the group to cultural standards; communicative, or exchange of meanings throughout the group; and functional, or interdependence in the group through exchange of services."

The internal consistency of values, norms, and standards of the community is a sign of cultural integration. An important dimension of cultural integration within a community is the degree to which the cultural aspects of a community correspond to those of mainstream society. Normative integration focuses on the extent to which community residents conform to cultural standards. Measurement of positive integration is illustrated by an indicator such as "giving to charity" patterns. An indicator of negative integration is the rate of crime and other deviant behavior in a community. Various subsystems within a community, especially the political, educational, and religious-community systems, establish standards, with normative integration representing the conformity of members of a community to these standards. All of the community subsystems serve as sources of communicative and functional integration. The "multiple communities" of place, as well as communities of interest and identification, offer members opportunities for communication and interdependence, with considerable variation in levels of integration among various types of communities. A special case of social integration involves the segregation and integration of ethnic minority and social class groups.

The major focus of this chapter is on communicative and functional social integration, that is, the extent to which individuals participate in and use the resources of the local community, as well as the level of social contacts and social interaction of residents within a personal community. The concept of social network is used to examine the individual's social integration into a community. This is followed by examination of how communities of interest foster social integration on the part of their members. One especially significant example of a community of interest which carries out integrative functions is membership in a religious group. Less obvious sources of integration, such as recreation, sports spectatorship, eating and drinking establishments, are also examined. Finally, attention is directed to groups of individuals who have difficulty integrating or reintegrating into communities.

SOCIAL NETWORKS

A major source of social integration is an individual's social network. This network includes one's significant others, often drawn from family, kinship, friendship, neighborhood, voluntary association, and work-related groups (Maguire 1983). Rather than thinking of these discrete groups as separate sources of community integration, social network analysis identifies a configuration of social relationships which constitutes a mixture of individuals from these groups. Social networks differ by virtue of a number of dimensions, such as "the size of the network, frequency of contacts among members, strength of ties, homogeneity (similarities in the network with regard to gender, age, religion, race, or ethnicity), geographic distance, and the symmetry of contacts" (Greenblatt et al., 1983). The relationships in social networks may be supportive, warm, and helpful or hostile, cold, and disapproving. The nature of one's social network is closely related to the provision of social support, such as emotional, physical, economic, and informational support. One's social network not only provides access to resources, but, in doing so, also serves to integrate the individual into the local community.

Since social networks are likely to include a mixture of individuals, such as family members, friends, relatives, neighbors, and coworkers, it is natural that some ties with these individuals will be stronger than others. Granovetter (1973) has highlighted the fact that both strong and weak network ties can be functional for individuals. In fact, weak ties often serve to hold people in urban communities together, providing links which help individuals find employment, relate to others in the workplace, gain occupational and social mobility, and connect to the resources of the larger community. Choldin (1985) extends this idea to the metropolitan community, concluding that "Social networks play a part in tying together large populations and subsystems of the metropolis. Individuals in disparate networks may have weak ties with each other, which form bridges between different subsystems. Thus the metropolis may be seen as a network of networks."

COMMUNITIES OF IDENTIFICATION AND INTEREST

Individuals and groups are often affiliated with "non-place" communities, that is, communities of interest and identification. These communities provide avenues for integration and attachment to the local community of place, while at the same time providing identification with a "community" that may have no geographical bounds. Terms such as "we-feeling," community sentiment, common bonds, values, psychological identification, and cultural ties are used to describe the major dimensions of these non-place communities.

Examples of these communities of interest include the professions, social classes, and groups identified in terms of race, ethnicity, and religious affiliation. In the case of professions, individuals often identify themselves with membership in an occupational group, such as the legal community, the medical community, the social work community, or the ministry. In most cases, these memberships provide opportunities for social, educational, and professional activities and serve to integrate their members into the local "place" community. At the same time, individual professionals often also identify with their profession at state, national, and/or international levels. Membership in a professional group may substitute for local ties, thus reducing community integration by inhibiting individuals from participating in the activities of the local community.

As we noted in our discussion of the stratification of communities, for some people a social class may constitute a social community (Jackman and Jackman, 1983). Class awareness may be a powerful force in determining negative or positive feelings and attachments to a local community. For example, individuals in the lower classes may have negative feelings toward a community if it does not offer opportunities for upward mobility, does not provide services for their neighborhoods, does not offer good educational programs, or does not control crime. On the other hand, middle-class and upper-class individuals may identify positively with their local community because they perceive that the community reinforces their values, protects their property, and provides cultural opportunities for them.

Membership in racial and ethnic groups is a prime example of a community of identification. Oftentimes membership in one of these groups coincides with the place of residence, such as in some Italian, Polish, Irish, Jewish, Catholic, African American, Hispanic, or Asian American communities in large urban areas. As noted in the previous discussion of ethnic minority neighborhoods, a member of a specific group may change residence and still retain psychological identification with the old neighborhood group. In these types of communities, individuals most often develop a sense of belonging to the local community as well as a sense of membership in a much broader, even worldwide, group. Again, attachment to the local geographic community is often determined by involvement in local activities emerging from membership in these non-place communities.

RELIGION AND COMMUNITY INTEGRATION

For many Americans, religious affiliation is the basis for a community of identification. While many religious groups have churches, synagogues, mosques, or other places of worship in local community areas, their members generally identify with their religion on a basis that does not have geographic bounds. This is most vividly highlighted by the response to religious appeals for funds for local community, national, and international needs and projects. Religion serves to link its membership to the community through participation in religious services, social and educational activities, and volunteer services.

While membership in churches and other religious organizations serves as a mechanism for integration into the local community, such membership may also lead to community conflict and controversy. Inasmuch as those who belong to religious organizations often identify with a specific set of norms and values, they may find these values to be at odds with those of other members of the community. Controversial issues that relate to the values of religious groups include sex education, prayer in public schools, abortion, sale and use of liquor, and enforcement of laws on pornography.

From a social systems perspective, religious institutions comprise one of the major types of voluntary associations in the community. Religious organizations function as instruments of socialization, education, social control, and mutual support. As a result, religion offers a number of avenues, formal and informal, for individuals and families to develop attachments and social interactions with people in the local community. Some of the major formal ways in which religious organizations facilitate community integration include religious-oriented schools, social agencies, and volunteer groups. For example, schools establish a basis for the development of child and adult ties to religious and school communities and serve to integrate families into the local community. Members of religious organizations often participate in volunteer services under the direction of sectarian social welfare and health care organizations. In addition, some religious organizations create their own volunteer groups, with goals of assisting members of the community. Finally, informal relationships may be developed between members of religious organizations, leading to mutual aid and social supports among families connected to a religious congregation.

THE INFLUENCE OF RESIDENCE IN A MASS SOCIETY

It is generally recognized that local American communities operate within a larger context, sometimes labeled a national "mass society." There is little agreement as to the influence of a national society on local communities and their residents. Some social scientists suggest a coexistence, stressing the importance of both the national society and the local community. Others suggest that the local community has diminished in influence and as a source of social integration. The issues center around the nature of a "mass society," a society which has emerged from the social processes of urbanization, bureaucratization, and industrialization. Among the features of "mass society" are an increase in secondary over primary group relations (a movement from Gemeinschaft to Gesellschaft relationships), the development of mass media, large-scale bureaucratic institutions, high levels of residential mobility, and an increase in the size and density of urban populations. The claim is made that these societal features have negative effects on residents, increasing their sense of isolation, alienation, and anomie. Under this formulation, social residence is said to be a relatively unimportant source of social integration. With this perspective, the social significance of the local geographic community is considered to be minimal, at least in terms of local social bonds and community sentiments.

A contrasting model of mass society vis-a-vis local communities, has emerged over time from studies of American communities. This model, which may be characterized as the "community of limited liability" (Janowitz, 1978), is based on the proposition that participation in local institutions and local attachments do persist within the larger society, although they are more limited than in previous traditional forms of community. The concept of "community of limited liability" suggests that personal community involvement is partial and voluntary in relation to primary group friendship, kinship, and neighboring bonds (Kasarda and Janowitz, 1974). The same is true of participation in voluntary associations, formal organizations, and informal and formal local social activities. These latter kinds of relationships appear to reinforce the primary contacts rather than replace them.

In short, the qualities associated with a good community, such as citizen involvement, participation, commitment, and local attachment, appear to be possible within a "mass society." This does not mean that there are many communities that resemble the traditional autonomous community of yesteryear (Keillor, 1985), but it does mean that citizens of contemporary mass society can have local sentiments and involvements which integrate them into the local community. However, the degree of social integration appears to vary among social classes, ethnic and racial groups, and occupational groups. A number of barriers, such as residential segregation, work against the social integration of ethnic minorities into municipal and metropolitan communities. Ties to these communities are also affected by factors such as residential mobility, length of residence, and stage in the life-cycle (Kasadra & Janowitz, 1974). Some observers suggest that continued urbanization and deconcentration of populations make integration into local communities increasingly problematic. Louv (1985), for example, in *American II*, suggests that "the chief psychosocial issue of America II is one of affiliation. Most of us need a feeling of belonging, a sense of being protected. We need to feel a part of a group, a community, or a company."

OBVIOUS AND LESS OBVIOUS SOURCES OF INTEGRATION

Traditionally, religious, educational, and economic institutions have been the major forces for cohesion and integration of citizens into their communities. These institutions, especially through their related voluntary associations, continue to serve integrative functions for a large portion of the population of a community. However, less obvious forces outside the customary social institutions also serve important integrative functions. There are a number of such examples, such as local newspapers, disc jockeys, radio personalities, talk shows, meals-on-wheels for the elderly, suburban neighborhood swimming pools, neighborhood ethnic restaurants, country clubs, golf courses, youth recreational programs, libraries, community colleges, shopping malls, food markets, and street corners. A discussion of drinking and eating establishments and local sports events is used to illustrate these sources of community integration.

BARS, TAVERNS, COFFEE HOUSES, LOUNGES

Bars, coffee houses, and local neighborhood restaurants serve integrative functions for their patrons by promoting a sense of community. In Kornblum's (1975) study, *Blue Collar Community*, he noted that "the tavern is among the most important of neighborhood institutions where people can form and maintain friendships with others whom they know well but may not associate with at home." In some cases the same people keep showing up at the same location, to hang out, to drink, eat, and socialize. It is clear that patrons develop loyalties to particular locations and that their social contacts provide links to the local community. More often than not, drinking and eating places develop personalities of their own, due to the atmosphere of the place, the patrons, and the personnel. These establishments take on identifications, based on their clientele, as gathering places for certain social classes, racial or ethnic groups, "singles," people of gay or lesbian orientation, sports figures, neighborhood residents. Descriptions of drinking/eating establishments illustrate these sources of social contact and community integration.

Sports Bars

Bars located near baseball and/or football stadiums in large cities serve a varied clientele. During the nongame days and noontime periods, the "Bar & Grill" tends to draw patrons from the surrounding neighborhood areas. On game days, some of the old crowd come in, but the size of the crowd is swelled by outsiders, many of whom identify themselves with the bar.

Ethnic/Racial Bars

Neighborhood bars often are ethnic or racial in terms of their patrons. They tend to be in working-class neighborhoods and, often, ghetto areas. Bars and restaurants are places for socializing, and they assist newcomers in becoming a part of a neighborhood group community.

Singles Bars

Singles bars seem to be everywhere, in downtown areas of large cities, in neighborhoods, in restaurants, in motels. The clientele ranges from college-age young adults to young urban professionals, to middle-aged men and women who are single, married, or divorced. For some, especially college students, "the bar" is a place for hanging out, listening to music, and socializing.

Gay and Lesbian Bars

Communities vary as to how easy or difficult it is for people with gay and lesbian orientations to integrate into the social activities of the local area. In some communities, gay bars are among the few places in which gay and lesbian persons can congregate comfortably. These bars, lounges, and clubs, found especially in communities with large populations of gay and lesbian individuals, serve to link their patrons to each other and to the local community.

Cheap Bars, Dives

These bars are usually found in deteriorated areas of large urban areas, in ghetto neighborhoods, on "mean streets." They generally offer a place to hang out for unemployed men and women, homeless people, prostitutes, and pimps. They often provide a location for illegal activities, such as the sale of drugs and gambling.

Drinking and eating establishments in American communities serve integrative functions for their patrons because people feel comfortable in these places, get to know the staff and other patrons, and develop primary group relationships with them. For some local residents, these places have negative consequences if they lead to alcoholism or other illness. For some, these places provide the primary source of social contact and identification with the community. The theme song for the TV series *Cheers* expressed one meaning of these experiences, that is, the "sense of community" which comes from being "where everybody knows your name" (Portnoy and Angelo, 1982).

SPORTS TEAMS AND COMMUNITY ATTACHMENT

Organized sports provide mechanisms for citizens to identify with their home communities, their neighborhood schools, their local colleges, and their cities and metropolitan areas. Communities become known for the successes and failures of their sports teams, and residents take pride in winning teams. Sports fans follow their teams by newspaper, radio, and TV and by attending games. The sports pages make up a major section of any community newspaper. A winning team increases the sense of belonging and pride in the community. At the same time, a losing team may still engender loyal fans and an identification with the underdog, as illustrated by the early years of the New York Mets baseball team.

Both spectator and participant sports serve to link individuals to their local community. Participation in sports, especially team sports, and other recreation activities builds ties to local communities. Summer baseball and softball teams for all ages, bowling leagues, pool rooms, informal sports in parks, lake areas, cross country ski areas, all play integrative roles for community residents.

REINTEGRATION INTO COMMUNITIES

A special dimension of social integration is the movement back into the community of persons who have been institutionalized. Major treatment goals for these persons often includes their reintegration into their own communities. Reintegration has a variety of meanings, especially in terms of differences in the needs of the clientele, who may be adult mental patients, adult drug abusers, retarded adults, homeless adults, or adults in work-release programs of correctional facilities (Davidson, 1975). Children and adolescents, including neglected children, developmentally disabled children, juvenile delinquents, and children in foster care, may require reintegration into the community. Reintegration usually means that persons are able to become involved in everyday experiences within the community, developing acceptable behaviors, participating in social networks, and using local resources.

Our conception of "multiple communities," both geographical and identificational, can be applied to the community reintegration of special populations, such as mentally ill persons (Fellin, 1993). From this perspective, patients returning from institutional care to community-based care have a range of "communities" to which they can derive the benefits of group membership, such as social interaction, collective identity, shared interests, and social resources. Within this context, a personal community serves as a context for the development of treatment and social service goals. Thus, a personal community may include people in informal and formal helping networks, such as families, kinship and friend groups, self-help groups, daytime drop-in centers, club-house programs, church groups, recreational groups, and mental health and social welfare organizations (Fellin, 1993).

Most communities have social service programs which assist individuals in community reintegration. These programs include different types of community-based treatment centers (Davidson, 1981, 1982). Treatment programs range from halfway houses and group homes to congregate-apartment living arrangements, all involving "least restrictive environments" compared to institutionalization. The major problem these programs encounter is community opposition to their location in residential areas. This opposition is less pronounced in programs for children than for adults, and less pronounced for the aged than for the mentally ill or criminal offenders.

In his study of community-based treatment centers, Davidson (1982) found that neighborhoods with resources for adults were low-resistance neighborhoods, since centers were mainly located in "transitional" and deteriorating neighborhood areas in the central city. The major limitations of such locations is the existence of crime and other social problems, which restricts free movement within the community. Potential positive social networks are often limited in these areas. Residents in neighborhoods that are free of these limitations are usually opposed to community-based treatment centers, and negative attitudes of residents are likely to limit reintegration.

Another obstacle to reintegration may be the failure of social practitioners to recognize the most relevant part of the community for the client (Kirk and Thirren, 1975). For example, an ethnic minority person may be located in living facilities at some distance from individuals of the person's own cultural group, thereby limiting opportunities for reintegration and social interaction. In such cases the client/patient is returned to the community but is not within a relevant local community area, such as an ethnic neighborhood. Another example is elderly persons who are in nursing homes in the community but isolated by rules and restrictions from social interactions with neighbors, family, and friends.

SOCIAL INTEGRATION AMONG THE HOMELESS

One of the major social characteristics associated with homeless persons is their lack of social integration and attachment to the community. They are pictured as lacking in normative integration in that their lifestyles are inconsistent with the standards and expectations of mainstream society. Communicative and functional integration are viewed as minimal among the homeless in that these persons are characterized as disaffiliated, uprooted, socially isolated, and lacking in social networks and social supports. In fact, homelessness has been defined as "both the lack of adequate and permanent shelter and the absence of community and social ties" (ADAMHA, 1983).

Sociological and anthropological studies present a picture of three major levels of social integration among homeless persons. The majority of homeless persons are disaffiliated from family, relatives, friends, and the community, with a weak system of social supports (Leshner, 1992). This condition is especially prevalent among the homeless mentally ill (Segal and Baumohl, 1980; Lamb, 1984; Rossi, 1989). A second level of integration is found among some homeless people, especially women, who have limited social integration through social contacts and supports from their social networks in the community (Koegel, 1987). A third level of social integration is derived from membership of some homeless persons in subcultures of homelessness. These subcultures include skid row culture, street culture, and shelter culture.

An exemplar of skid-row culture is the Bowery in New York City. Integration into this culture is described by Giamo (1989), who found homeless Bowery men to belong to an ordered community, with an identity, structure, and affiliative network of supports. Thus, he indicates that as Bowery men find food, shelter, and alcohol in this place, they become "enculturated into their subculture . . . integrated within their community and have daily attachments to bars, restaurants, flops, liquor stores, social agencies, missions, used clothing stores, and bottlegang groups."

Many homeless people live in public places, while others are sheltered on a temporary basis and spend most of the daylight hours on the streets and in drop-in centers. These individuals handle day-to-day living in ways which can be termed a "street culture," that is "a loose sense of cohesiveness and an irregular but often effective communication network" (Sosin et al., 1988). This group of homeless people usually has a strong resistance to institutional living arrangements and to health and welfare services. Whether they have regular contacts with other street people, pedestrians, and merchants or are "loners" who shy away from social relationships, over time they develop a minimal level of social integration through their street culture.

With the increased use of homeless shelters into the 1990s, a form of social integration has developed through "shelterization" (Grunberg and Eagle, 1990; Gounis and Susser, 1990). Some shelter residents begin to "attach and adapt" to shelter life in order to survive, with an increase in dependency on the providers. While these homeless persons may come into a shelter with a high degree of disaffiliation, they soon affiliate with shelter residents, incorporate the lifestyle of the shelter, and become more isolated from the outside world. Residents become concerned about how to improve life within the shelter, rather than a concern with using the shelter as a bridge to permanent housing.

Social welfare agencies and other community groups concerned with housing of the homeless encounter strong resistance within the community with regard to the location of emergency shelters, to transitional housing, and to the development of permanent low-cost affordable housing. Resistance is particularly strong when homeless persons have been involved with the mental health system or the criminal justice system. As a consequence, integration and reintegration of homeless persons into the local community is a complex task, one that requires cooperation of organizations within the various subsystems of a community. Multidimensional networking on the part of service providers to homeless people, along with new models of intensive case management, represent examples of innovative approaches to overcoming the lack of community integration (Hutchinson et al., 1986; Leshner, 1992).

REVIEW

Social integration of local communities and their residents is a sign of a competent community. Integration of individuals is facilitated by their social networks through involvements with family members, kin, friends, neighbors, coworkers, and social groups. People in the social networks of individuals come from a variety of local communities, such as neighborhoods, community areas, and municipalities, as well as from communities of interest. An important community of interest is religious affiliation, through which social integration is generated by way of religious services, volunteer activities in social welfare, and educational programs.

It is clear that social integration usually comes from involvements and ties to "multiple communities" of place and interest, and that for many residents the importance of some of these communities has diminished due to the emergence of a "mass society." Thus, for many people the neighborhood no longer plays as strong an integrative role as in the past. At the same time, other communities, such as school systems and religious groups, continue to serve as avenues for social integration. Less obvious sources of social integration have been identified, including drinking and eating establishments and sports participation and spectatorship.

The integration and reintegration of special populations in American communities is of particular concern to human service professionals. Mentally ill persons and homeless persons stand out among these populations, especially due to the negative attitudes toward these individuals on the part of neighborhood and local community residents. Human service professionals in health and social welfare service areas, as well as in housing and income maintenance programs, have countered with renewed efforts to serve these special client groups.

SUGGESTED READINGS

Fellin, Phillip (1993). "Reformulation of the Context of Community Based Care." *Journal of Sociology and Social Welfare* 20:2.

Grunberg, J. and P. F. Eagle (1990). "Shelterization: How the Homeless Adapt to Shelter Living." *Hospital and Community Psychiatry* 41:5.

Leshner, A. I. (1992). *Outcasts on Main Street*. Washington: Interagency Council on the Homeless (ADM) 92-1904.

Taylor, Robert J. and Linda M. Chatters (1988). "Church Members as a Source of Informal Social Support." *Review of Religious Research* 30:2.

CHAPTER 14

The Community and Social Work Practice

In this final chapter we provide illustrations of how knowledge about communities in American society can inform social work practice. Major themes of the book are used as a framework for guiding the reader in the reexamination of the news reports and suggested readings used as exercises in previous chapters. Special attention is given to the macro level of practice and its focus with the development of strategies for social planning, community development, and social action.

DEFINING COMMUNITIES AND COMMUNALITY COMPETENCE

Communities have traditionally been viewed as locality-based, geographic entities which serve residents as a source of sustenance, social interaction, and collective identity. A definitional issue related to social work practice concerns the need for expansion of the meaning of the concept of community. Thus, we introduce the idea of multiple communities, which includes not only the several geographic areas clients may belong to (neighborhoods, community areas, municipalities, metropolitan areas), but also "non-place" communities of identification and interest. This leads to the concept of a personal community, which includes all of the interactions and identifications a person has with individuals, informal groups, and formal organizations through membership in multiple communities.

The concept of a personal community serves as a context for the development of clinical treatment and social service goals in the interpersonal practice of social work. From this perspective, to be effective the social worker must ascertain the nature of the client's membership in multiple communities. For the practice of social work at community and/or administrative levels, recognition of these multiple communities provides a more comprehensive focus for community organizing, community planning, and social policy development. Thus reformulations of the concept of community are related to both micro and macro social work practice, since practice at both these levels seeks to mobilize informal and formal resources on behalf of individuals, families, and other groups in need of service.

The extent to which communities function well for the benefit of their membership is captured by the concept of community competence. Community social workers in particular involve themselves in identifying the problems, needs, and interests of communities, in working to enhance the process of competence, and in creating conditions which lead to a positive social environment. One of these conditions which has particular relevance for ethnic minorities, women, and other populations at risk, is empowerment, defined as the capacity to use existing resources and to create opportunities for self and group fulfillment.

Reread the news report at the close of Chapter 1 entitled, "Detroit Ghetto Area Tries Self-Reliance, and Learns Its Limits" (Bussey, 1989), in order to once again examine the concepts of community and community competence. After identifying the boundaries of the community, identify ways in which the residents have joined together to improve the social and physical environment of their neighborhood. Explore possible roles for social workers in this community, such as direct practice with individuals and families in this poverty area, as well as group leadership roles in the block clubs and church related associations.

You may also wish to examine implications for social work practice by reading the following news reports: "A South Bronx Street Rises Through the Toil of Poor Homesteaders" (Graham and Boyce, 1989, Chapter 5); "Cleveland Suburbs Work to Achieve a Racial Balance" (Pepper, 1990, Chapter 6); "District Finds Way to End Segregation and Restore Neighborhood Schools" (Celis, 1991, Chapter 9). In reading these reports again, give attention to how social workers might meet their professional responsibilities to society, as identified in the social work profession's Code of Ethics. This Code calls upon social workers to assist in reducing the barriers to community competence, to improve social conditions, and to promote social justice, especially for special population groups historically subjected to oppression and discrimination.

SYSTEMS PERSPECTIVES FOR UNDERSTANDING COMMUNITIES

A principal issue related to the understanding of communities centers around the lack of fully developed theoretical perspectives of community structure and function. While the nature of communities does not allow for a perfect match to ecological and social systems theories, these perspectives provide a useful set of concepts to guide social work practice. Of special relevance to social workers is the focus of the ecological perspective on the spatial organization of the community—that is, the characteristics, distribution, and interdependence of the population and services in a locality-based community. This perspective can be used to explore the demographic development and social stratification of communities, with special attention to social class, race and ethnicity, migration and immigration.

Reread the news report in Chapter 4, "Influx of Asians Brings Prosperity to Flushing, a Place for Newcomers" (Wysocki, 1991), which describes how a New York community has absorbed new immigrants and has been transformed physically, culturally, and economically. Note the ways in which cultural clashes occur within the community. Assess this community in terms of possible roles social workers may play in helping to resolve community conflicts. Examine how descriptive demographic data on residents in local communities such as Flushing, New York, can provide a foundation for the assessment of the social welfare services and resources needed within a community, and for policymaking and planning activities directed to the acquisition and allocation of these resources.

The demographic changes which have occurred in the inner-city neighborhood areas of major metropolitan areas have special significance for social work practice. Residents in these areas are viewed as needing a wide range of health and social welfare services, many of which are provided through social programs staffed by social workers. Read articles by Wilson (1989) on "The Underclass: Issues, Perspectives, and Public Policy" and Coulton, Pandey, and Chow (1990), "Concentration of Poverty and the Changing Ecology of Low-Income, Urban Neighborhoods" as a foundation for considering the practice roles of social workers vis-a-vis residents of urban inner-city communities. Focus on the needs of the residents in these communities who are dislocated from mainstream society and trapped in an underclass ghetto environment. Consider ways in which social workers can intervene in order to enhance the empowerment of these inner-city residents. Examine practice models which include attention to culturally sensitive interventions with ethnic minorities in these neighborhood communities.

The ecological perspective of communities guides the social worker in the consideration of various dimensions of neighborhoods in American society, especially those identified with specific social classes and ethnic, racial, and cultural groups. Neighborhood communities may enhance or detract from community and interpersonal competence. Read the news report in Chapter 5, "A South Bronx Street Rises Through the Toil of Poor Homesteaders" (Graham and Boyce, 1989), which shows how community associations can promote citizen participation, neighborhood stability, and rejuvenation. Consider possible roles for social workers in relation to these associations and residents in changing the social conditions of the neighborhood, particularly drug traffic, school problems, lack of safety, and the lack of social services.

Several models for evaluating the nature of neighborhoods are provided in Chapter 5, with the implications of these models for social work practice identified through reference to the social work literature. Our discussion of the emergence of social class and ethnic minority neighborhoods highlights the application of the ecological concepts of residential segregation and integration in relation to social work practice in a multicultural society. A number of communities have developed strategies for creating and/or maintaining racial diversity. Read the news report in Chapter 6, "Cleveland Suburbs Work to Achieve a Racial Balance" (Pepper, 1990) in order to examine the potential for social work practice in the creation of community goals and the development of intervention strategies for suburban communities.

SOCIAL SYSTEMS PERSPECTIVES

The social systems perspective contributes to our understanding of the competence of a community by focusing on the extent to which the various subsystems of a community meet the functional needs of residents. This view of a locality based community is particularly salient to social work practice, as one of the major community subsystems is social welfare and health care. However, social workers also play significant roles in the political, economic, and educational community subsystems. A major issue of social work practice is how well the social welfare and health care systems operate in a given geographic community and the extent to which their interdependencies with other subsystems result in a competent community. Read the work of Norton Long (1958) in order to examine how social workers might use a "community as games" framework to examine professional leadership roles in local community subsystems. Use this perspective to examine the health and welfare "game" in relation to other "games" being played in your local community, and consider how this approach gives direction to strategies for community change.

Our examination of the local community from a social systems perspective discusses the nature and role of voluntary associations in American society. Voluntary associations occupy a prominent place in helping networks, in providing links for residents to the larger community, in serving people in need of social supports through self-help groups, and as a mechanism for empowerment. Of special concern to social workers is the relationship of self-help and mutual aid voluntary associations to the formal structure of social welfare service delivery. Practice examples of this concern are provided in the suggested readings listed at the close of Chapter 7, particularly Wolf (1985), "Professionalizing Volunteer Work in a Black Neighborhood"; Gutierrez, Ortega, and Suarez (1990), "Self-Help and the Latino Community"; and Neighbors, Elliott, and Gant (1990), "Self-Help and Black Americans: A Strategy for Empowerment." Relate these readings to the leadership roles of social workers with voluntary associations discussed in "Educating Leadership for Effecting Community Change Through Voluntary Associations" (Theilen and Poole, 1986). You may also explore these practice roles through reading of the news report presented in Chapter 7, "Volunteers' Distress Cripples Huge Effort to Provide AIDS Care" (Chase, 1990).

COMMUNITY SOCIAL WELFARE AND HEALTH CARE SYSTEMS

Mutual support is provided within a community by formal human service organizations and by a variety of other social support systems, such as family, kin, neighbors, friends, and voluntary associations. Mutual support functions are shared by public and private formal organizations and by informal, lay helping systems. An important question concerning these shared functions involves the location of responsibility for care of people who cannot care for themselves. The public sectors of social welfare and health care have been delegated some responsibilities through local, state, and federal government legislation, policies, and practices.

Social workers who practice at community, administrative, and policy levels, can apply their knowledge of communities to the generation of a wide range of resources, from volunteers to fiscal resources. In our examination of the various fields of social welfare services, we noted that the delivery of services is influenced by the functioning of social workers in both direct service and planning agencies. Consider the kinds of knowledge needed for social workers to successfully engage in inter-organizational relations, through activities within communities, and through the extra-community political and economic environment. Read again the news report in Chapter 8, "Struggle over Hospital in Los Angeles Pits Minority vs. Minority" (Boyce, 1991). Examine how social workers can enhance the competent functioning of the social welfare and health care systems by advocating for community supports, qualified personnel, and development of institutional responses to the needs of local residents. As social workers participate in these systems, consider how they can advocate for special populations at risk, such as families and children in poverty, homeless people, and the mentally and physically disabled.

COMMUNITY EDUCATION SYSTEM

One of the principal indicators of a competent community is the functioning of the local educational system. Using Long's (1958) view of the community as an ecology of games, there are a number of ways in which residents can "keep score" of how well the community educational system is functioning. Important indicators include test scores, dropout rates, graduation rates, student per capita funding, and quality of teachers. An important issue with regard to community educational systems concerns the discrepancies between communities in terms of funding and student performance, especially in relation to the quality of education provided in inner-city schools as compared to those in suburban communities. In order to examine the relationship between residential patterns and education, read the news report in Chapter 9, "District Finds Way to End Segregation and Restore Neighborhood (Celis, 1991). Consider what roles social workers might play in relation to desegregation efforts and their impact on school systems.

It is clear that the lack of educational opportunities contributes to the social problems of people of color. For a discussion of possible roles of social workers in the educational system to overcome this lack, read the articles by Williams (1990) and Allen-Meares (1990) cited in Chapter 9. For example, Williams (1990) explores the nature of discrimination in education and suggests that the social work profession has not made a significant contribution to the education of minorities. He challenges individuals who practice social work in schools to become more involved in "client advocacy, political and organizational change, and community development and involvement."

THE COMMUNITY ECONOMIC SYSTEM

The practice of social work is connected to the economic system in a variety of ways. As we discussed in Chapter 10, social welfare programs are a part of the economic system, providing income and other benefits to eligible community residents. These programs provide economic benefits for families and children and for people who are retired, unemployed, and/or disabled. Social workers play important roles in the delivery of these welfare and health care services. Increasingly, social workers are employed in workplaces, are involved in employee assistance programs, and have practiced roles related to emerging programs under the Americans with Disabilities Act of 1990. Social workers in community direct-service agencies work with clients who have problems related to the economic system, such as equal employment, unemployment, need for job training, sexual harassment, and entitlements related to disabilities. A basic understanding of the community economic system is especially necessary for social workers who are active in community organizing, services planning, and resource development in economically disadvantaged neighborhood communities. Read the news report, "Inner-City Capitalists Push to Start a Bank for Their Community" (Bacon, 1993), and explore the question, what roles might social workers play in working with leaders in "transitional" inner-city neighborhoods in order to promote empowerment through community development institutions?

THE COMMUNITY POLITICAL SYSTEM

In most communities the representation of social workers in political positions, such as official officeholders and city or county council members, is minimal. However, social workers develop contacts with elected officials in order to influence the political community in providing resources for meeting social welfare and health care needs. Social workers in elected and appointed positions within the political structure, as well as social welfare agency executives, are in strategic positions for seeking support for social welfare programs from other community leaders. Our discussion of the community political system in Chapter 10 alerts the social worker to important sources of support for social welfare programs, including political and economic system leaders, as well as leaders in grass roots organizations and voluntary associations, particularly neighborhood, ethnic, and religious organizations.

Our view of community power from an organizational perspective is relevant to the practice of social work at community and organizational levels. While individual social welfare organizations may be limited in community influence, membership of such agencies in community decision organizations such as United Way, agency coalitions, and national organization affiliations, increases the opportunities for gaining support within the political system. Influence on the part of clients of the social welfare system is gained through empowerment, a process which can be facilitated by social workers, especially in their work with populations at risk.

COMMUNITY CONFLICT AND COMMUNITY INTEGRATION

Several examples of community conflict discussed in Chapter 12—for example, controversies over community-based treatment centers, homeless shelters, and group homes for mentally and physically disabled persons—are relevant to the practice of social work. An example of such a controversy is presented in Chapter 12, "House Divides Grand Rapids Neighbors" (George, 1992). The implications for social work practice of these controversies can be discussed in terms of the social integration needs of consumers of social welfare, health, and mental health services. To this point, read the article, "Reformulation of the Context of Community Based Care" (Fellin, 1993), which focuses on planning for community based care for mentally ill persons. This discussion explores various levels of social integration and their relationship to social work intervention at the community level.

For a synthesis of knowledge about social integration and social conflict related to social work practice, read the article, "An Approach to Teaching about Diversity in American Communities" (Fellin, 1992). This discussion focuses on community competence and empowerment, community social integration/segregation, community conflict, and socio-demographic structure of communities. These topics provide a framework for understanding social work roles related to communities of identification/interest, especially communities displaying ethnic, racial, cultural, and social diversity.

REVISITING COMPETENT COMMUNITIES

Community competence may be viewed in terms of the community acting as a whole system and through its subsystems on behalf of its members. Another dimension of competence involves the activities of individuals and groups in relating to and using the resources of the community for their own betterment. Social workers can contribute to both these dimensions of competence by participating in the activities which make for improved functioning of communities as systems and their component subsystems, as well as by helping individuals and groups gain access to and utilize community resources. A major role for social workers is to be involved in reducing and eliminating barriers to community competence. In order to gain further knowledge and skill in community assessment, social workers may wish to reread Chapters 1 and 2 as a foundation for applying social work practice strategies, tasks, and experiences to the communities they serve in their professional practice.

REFERENCES

Aiken, M., and Alford, R. (1970). Community structure and innovation: The case of urban renewal. *American Sociological Review* 35:4.

Alcohol, Drug Abuse, and Mental Health Administration (1983). *Problems of the homeless.* Proceedings of a roundtable. Rockville, MD.

Aldrich, H. (1975). Ecological succession: A review of the literature. *Urban Affairs* 10:1.

Aldrich, H., and Reiss, A. J. (1976). Continuities in the study of ecological succession: Changes in the race composition of neighborhoods and their business. *American Journal of Sociology* 81:4.

Allen-Meares, P. (1990). Educating Black youths: The unfulfilled promise of equality. *Social Work* 35:3.

Allen-Meares, P., Washington, R. O., and Welsh, B. L. (1986). *Social work services in schools.* Englewood Cliffs, NJ: Prentice-Hall.

Americans with Disabilities Act of 1990 (P.L. 101-336).

Anderson, J. (1981). That was New York: Harlem. *New Yorker*, 6/29, 7/6, 7/13, 7/20.

Anderson, E. (1990). *Streetwise: Race, class, and change in an urban community.* Chicago: University of Chicago Press.

Anderson, R. E., and Carter, I. (1978). *Human behavior in the social environment*, 2nd ed. New York: Aldine.

Auerbach, J. (1985). The Poletown dilemma. *Harvard Business Review* 63:3.

Auletta, K. (1981). A reporter at large: The underclass. *New Yorker*, 11/16, 11/23, 11/30.

Bacon, K. H. (1993). Clinton is to unveil two-part program to boost lending in poor communities. *Wall Street Journal*, 5/19.

Bacon, K. H. (1993). Inner-city capitalists push to start a bank for their community. *Wall Street Journal*, 1/19.

Bane, M. J., and Ellwood, D. T. (1991). Is American business working for the poor? *Harvard Business Review* 69:5.

Bane, M. J., and Ellwood, D. T. (1983). *Slipping into and out of poverty: The dynamics of spells.* Cambridge, MA: National Bureau of Economic Research Working Paper #1199.

Barbarin, O., Good, P. R., Pharr, O. M., and Siskind, J. A., eds. (1981). *Institutional racism and community competence*. U.S. Department of Health and Human Services, publication number (ADM) 81-907. Washington, DC: U.S. Government Printing Office.

Barker, R. (1987). Private and proprietary services. In A. Minahan, ed., *Encyclopedia of Social Work*, 18th ed. Silver Spring, MD: NASW Press.

Barrett, P. M. (1992). Justices ease rules on school desegregation. *Wall Street Journal*, 4/1.

Barrett, P. M. (1993). Court's ruling on help for deaf student cheers backers of parochial-school aid. *Wall Street Journal*, 6/21.

Barrett, P. M. (1993). School policy on religion is struck down. *Wall Street Journal*, 6/8.

Barringer, F. (1991). Census shows profound change in racial makeup of the nation. *New York Times*, 3/11.

Barringer, F. (1991). Immigration brings new diversity to Asian population in the U.S. *New York Times*, 6/12.

Barringer, F. (1993). Ethnic pride confounds the census. *New York Times*, 5/9.

Barringer, F. (1993). Population grows in rural America, studies say. *New York Times*, 5/25.

Barron, J. (1990). Society on high. *Detroit Monthly* 13:10.

Bell, W., and Robinson, R. V. (1980). Cognitive maps of class and racial inequalities in England and the U.S. *American Journal of Sociology* 86:2.

Bellah, R. N., Madsen, R., Sullivan, W. M., Swidler, A., and Tipton, S. M. (1985). *Habits of the heart*. Berkeley: University of California Press.

Berger, J. (1993). For many Hispanic immigrants, a search for opportunities skirts the cities. *New York Times*, 7/28.

Bernal, M. E. (1990). Ethnic minority mental health training trends and issues. In F. C. Serafica et al., eds., *Mental health and ethnic minorities*. New York: Praeger.

Birnbaum, J. H. (1993). Clinton unveils anti-crime bill calling for tighter gun controls, more police. *Wall Street Journal*, 8/12.

Bleakley, F. R. (1992). How groups pressured one bank to promise more inner-city loans. *Wall Street Journal*, 9/22.

Boles, J. K. (1991). American feminism; new issues for a mature movement. *Annals* 515, Sage Publications.

Bonjean, C., and Olson, D. (1966). Community leadership. In R. Warren, ed., *New Perspectives on the American community*. Chicago: Rand McNally.

Boston, T. D. (1988). *Race, class and conservatism*. Boston: Unwin Hyman.

Boyce, J. N. (1991). Struggle over hospital in Los Angeles pits minority vs. minority. *Wall Street Journal*, 4/1.

Boyce, J. N. (1990). More Blacks embrace self-help programs to fight urban ills. *Wall Street Journal*, 2/26.

Breindel, E. (1993). Autopsy of a riot. *Wall Street Journal*, 7/22.

Brieland, D., Costin, L. B., and Atherton, C. R. (1985). *Contemporary social work*. New York: McGraw Hill.

Brooks, A. (1983). Among volunteers, change in the suburbs. *New York Times*, 10/28.

Bussey, J. (1989). Detroit ghetto area tries self-reliance, and learns its limits. *Wall Street Journal*, 4/7.

Cannon, A. (1990). A new town within a city for Detroiters. *Detroit News*, 9/30.

Celis, W., 3rd (1993). Uneven progress in decade of school reform. *New York Times*, 4/28.

Celis, W., 3rd (1991). District finds way to end segregation and restore neighborhood. *New York Times*, 9/4.

Celis, W., 3rd (1993). The fight over national standards. *New York Times*, 8/1.

Chafets, Ze'ev (1990). *Devil's Night and other true tales of Detroit*. New York: Random House.

Chase, M. (1990). Volunteers' distress cripples huge effort to provide AIDS care. *Wall Street Journal*, 3/12.

Chess, W. A., and Norlin, J. M. (1988). *Human behavior and the social environment*. Boston: Allyn and Bacon.

Chira, S. (1990). Preschool aid for the poor: How big a Head Start? *New York Times*, 2/14.

Chira, S. (1993). Clinton to offer plan for change in U.S. schools. *New York Times*, 4/21.

Chira, S. (1991). The rules of the marketplace are applied to the classroom. *New York Times*, 6/12.

Chira, S. (1993). Schools open soon (with luck), to more trouble than usual. *New York Times*, 9/5.

Choldin, H. (1978). Retrospective review essay: Neighborhood life and urban environment. *American Journal of Sociology* 84:2.

Choldin, H., Hanson, C., and Bobrer, R. (1980). Suburban status instability. *American Sociological Review* 45:6.

Choldin, H. M. (1985). *Cities and suburbs*. New York: McGraw-Hill.

Chubb, J. E., and Moe, T. M. (1990). *Politics, markets, and America's schools*. Washington, DC: The Brookings Institution.

Clark, K. (1965). *Dark ghetto*. New York: Harper & Row.

Clark, T. N. (1973). *Community power and policy outputs: A review of urban research*. Beverly Hills: Sage Publications.

Coleman, J. (1957). *Community conflict*. New York: Free Press.

Coleman, J. (1983). The dynamics of community conflict. In R. Warren, and L. Lyon, eds., *New perspectives on the American community*. Homewood, IL: The Dorsey Press.

Coleman, J. S., and Hoffer, T. (1987). *Public and private high schools*. New York: Basic Books.

Coleman, J. S., Hoffer, T., and Kilgore, S. (1992). *High school achievement*. New York: Basic Books.

Constable, R. T., and Flynn, J. P. (1982). *School social work*. Homewood, IL: Dorsey Press.

Coser, L. (1956). *The functions of social conflict*. Glencoe, IL: Free Press.

Coser, L. (1970). *Continuities in the study of social conflict*. Glencoe, IL: Free Press.

Cottingham, C., ed. (1982). *Race, poverty and the urban underclass*. Lexington: Lexington Books.

Cottrell, L. S. Jr. (1983). The competent community. In R. Warren, and L. Lyon, eds., *New perspectives on the American community*. Homewood, IL: The Dorsey Press.

Coulton, C., Pandey, S., and Chow, J. (1990). Concentration of poverty and the changing ecology of low-income, urban neighborhoods: An analysis of the Cleveland area. *Social Work Research and Abstracts* 26:4.

Council on Social Work Education. (1988, 1992). *Curriculum Policy Statement*. Alexandria, VA: Council on Social Work Education.

Cox, F. M. (1987). Communities: Alternative conceptions of community. In F. M. Cox, J. L. Erlich, J. Rothman, and J. E. Tropman, eds., *Strategies of Community Organization*, 4th ed. Itasca, IL: F. E. Peacock Publishers.

Cox, F. M., Erlich, J. L., Rothman, J., and Tropman, J. E. (1987). *Strategies of community organization*. Itasca, IL: F. E. Peacock Publishers.

Darden, J. T. (1987). Choosing neighbors and neighborhoods: The role of race in housing preference. In G. A. Tobin, ed., Divided neighborhoods: Changing patterns of racial segregation. *Urban Affairs Annual Reviews* 32.

Data Research. (1988). *Deskbook encyclopedia of American school law.* Rosemount, MN: Data Research Inc.

Davidson, J. (1981). Location of community based treatment centers. *Social Service Review* 55:2.

Davidson, J. (1982). Balancing required resources and neighborhood opposition in community based treatment center neighborhoods. *Social Service Review* 56:1.

Davidson, J. (1987). Melting pot boils as influx of Asian merchants into Black neighborhoods is greeted grimly. *Wall Street Journal,* 7/31.

de Rothschild, G. (1985). *The whims of fortune.* New York: Random House.

de Tocqueville, A. (1947). *Democracy in America.* New York: Oxford University Press.

Delgado, M., and Humm-Delgado, D. (1982). Natural support systems: Sources of strength in Hispanic communities. *Social Work* 27:1.

DeParle, J. (1993). Housing secretary carves out role as a lonely clarion against racism. *New York Times,* 7/8.

Devine, J. A., and Wright, J. D. (1993). *The greatest of evils: Urban poverty and the American underclass.* New York: Aldine De Gruyter.

Dillman, D. A., and Tremblay, K. (1977) The quality of life in rural America. *The American Academy of Political and Social Science* 429:19.

Dixon, J. (1993). Health secretary to review Head Start. *Associated Press,* 5/7.

Dozier, M. (1993). Fund to boost Oakland integration. *Detroit Free Press,* 4/23.

Durkheim, E. (1932). *De la division du travail social.* Paris.

Eastland, T. (1992). Weed and seed: Root out crime, nurture poor. *Wall Street Journal,* 5/14.

Elliott, S. (1993). Advertising. *New York Times,* 6/1.

Epstein, A. (1993). High court allows church groups to hold meetings in public schools. *Detroit Free Press,* 6/8.

Equal Employment Opportunity Commission. Guidelines on Discrimination because of Sex, Title VII, Sec. 703. *Federal Register,* 45, 4/11/1980.

Etzioni, A. (1992). Do fence me in. *Wall Street Journal,* 12/1.

Farhi, P. (1990). Living on the edge in Mount Pleasant. *Washington Post,* 10/7.

Farley, J. E. (1987). Segregation in 1980: How segregated are America's metropolitan areas? In G. A. Tobin, ed., Divided neighborhoods: Changing patterns of racial segregation. *Urban Affairs Annual Reviews* 32.

Farley, R. et al. (1994). The causes of continued racial residential segregation: Chocolate city, vanilla suburbs revisited. *Journal of Housing Research* 4:1.

Farley, R., and Frey, W. H. (1994). Changes in the segregation of whites from blacks during the 1980's: Small steps toward a more integrated society. *American Sociological Review* 59:1.

Farley, R., Bianchi, S., and Colasanto, D. (1979). Barriers to the racial integration of neighborhoods: The Detroit case. *The American Academy of Political and Social Science* 441.

Farney, D. (1992). Can big money fix urban school systems? A test is under way. *Wall Street Journal,* 1/7.

Fears, D. (1989). Neighborhood group turns 15, flexes muscles. *Detroit Free Press,* 11/5.

Fellin, P. (1992). An approach to teaching about diversity in American communities. *Journal of Teaching in Social Work* 6:1.

Fellin, P. (1993). Reformulation of the context of community based care. *Journal of Sociology and Social Welfare* 20:2.

Fellin, P., and Litwak, E. (1963). Neighborhood cohesion under conditions of mobilization. *American Sociological Review* 28:3.

Fellin, P., and Litwak, E. (1968). The neighborhood in urban American society. *Social Work* 13:3.

Felsenthal, E. (1990). New Jersey's public school financing is struck down by state's highest court. *Wall Street Journal*, 6/6.

Ferguson, R., and Carlson, E. (1990). Distant communities promise good homes but produce malaise. *Wall Street Journal*, 10/25.

Ferguson, T. W. (1992). California feels anti-immigrant tremors. *Wall Street Journal*, 12/29.

Figueira-McDonough, J. (1991). Community structure and delinquency: A typology. *Social Service Review* 65:1.

Finch, W. A. (1990). The immigration reform and control act of 1986: A preliminary assessment. *Social Service Review* 64:2.

Finn, C. E. (1990). The radicalization of school reform. *Wall Street Journal*, 2/2.

Finn, C. E. (1992). Fear of standards threatens education reform. *Wall Street Journal*, 3/23.

Finnegan, W. (1990). A reporter at large: Out there. *New Yorker*, 9/10.

Fischer, C. (1978). Urban to rural diffusion of opinions in contemporary America. *American Journal of Sociology* 84:1.

Fischer, C. (1981). The public and private worlds of city life. *American Sociological Review* 46:3.

Fischer, C. (1984). *The urban experience.* New York: Harcourt Brace Jovanovich.

Fliegel, S. (1992). Public school choice works . . . look at East Harlem. *Wall Street Journal*, 10/29.

Freeman, D. (1991). A different wave of immigrants. *Wall Street Journal*, 9/9.

Freudenheim, M. (1991). New law to bring wider job rights for mentally ill. *New York Times*, 9/23.

Frey, W. H. (1993). Newhouse study. *Newhouse News Service*, 8/23.

Fusfeld, D. R. (1973). *The basic economics of the urban racial crisis.* New York: Holt, Rinehart and Winston.

Fusfield, D., and Bates, T. (1984). *The political economy of the urban ghetto.* Carbondale, IL: Southern Illinois University Press.

Gamson, W. (1966). Rancorous conflict in community politics. *American Sociological Review* 31:1.

Gann, J. L., Jr. (1993). Main Street vs. Wal-Mart. *Wall Street Journal*, 8/30.

Garcia, P. (1985). Immigration issues in urban ecology: The case of Los Angeles. In L. Maldonado, and J. Moore, eds., Urban ethnicity in the United States. *Urban Affairs Annual Reviews* 29.

Garreau, J. (1991). *Edge city.* New York: Doubleday.

Gartner, A. (1985). A typology of women's self-help groups. *Social Policy*, Winter, 25-30.

Garvin, C. D., and Tropman, J. E. (1992). *Social work in contemporary society.* Englewood Cliffs, NJ: Prentice-Hall.

Gates, H. L. Jr. (1993). Black intellectuals, Jewish tensions. *New York Times*, 4/14.

Gaventa, J. (1980). *Power and powerlessness.* Chicago: University of Illinois Press.

George, M. (1992). House divides Grand Rapids neighborhood. *Detroit Free Press*, 12/3.

Germain, C. (1979). *Social work practice: People and environments.* New York: Columbia University Press.

Germain, C. B. (1989). *Human behavior in the social environment.* New York: Columbia University Press.

Giamatti, A. (1989). *Take time for paradise: Americans and their games.* New York: Simon and Schuster.

Giamo, B. (1989). *On the bowery: Confronting homelessness in American society.* Iowa City: University of Iowa Press.

Giese, J. (1990). A communal type of life with dinner for all and day care, too. *New York Times,* 9/27.

Gilbert, D. (1993). Not in my backyard. *Social Work* 38:1.

Gilbert, N., Specht, H., and Brown, C. (1974). Demographic correlates of citizen participation: An analysis of race, community size, and citizen influence. *Social Service Review* 48:4.

Glasgow, D. (1981). *Black underclass.* New York: Vintage Books.

Glazer, N. (1983). *Ethnic dilemmas.* Cambridge: Harvard University Press.

Goldberg, R. (1993). Portraits of urban violence. *Wall Street Journal,* 4/26.

Goldsmith, B. (1993). Women on the edge. *New Yorker,* 4/26.

Gonzalez, D. (1992). Dominican immigration alters Hispanic New York. *New York Times,* 9/1.

Gounis, K., and Susser, E. (1990). Shelterization and its implications for mental health services. In N. Cohen, ed., *Psychiatry takes to the streets.* New York: Guilford Press.

Graham, E., and Boyce, J. N. (1989). A South Bronx street rises through the toil of poor homesteaders. *Wall Street Journal,* 8/22.

Granovetter, M. (1973). The strength of weak ties. *American Journal of Sociology* 78:5.

Green, J. W. (1982). *Cultural awareness in the human services.* Englewood Cliffs, NJ: Prentice-Hall.

Green, W. E., and Marcus, A. D. (1989). Texas school funding is unconstitutional. *Wall Street Journal,* 10/3.

Greenblatt, M., Becerra, R. M., and Serafetinides, E. A. (1983). Social networks, adaptability to stress, and recovery from psychiatric illness. *Directions in psychiatry.* New York: Hatherleigh Company.

Grunberg, J., and Eagle, P. F. (1990). Shelterization: How the homeless adapt to shelter living. *Hospital and Community Psychiatry* 41:5.

Grzywinski, R. (1991). The new old-fashioned banking. *Harvard Business Review* 69:3.

Gulati, P. (1982). Consumer participation in administrative decision making. *Social Service Review* 56:1.

Gutierrez, L. (1990). Working with women of color: An empowerment perspective. *Social Work* 35:2.

Gutierrez, L. (1992). Macro practice for the 21st Century: An empowerment perspective. Ann Arbor, MI: The University of Michigan School of Social Work.

Gutierrez, L., Ortega, R. M., and Suarez, Z. E. (1990). Self-help and the Latino Community. In T. Powell, ed., *Working with self-help.* Silver Spring, MD: NASW Press.

Hagerty, B. (1993). Trainers help expatriate employees build bridges to different cultures. *Wall Street Journal,* 6/14.

Harrison, R. J., and Weinberg, D. H. (1992). *Racial and ethnic segregation in 1990.* Washington, DC: U.S. Bureau of the Census, April.

Hasenfeld, Y. (1983). *Human service organizations.* Englewood Cliffs, NJ: Prentice-Hall.

Hasenfeld, Y., and Gidron, B. (1993). Self-help groups and human service organizations: An interorganizational perspective. *Social Service Review* 67:2.

Hawley, A. (1950). *Human ecology: A theory of community structure.* New York: Roland Press.

Hawley, A. (1986). *Urban ecology.* Chicago: University of Chicago Press.

Hawley, A. (1978). Urbanization as process. In D. Street, ed., *Handbook on contemporary urban life.* San Francisco: Jossey Bass.

Hayden, D. (1980). What would a nonsexist city be like? *Signs: Journal of Women in Culture and Society* 5:3 Supplement.

Hayes, A. S. (1990). Is town's housing plan the key to integration or a form of racism? *Wall Street Journal*, 10/4.

Hayes, A. S. (1990). Judge clears way for students to conduct graduation prayer. *Wall Street Journal*, 5/24.

Hechinger, F. M. (1989). About education. *New York Times,* 5/24.

Hernandez, J. (1985). Improving the data: A research strategy for new immigrants. In L. Maldonado, and J. Moore, eds., Urban ethnicity in the United States. *Urban Affairs Annual Reviews* 29.

Hetter, K. (1993). States move to allow prayer in schools. *Wall Street Journal*, 8/18.

Hicks, D. A., and Rees, J. (1993). Cities and beyond: A new look at the nation's urban economy. In J. Summer and D. A. Hicks, eds., *Rediscovering urban America.* Washington, DC: U.S. Dept. of Housing and Urban Development.

Hill, P. T., Wise, A. E., and Shapiro, L. (1980). *Educational progress: Cities mobilize to improve their schools.* Santa Monica, CA: Rand Corporation.

Hirsch, J. S. (1992). Columbia, Md. at 25, sees integration goal sliding from its grasp. *Wall Street Journal*, 2/27.

Hirsch, J. S. (1991). Planned communities promise a new calm with the new home. *Wall Street Journal*, 5/9.

Hiss, J. (1993). The end of the rainbow. *New Yorker*, 4/12.

Holden, B. A. (1993). Los Angeles 'Hood, a blend of races, strives to get along. *Wall Street Journal*, 4/8.

Holly, D. (1993). Neighborhood battles adult entertainment. *Detroit Free Press,* 3/28.

Holly, D. (1993). Neighbors come apart on blockade. *Detroit Free Press*, 3/26.

Holly, D. (1993). Neighbors join in an effort to keep out other Detroiters. *Detroit Free Press*, 3/5.

Hood, J. (1993). What's wrong with head start? *Wall Street Journal*, 2/1.

Hunter, A. (1975). The loss of community: An empirical test through replication. *American Sociological Review* 40:5.

Hunter, F. (1953). *Community power structure.* Chapel Hill: University of North Carolina Press.

Hutchinson, W. J. et al. (1986). Multidimensional networking: A response to the needs of homeless families. *Social Work* 31:6.

Hymowitz, K. S. (1993). Multiculturalism is anti-culture. *New York Times*, 3/25.

Jackman, M., and Jackman, R. (1983). *Class awareness in the United States.* Berkeley: University of California Press.

Jacobs, C. and Bowles, D., eds. (1988). *Ethnicity and race: Critical concepts in social work.* Silver Spring, MD: NASW Press.

Jacobs, J. (1961). *The death and life of great American cities.* New York: Random House.

James, D. (1992). Big immigrant wave swamps assimilation. *Wall Street Journal*, 7/2.

Janowitz, M. (1967). *The community press in an urban setting.* Chicago: University of Chicago Press.

Janowitz, M. (1978). *The last half century societal change and politics in America.* Chicago: University of Chicago Press.

Jeffrey, N. A. (1991). Our time is now, city Hispanic community says. *Detroit Free Press,* 5/4.

Jencks, C., and Peterson, P. E. (1991). *The urban underclass.* Washington, DC: The Brookings Institution.

Jenkins, S. (1980). The ethnic agency defined. *Social Service Review* 54:2.

Johnson, D. (1993). Blow dealt to Colorado anti-gay law. *New York Times,* 7/20.

Johnson, D. L. (1993). The best defense against workplace violence. *Wall Street Journal,* 7/19.

Johnson, H. W. (1990). *The social services,* 3rd ed. Itasca, IL: F. E. Peacock Publishers.

Jones, L. (1990). Balancing act. *Detroit Free Press,* 9/29.

Kaczor, B. (1993). Pensacola's gay riviera coming out of the closet. *Associated Press,* 7/14.

Karr, A. R. (1993). Consumer group finds marketing bias in mortgage lending in 16 large cities. *Wall Street Journal,* 8/13.

Kasarda, J., and Janowitz, M. (1974). Community attachment in mass society. *American Sociological Review* 39:3.

Kasarda, J. D. (1989). Urban industrial transition and the underclass. *Annals* 501.

Kasarda, J. D. (1992). Why Asians can prosper where Blacks fail. *Wall Street Journal,* 5/28.

Keillor, G. (1985). *Lake Wobegon days.* New York: Viking Penguin.

Kemp, J. (1990). Liberate America's other economy. *Wall Street Journal,* 6/12.

Kennedy, R. (1993). Still a pigmentocracy. *New York Times,* 7/21.

Kettner, P., Daley, J. M., and Nichols, A. W. (1985). *Initiating change in organizations and communities.* Monterey, CA: Brooks/Cole Publishing Co.

Kiesler, C. A. (1992). U.S. Mental Health Policy. *American Psychologist* 47:9.

Kilborn, P. G. (1990). Labor department wants to take on job bias in the executive suite. *New York Times,* 7/30.

Kilborn, P. T. (1993). Law failed to stem illegal immigration, panel says. *New York Times,* 2/11.

Kilpatrick, L. (1990). In Ontario, equal pay for equal work becomes a reality, but not very easily. *Wall Street Journal,* 3/9.

Kim, C. H. (1993). We're too busy to fight a "mommy war". *Wall Street Journal,* 8/23.

Kinkead, G. (1991). A reporter at large: Chinatown. *New Yorker,* 6/10, 6/17.

Kirk, S., and Therrien, M. (1975). Community mental health myths and the fate of former hospitalized patients. *Psychiatry* 38:8.

Klibanoff, H. (1984). Chicago suburb actively seeks racial diversity. *Detroit Free Press,* 10/8.

Knoke, D. (1981). Commitment and detachment in voluntary associations. *American Sociological Review* 46:2.

Kobrin, S. (1958). The conflict of values in delinquency areas. In H. Stein, and R. Cloward, eds., *Social perspectives on behavior.* New York: Free Press.

Koegel, P. (1987). *Ethnographic perspectives on homeless and homeless mentally ill women.* Los Angeles: University of California.

Kornblum, W. (1975) *Blue collar community.* Chicago: University of Chicago Press.

Krauss, C. (1991). Latin immigrants in capital find unrest a sad tie to past. *New York Times*, 5/8.

Krupat, E. (1985). *People in cities.* Cambridge: Cambridge University Press.

Lam, T. (1993). Residents, topless bar owners reach pact. *Detroit Free Press*, 2/10.

Lamb, H. R., ed. (1984). *The homeless mentally ill.* Washington, DC: American Psychiatric Association.

Lambert, S. (1993). Workplace policies as social policy. *Social Service Review* 67:2.

Landecker, W. S. (1951). Types of integration and their measurement. *American Journal of Sociology* 56:4.

Lardner, J. (1993). A new kind of cop. *Wall Street Journal*, 7/5.

Lee, M. (1993). Diversity training brings unity to small companies. *Wall Street Journal*, 9/2.

Lemann, N. (1991). *The promised land: The great black migration and how it changed America.* New York: Knopf.

Leshner, A. I. (1992). *Outcasts on main street.* Interagency Council on the Homeless, publication number (ADM) 92-1904. Washington, DC: U.S. Government Printing Office.

Levin, M. J. (1986). A classless society. *Detroit Free Press*, 9/5.

Levine, H., and Harmon, L. (1992). *The death of an American Jewish community.* New York: Free Press.

Levine, R. (1990). Young immigrant wave lifts New York economy. *New York Times*, 7/30.

Liebow, E. (1967). *Tally's corner.* Boston: Little, Brown and Co.

Lief, B. J., and Goering, S. (1987). The implementation of the Federal mandate for fair housing. In G. A. Tobin, ed., Divided neighborhoods: Changing patterns of racial segregation. *Urban Affairs Annual Reviews* 32.

Lipsky, M., and Smith, S. R. (1989). When social problems are treated as emergencies. *Social Service Review* 63:1.

Litwak, E. (1961). Voluntary associations and neighborhood cohesion. *American Sociological Review* 26:2.

Litwak, E. (1985). *Helping the elderly.* New York: Guilford Press.

Liu, W. T., and Yu, E. S. H. (1985). Ethnicity, mental health, and the urban delivery system. In L. Maldonado, and J. Moore, eds., Urban Ethnicity in the United States. *Urban Affairs Annual Reviews* 29.

Logan, A. (1993). Cry the beloved community. *New Yorker*, 4/26.

Logan, J. (1978). Growth, politics and the stratification of places. *American Journal of Sociology* 84:2.

Long, N. E. (1958). The local community as an ecology of games. *American Journal of Sociology* 64:3.

Longres, J. F. (1990). *Human behavior and the social environment.* Itasca, IL: F. E. Peacock Publishers.

Louv, R. (1985). *America II.* New York: Penguin Books.

Lubman, S. (1992). Santa Monica grows hostile to the homeless who consider it home. *Wall Street Journal*, 11/9.

Lynd, R. S., and Lynd, H. M. (1929). *Middletown: A study in contemporary American culture.* New York: Harcourt Brace.

MacGuire, J. (1992). The Carnegie assault on school choice. *Wall Street Journal*, 11/25.

MacKinnon, C. A. (1979). *Sexual harassment of working women: A case of sex discrimination.* New Haven, CT: Yale University Press.

Magill, R. S. (1985). Ethnicity and social welfare in American cities: A historical view. In L. Maldonado, and J. Moore, eds., Urban ethnicity in the United States. *Urban Affairs Annual Reviews* 29.

Maguire, L. (1983). *Understanding social networks*. Beverly Hills: Sage Publications.

Maldonado, L., and Moore, J. (1985). *Urban ethnicity in the United States*. Beverly Hills: Sage Publications.

Malekoff, A., Levine, M., and Quaglia, S. (1987). An attempt to create a new old neighborhood: From suburban isolation to mutual caring. *Social Work With Groups* 10:3.

Martin, P. (1993). Turn ailing thrifts into community banks. *Wall Street Journal*, 7/6.

Martinez-Brawley, E. E. (1990). *Perspectives on the small community*. Silver Spring, MD: NASW Press.

Massey, D. (1981). Social class and ethnic segregation. *American Sociological Review* 46.

Mathews, L. (1993). Grosse Pointe Park closes street to Detroit. *Detroit Free Press*, 4/13.

Maypole, D. E., and Skaine, R. (1983). Sexual harassment in the workplace. *Social Work* 28:5.

Maypole, D. E. (1987). Sexual harassment at work: A review of research and theory. *Affilia* 2:1.

McCaughey, E. (1993). Court deals a blow to racial gerrymandering. *Wall Street Journal*, 6/30.

McClure, J. (1974). Black community structure and participation: An analysis of the state of the art. In L. E. Gary, ed., *Social research and the Black community*. Washington, DC: Howard University.

McGinley, L. (1993). Some advocates of enterprise-zone concept find little to cheer in Democrats' legislation. *Wall Street Journal*, 8/9.

McGroarty, D. (1993). A prayer for a better education. *Wall Street Journal*, 10/1.

McKenzie, R. D. (1926). The scope of human ecology. *American Journal of Sociology* 32.

Mead, L. M. (1989). The logic of workfare: The underclass and work policy. *Annals* 501.

Merton, R. (1983). Local and cosmopolitan influentials. In R. Warren, and L. Lyon, eds., *New Perspectives on the American community*. Homewood, IL: The Dorsey Press.

Merton, R. K. (1949). Types of influentials: The local and the cosmopolitan. In P. Lazarsfeld, and F. Stanton, eds., *Communications research*. New York: Harper and Row.

Meyer, C. (1983). *Clinical social work in the eco-systems perspective*. New York: Columbia University Press.

Miller, J. J. (1993). The rest of the rainbow curriculum. *Wall Street Journal*, 2/10.

Moilanen, K. A. (1993). Family leave won't bring major change. *Ann Arbor News*, 8/1.

Montana, C. (1986). Latino schism: Hispanic communities in U.S. are divided by influx of Mexicans. *Wall Street Journal*, 10/1.

Morgenthaler, E. (1993). Old-style towns where people walk have modern backers. *Wall Street Journal*, 2/1.

Morris, B. (1982). Scoring a home run: A small town builds its baseball stadium. *Wall Street Journal*, 8/17.

Murray, K. (1993). The unfortunate side effects of "Diversity Training". *New York Times*, 8/1.

Nathan, J. (1993). School choice works in Minnesota. *Wall Street Journal*, 4/22.

Nathan, R. P. (1991). Where the minority middle class lives. *Wall Street Journal*, 5/22.

National Commission on Educational Excellence. (1988). *A nation at risk*. Washington, DC.

Naylor, R. (1993). Clinton proposes national standards for schools. *Associated Press*, 4/22.

Neighbors, H. W., Elliott, K. A., and Gant, L. M. (1990). Self-help and Black Americans: A strategy for empowerment. In T. Powell, ed., *Working with self-help.* Silver Spring, MD: NASW Press.

Nes, J. A., and Iadicola, P. (1989). Toward a definition of feminist social work. *Social Work* 34:1.

Netting, F. E., Kettner, P. M., and Mc-Murtry, S. L. (1993). *Social work macro practice.* New York: Longman.

Newman, K. S. (1988). *Falling from grace.* New York: Free Press.

Newman, K. S. (1993). Declining fortunes: *The withering of the American dream.* New York: Basic Books.

Newman, S. J. (1981). *Residential crowding: A study of definitions.* Ann Arbor, MI: Institute for Social Research.

New Yorker. (1993). The wobbly blue line. 7/5.

New York Times. (1991). Study finds bias in house hunting. 9/1.

Olofson, C. E. (1989). Management women: Debating the facts of life. *Harvard Business Review* 67:3.

Padilla, Y. C. (1990). Social science theory on the Mexican American experience. *Social Service Review* 64:2.

Park, R., Burgess, E. W., and McKenzie, R. D., eds. (1925). *The city.* Chicago: University of Chicago Press.

Parsons, T. (1951). *The social system.* Glencoe, IL: Free Press.

Parsons, T. (1960). *Structure and process in modern societies.* New York: Free Press.

Pepper, J. (1990). Common ground: Cleveland suburbs work to achieve a racial balance. *Detroit News*, 8/19.

Perlman, R., and Gurin, A. (1972). *Community organization and social planning.* New York: Wiley.

Perrucci, R., and Pilisuk, M. (1970). The interorganizational bases of community power. *American Sociological Review* 35:6.

Perry, J. M. (1993). As prospects improve for passage of Brady bill, NRA, opponents debate what should come next. *Wall Street Journal,* 8/11.

Pildes, R. H., and Niemi, R. G. (1993). Expressive harms, "bizarre districts," and voting rights: Evaluating election-district appearances after Shaw v Reno. *Michigan Law Review* 92:3.

Poplin, D. (1979). *Communities: A survey of theories and methods of research,* 2nd ed. New York: Macmillan.

Portnoy, G., and Angelo, J. H. *Cheers.* Addax Music Co., Inc.

Powell, T. (1979). Comparisons between self-help groups and professional services. *Social Casework* 60:11.

Powell, T. (1987). *Self-help organizations and professional practice.* Silver Spring, MD: NASW Press.

Powell, T. (1990). *Working with self-help.* Silver Spring, MD: NASW Press.

Putka, G. (1990). Wisconsin to allow some students to use education vouchers at private schools. *Wall Street Journal,* 3/26.

Quintanilla, C. (1993). Disabilities act helps. *Wall Street Journal,* 7/19.

Radin, N. (1989). School social work practice: Past, present, and future trends. *Social Work in Education* 11:4.

Redfield, R. (1947). The folk society. *American Journal of Sociology* 52:4.

Reeves, R. (1981). Boyle Heights and beyond. *New Yorker,* 9/14.

Reischauer, R. D. (1989). Immigration and the underclass. *Annals* 501.

Reissman, R. (1987). Foreword. In T. Powell, *Self-help organizations and professional practice.* Silver Spring, MD: NASW Press.

Rigdon, J. E. (1993). Three decades after the equal pay act, women's wages remain far from parity. *Wall Street Journal*, 6/9.

Rimer, S. (1991). New immigrant group displays its enterprise. *New York Times*, 9/16.

Rivera, F. G., and Erlich, J. L. (1992). *Community organizing in a diverse society*. Boston: Allyn and Bacon.

Roberts, S. (1993). Crown heights report leaves lingering questions. *New York Times*, 7/25.

Rohter, L. (1992). Judge orders safe zones for homeless. *New York Times*, 11/18.

Rose, H. (1976). *Black suburbanization*. Cambridge, MA: Ballinger.

Rossi, P. H., and Wright, J. D. (1989). The urban homeless: A portrait of urban dislocation. *Annals* 501.

Rossi, P. H. (1989). *Down and out in America*. Chicago: University of Chicago Press.

Rothman, J. (1974). *Planning and organizing for social change*. New York: Columbia University Press.

Rothman, J. (1982). Taking account of workplace in community organizational practice. In S. H. Akabas, and P. A. Kunzman, eds., *Work, workers and work organizations*. New York: Prentice-Hall.

Rothman, J. (1979). Three models of community organization practice, their mixing and phasing. In F. M. Cox, J. L. Erlich, J. Rothman, and J. E. Tropman, eds., *Strategies of community organization*. Itasca, IL: F. E. Peacock Publishers.

Rowan, C. (1993). Parity must be the goal in funding schools. *North America Syndicate*, 4/25.

Rusk, D. (1993). *Cities without suburbs*. Baltimore: Johns Hopkins University Press.

Saltman, J. (1991). Maintaining racially diverse neighborhoods. *Urban Affairs Quarterly* 26:3.

Sandefur, G. D., and Tienda, M. (1988). *Divided opportunities: Minorities, poverty, and social policy*. New York: Plenum Press.

Saxton, P. (1991). Comments on social work and the psychotherapies. *Social Service Review* 65:2.

Schlesinger, A. M. (1992). *The disuniting of America: Reflections on a multicultural society*. New York: Norton and Company.

Schmidt, B. C. (1992). Educational innovation for profit. *Wall Street Journal*, 6/5.

Schwartz, F. N. (1989). Management women and the new facts of life. *Harvard Business Review* 67:1.

Schwartz, F. N. (1992). Women as a business imperative. *Harvard Business Review* 70:2.

Segal, S. P., and Baumohl, J. (1980). Engaging the disengaged: Proposals on madness and vagrancy. *Social Work* 25:5.

Shanker, A. (1993). Lewd or rude? *New York Times*, 8/1.

Sharpe, R. (1993). Clinton package for schools has chance to pass. *Wall Street Journal*, 4/16.

Shellenbarger, S. (1993). So much talk, so little action. *Wall Street Journal*, 6/21.

Shellenbarger, S. (1993). Work-force study finds loyalty is weak, divisions of race and gender are deep. *Wall Street Journal*, 9/3.

Shellenbarger, S. (1993). Executive women make major gains in pay and status. *Wall Street Journal*, 6/30.

Shellenbarger, S. (1993). Longer commutes force parents to make tough choices on where to leave the kids. *Wall Street Journal*, 8/18.

Shevky, E., and Bell, W. (1955). *Social area analysis: Theory, illustrative application and computational procedures*. Stanford, CA: Stanford University Press.

Shils, E. A. (1962). The theory of the mass society. *Diogenes* 39.

Shipp, E. R. (1991). New districts revive debate: Where and what is Harlem? *New York Times*, 5/8.

Shlay, A., and Rossi, P. (1981). Keeping up the neighborhood: Estimating net effects of zoning. *American Sociological Review* 46:6.

Shribman, D. (1993). Migration to suburbs will transform character of legislative bodies and alter funding patterns. *Wall Street Journal*, 6/19.

Shribman, D. (1991). Census '90 indicate a new megalopolis. *Wall Street Journal*, 6/19.

Simkus, A. (1978). Residential segregation by occupation and race in ten urbanized areas, 1950–1970. *American Sociological Review* 43:2.

Simon, J. L. (1990). Bring on the wretched refuse. *Wall Street Journal*, 1/26.

Simon, J. L. (1993). The nativists are wrong. *Wall Street Journal*, 8/4.

Slevin, C. A. E. (1993). Here's a time share that's music to thousands living in small towns. *Wall Street Journal*, 9/24.

Snipp, C. M. (1989). *American Indians: The first of this land*. New York: Russell Sage.

Soifer, S. (1991). Infusing content about Jews and about anti-semitism into the curricula. *Journal of Social Work Education* 27:2.

Solomon, B. (1976). *Black empowerment: Social work in oppressed communities*. New York: Columbia University Press.

Solomon, J. (1989). Schwartz of mommy track notoriety prods firms to address women's needs. *Wall Street Journal*, 9/11.

Solomon, J. (1990). As cultural diversity of workers grows, experts urge appreciation of differences. *Wall Street Journal*, 9/12.

Sorkin, A. (1978). *The urban American Indian*. Toronto: Lexington Books.

Sosin, M. R., Colson, P., and Grossman, S. (1988). *Homelessness in Chicago*. Chicago: The Chicago Community Trust.

Specht, H. (1990). Social work and the popular psychotherapies. *Social Service Review* 64:3.

Specht, H. (1992). A less complex statement of social work's mission. *Social Service Review* 66:1.

Statistical Abstracts. (1992). Washington, DC: U.S. Bureau of the Census.

Steggert, F. (1975). *Community action groups and city government*. Cambridge, MA: Ballinger.

Stogdill, R. (1974). *Handbook of leadership*. New York: Free Press.

Stout, H. (1992). School choice programs do not lead to improved education, report finds. *Wall Street Journal*, 10/26.

Street, D. (1978). *Handbook on contemporary urban life*. San Francisco: Jossey-Bass.

Sullivan, S. (1993). Wife-beating N the hood. *Wall Street Journal*, 7/6.

Summer, J. (1993). Renewing a dialogue on urban America. In J. Summer, and D. A. Hicks, eds., *Rediscovering urban America*. Washington, DC: U.S. Dept. of Housing and Urban Development.

Summer, J., and Hicks, D. A., eds. (1993). *Rediscovering urban America*. Washington, DC: U.S. Dept. of Housing and Urban Development.

Suro, R. (1991). Where America is growing: The suburban cities. *New York Times*, 2/23.

Suttles, G. (1968). *The social order of the slum*. Chicago: University of Chicago Press.

Swasy, A. (1993). Stay-at-home moms are fashionable again in many communities. *Wall Street Journal*, 7/23.

Taub, R., et al. (1977). Urban voluntary associations, locality based and externally induced. *American Journal of Sociology* 83:2.

Taub, R. P., Taylor, D. G., and Dunham, J. D. (1984). Paths of neighborhood change: Race and crime in urban America. Chicago: University of Chicago Press.

Taube, C. A., Mechanic, D., and Hohmann, A., eds. (1989). The future of mental health services research. U.S. Department of Health and Human Services, publication number (ADM) 89-1600. Washington, DC: U.S. Government Printing Office.

Taylor, B., and Taylor, A. (1989). Social casework and environmental cognition: Mobility training for community mental health services. Social Work 34:5.

Taylor, R. (1979). Black ethnicity and the persistence of ethnogenesis. American Journal of Sociology 84:6.

Taylor, R. J., and Chatters, L. M. (1988). Church members as a source of informal social support. Review of Religious Research 30:2.

Taylor, R. J., and Chatters, L. M. (1986). Patterns of informal support to elderly black adults: Family, friends, and church members. Social Work 31:6.

Teltsch, K. (1985). Atlanta's effort to cope with cut in federal aid. New York Times, 3/19.

Tessler, R. C., and Goldman, H. H. (1982). The chronically mentally ill: Assessing community support programs. Cambridge, MA: Ballinger.

Theilen, G. L., and Poole, D. L. (1986). Educating leadership for effecting community change through voluntary associations. Journal of Social Work Education 2.

Thernstgrom et al. (1980). Harvard encyclopedia of American ethnic groups. Cambridge: Harvard University Press.

Thomas, D. (1991). Young, rich and on a roll. Washington Post, 7/11.

Thomas, P. (1991). Mortgage rejection rate for minorities is quadruple that of whites, study finds. Wall Street Journal, 10/21.

Tilove, J., and Hallinan, J. (1993). A nation divided. Ann Arbor News, 8/22.

Tobin, G. A., ed. (1987). Divided neighborhoods: Changing patterns of racial segregation. Urban Affairs Annual Reviews 32.

Tomsho, R. (1993). Volunteers aid environmental agencies. Wall Street Journal, 7/27.

Tonnies, F. (1957). Community and society (translated and edited by Charles P. Loomis). East Lansing, MI: Michigan State University Press.

Trimer-Hartley, M. (1993). Chapter's just begun on accepting gays in school. Detroit Free Press, 4/23.

U.S. Bureau of the Census. (1985). Factfinder for the nation: Census geography-concepts and products. Washington, DC: Bureau of the Census.

Van Den Bergh, N., and Cooper, L. B. (1986). Feminist visions for social work. Washington, DC: National Association of Social Workers Press.

Verhovek, S. H. (1991). A New York panel urges emphasizing minority cultures. New York Times, 6/20.

Wacquant, L. J. D., and Wilson, W. J. (1989). The cost of racial and class exclusion in the inner city. Annals 501.

Wakefield, J. C. (1992). Why psychotherapeutic social work don't get no re-specht. Social Service Review 66:1.

Wald, M. L. (1984). Back offices disperse from downtowns. New York Times, 5/13.

Wall Street Journal. (1992). Mortgage gap on racial basis persisted in 1991. 10/1.

Wall Street Journal. (1993). Putting to the test views toward women. 2/22.

Ware, J. E., Jr. (1989). Measuring health and functional status in mental health services research. In Taube et al., eds., *The future of mental health services research.* U.S. Department of Health and Human Services, publication number (ADM) 89-1600. Washington, DC: U.S. Government Printing Office.

Warner, K. et al. (1982). Detroit's renaissance includes factories. *Urban Land.*

Warner, W. L., and Lunt, P. (1941). *The social life of a modern community.* New Haven, CT: Yale University.

Warren, D. (1975). *Black neighborhoods.* Ann Arbor: University of Michigan Press.

Warren, D. (1981). *Helping networks.* South Bend, IN: University of Notre Dame Press.

Warren, R. (1963). *The community in America.* Chicago: Rand McNally.

Warren, R. (1980). The good community revisited. *Social Development Issues* 4:3.

Warren, R. (1983). The good community: What would it be? In R. Warren, and L. Lyon, eds., *New perspectives on the American community.* Homewood, IL: Dorsey Press.

Warren, R., and Warren, D. I. (1977). *The neighborhood organizers handbook.* South Bend: University of Notre Dame Press.

Wartzman, R. (1993). New bus lines link the inner-city poor with jobs in suburbia. *Wall Street Journal,* 9/24.

Washington Post Writers Group. (1993). Cisneros, Bradley have what it takes to fix our aching cities. *Washington Post,* 4/12.

Wermiel, S. (1990). High court backs U.S. judge's authority to order funds for school desegregation. *Wall Street Journal,* 4/19.

West, C. (1993). How to end the impasse. *New York Times,* 4/14.

Whyte, W. H. (1988). *Rediscovering the center city.* New York: Doubleday.

Wilensky, H. L., and Lebeaux, C. N. (1965). *Industrial society and social welfare.* New York: Free Press.

Wilkerson, I. (1993). Chicago plans barriers to hinder street crime. *New York Times,* 1/22.

Williams, J., Babchuk, N., and Johnson, D. (1973). Voluntary associations and minority status: A comparative analysis of anglo, black, and Mexican-Americans. *American Sociological Review* 38:5.

Williams, L. F. (1990). The challenge of education to social work: The case for minority children. *Social Work* 35:3.

Williams, M. R. (1989). *Neighborhood organizing for urban school reform.* New York: Columbia University.

Williamson, A. D. (1993). Is this the right time to come out? *Harvard Business Review* 71:4.

Wilson, W. (1978). *The declining significance of race.* Chicago: University of Chicago Press.

Wilson, W. J. (1987). *The truly disadvantaged.* Chicago: University of Chicago Press.

Wilson, W. J. (1989). The underclass: Issues, perspectives, and public policy. *Annals* 501.

Wilson, W. J. (1993). *The new poverty and the problem of race.* O. C. Tanner Lecture. Ann Arbor: The University of Michigan.

Winters, W. G., and Eastor, F. (1983). *The Practice of social work in schools: An ecological perspective.* New York: Free Press.

Wirth, L. (1938). Urbanism as a way of life. *American Journal of Sociology* 44:1.

Wolf, J. H. (1985). Professionalizing volunteer work in a black neighborhood. *Social Service Review* 59:3.

Wong, G. (1985). Post-1965 immigrants: Demographic and socioeconomic profile. In L. Maldonado, and J. Moore, eds., Urban ethnicity in the United States. *Urban Affairs Annual Reviews* 29.

Wong, J. (1986). Bias against Orientals increases with rivalry of nations' economies. *Wall Street Journal*, 11/28.

Woolbright, L. A., and Hartmann, D. J. (1987). The new segregation: Asians and Hispanics. In G. A. Tobin, ed., Divided neighborhoods: Changing patterns of racial segregation. *Urban Affairs Annual Reviews* 32.

World Health Organization. (1948). Constitution of the World Health Organization. In *Basic Documents.* Geneva: WHO.

Wright, D. (1990). American, not African-American. *Wall Street Journal*, 10/30.

Wynter, L. E., and Solomon, J. (1989). A new push to break the glass ceiling. *Wall Street Journal*, 11/15.

Wysocki, B. (1991). Influx of Asians brings prosperity to Flushing, a place for newcomers. *Wall Street Journal*, 1/15.

Yankauer, A. (1987). Hispanic/Latino- What's in a name? *American Journal of Public Health* 77:1.

Zuravin, S. J., and Taylor, R. (1987). The ecology of child maltreatment: Identifying and characterizing high-risk neighborhoods. *Child Welfare* 56:6.

INDEX

The Community and the Social Worker, Second Edition
Composition by Point West, Inc.
Printing and binding by Braun-Brumfield, Inc.
The typeface is Melior

Second Edition

The Community